MARRIAGE, WIFE-BEATING AND
THE LAW IN VICTORIAN ENGLAND

Marriage, Wife-Beating and the Law in Victorian England

MAEVE E. DOGGETT

University of South Carolina Press

Copyright © 1993 University of South Carolina

Published in Columbia, South Carolina, by the
University of South Carolina Press

Manufactured in the United States of America

Doggett, Maeve E.
    Marriage, wife-beating and the law in Victorian England / Maeve E.
Doggett.
            p.   cm.
    Originally presented as the author's thesis (LLM—Osgood Hall Law
School, Toronto)
    Includes bibliographical references and index.
    ISBN 0–87249–967–7 (hard cover : acid-free paper)
    1. Wife abuse—Great Britain—History. 2. Husband and wife—Great
Britain—History. 3. Wife abuse—England—History—19th century.
I. Title.
KD7973.D64   1993
346.4201'63—dc20   93–14638
[344.206163]

CONTENTS

PREFACE

I have chosen in this study of marriage, wife-beating and the law to focus primarily on the nineteenth century. In some respects the book spans a much longer period; my examination of the origins of the fiction of marital unity, for example, takes me back to the twelfth century. However, the Victorian era was of pivotal significance in the history of the law relating to wife-beating. In 1891, after half a century of more or less persistent public concern about marital violence, *R.* v. *Jackson* was decided. *Jackson*, by abolishing the common law defences of reasonable chastisement and confinement, finally rendered it illegal for a husband to beat or imprison his wife. My central task has been to set this nineteenth-century development in its broader historical context and to explain and assess it. Why, in 1891, were centuries of established judicial authority so abruptly swept away? What had changed?

I am an academic lawyer. While researching and writing this book I often wished that I were also an historian and a sociologist. However, given the virtual impossibility of being all of these things simultaneously and the undoubted value of the interdisciplinary endeavour, I have not allowed myself to be deterred by this. If we are to develop a clearer understanding of the relationship between law and social and political change, we cannot afford to be timid about venturing beyond the boundaries of our individual disciplines.

This book started life as a thesis submitted in satisfaction of the LLM requirements at Osgoode Hall Law School in Toronto. I should like to take this opportunity to thank the Canadian Commonwealth Scholarship and Fellowship Committee for the financial assistance which made it possible for me to study in Canada. I should also like to thank my thesis supervisor, Professor Mary Jane Mossman, for her guidance and support, and the members of the examining committee, in particular Professor Douglas Hay, for their detailed and helpful comments.

As regards the transformation of my thesis into this book, thanks are due to Professor William Twining for his comments and advice, to Dr Ruth Paley for her patient attempts to initiate me into the very considerable mysteries of the Public Record Office, and to Professor Stephen Bailey for his assistance and support.

In the preface to *The World Turned Upside Down*, Christopher Hill observes that there are 'few activities more co-operative than the writing of history ... [The] whole enterprise depends on the preceding labours of others'. With this in mind, I should like to close by acknowledging my indebtedness to Norma Basch, Carole Pateman, Leonore Davidoff and Catherine Hall, just a few of the academics whose 'preceding labours' I have found so invaluable.

The Jackson Decision and the History of the Law on Wife-Beating

The Jackson Decision

It was a Sunday afternoon in March 1891. In Clitheroe in Lancashire Emily Jackson was attending church with her sister. As the service ended and the congregation began to emerge from the church, three men appeared. One of them had his face concealed in a black wrap. These men seized hold of Emily and started to force her into a waiting carriage. She tried to cling to her sister, Mrs Baldwin, but they were dragged apart. She was pushed on to the floor of the carriage with her legs sticking out of the door. One of the men took hold of her legs and shoved them in; the men jumped in themselves and the Clitheroe congregation watched as the carriage drove away.

The masked man was Emily's husband. They had married in Blackburn in November 1887. The ceremony took place without the knowledge of Emily's disapproving relatives; she was 46 at the time and of independent means and the family evidently suspected Edmund Jackson of being a gold-digger. Almost immediately after the marriage, Jackson had set sail for New Zealand, intending that his wife should join him there later. Emily went home to Clitheroe to live with her sisters and, after a time, she decided that she did not want to move to New Zealand. She and Jackson quarrelled in their letters. She urged him to return home but, when he did, in July 1888, she refused to live with him.

Jackson responded by obtaining a decree for restitution of conjugal rights. This had been the ecclesiastical remedy for desertion and was still available from the Probate and Divorce Division of the High Court.[1] It consisted of an order to the offending party to resume cohabitation with her spouse and treat him with conjugal affection. When Emily ignored the decree Jackson decided to take matters into his own hands.

Emily was taken to Jackson's uncle's house in Blackburn and kept there against her will. Her sisters and her brother-in-law soon arrived on the scene. The police were contacted but, when they discovered that Jackson had an order for restitution of conjugal rights, they refused to intervene. Periodically, a distressed and tearful Emily would be seen at the window. The family stationed themselves in the street outside the house and in a house across the road and took every opportunity of communicating with her. On one occasion, she was pulled back from the window and the blind was drawn down to prevent her from signalling to them.

All this attracted a great deal of attention. *The Times* reported that

[t]he excitement in the neighbourhood was very great ... a crowd of people watched every little incident. In the morning the milk and the papers were taken in by means of a string let down from one of the bedroom windows, and, later on, all kinds of provisions were obtained in the same way. At noon, a box of cigars was hoisted up to the garrison.[2]

Emily's family applied for a writ of *habeas corpus* – a remedy for wrongful imprisonment. The application was heard in the Queen's Bench Division of the High Court on March 16 1891. Cave and Jeune JJ. rapidly came to the conclusion that it should be rejected. The law required prima facie evidence of unlawful conduct and, in their view, this was lacking: 'the detention here is in no sense illegal, for, where the relations are those between husband and wife, there may be a detention which is not illegal'. They then went on to criticise the 'very mistaken conduct' of the sisters: instead of pursuing Jackson and 'besetting [his] house' they should have left 'the husband and wife alone for the purpose of settling their differences; and trying to live together as husband and wife should do'.[3]

However, the Court of Appeal took a very different view of the matter. On March 17 it ordered a writ of *habeas corpus* to issue. This meant that Jackson was obliged to bring his wife into court so that the legality of the detention could be scrutinised. On March 19 he complied.

Some of the decision's fame is attributable to the fact that the leading judgment was given by the Lord Chancellor, Lord Halsbury, who was then presiding over the Court of Appeal in an attempt to clear off arrears in the lists. The case is an illustration of the 'intransigent adherence to conviction for which he was to become celebrated'.[4]

Jackson's counsel, Henn Collins Q.C., sought to argue that a husband had a common-law right to the custody of his wife. Lord Halsbury L.C. and his fellow-judges were hostile to this argument from the beginning and repeatedly interrupted his speech with sharp and sarcastic questions:

[LORD ESHER : The husband, you say, has the right to take possession of her and to keep her?]
Yes.
[The LORD CHANCELLOR : By force?]
Yes, by force. . . . the authorities . . . do show the law to be so.
[The LORD CHANCELLOR : They also show that the husband may beat his wife. The same authorities show that as well as the other.]
That part of the authorities cannot be sustained.
[The LORD CHANCELLOR : You can hardly take one part of an authority and reject the rest. If it be an authority at all it is an authority for the whole.]
The authorities for the right to be beat do not show that it is any longer the law of England.
[LORD ESHER : It never was so.]
. . .
[The LORD CHANCELLOR : How is the supposed right [to custody] to be limited and restrained?]
He may do what is reasonably necessary for its exercise.
[The LORD CHANCELLOR : That is very loose and large, and might be deemed to justify beating to get her to go into his house.]
It must be admitted that it involves the use of violence.
[The LORD CHANCELLOR : To whatever extent may be necessary on the occasion?]
Yes.[5]

The Lord Chancellor and the Master of the Rolls emphatically repudi-
ated these propositions. They derived from 'quaint and absurd dicta'
which were no longer 'capable of being cited as authorities in a court
of justice in this or any civilised country'. These dicta did not represent
the law of England and, what was more, they never had done ; English
wives were not their husbands' abject slaves. They did not deny that
there were occasions when a man might exercise a limited right of
restraint − if he saw his wife in the act of going to meet a paramour,
he might seize her and pull her back; but a husband did not have a
right to the custody of his wife.[6]

These speeches were noted for their 'thunder-and-lightning rhetoric'.[7]
In contrast, Fry L.J. spoke in 'more measured and legal language'.[8]
He indicated the authorities which he considered to be relevant,
analysed them and concluded that Jackson's case must fail. Lord
Halsbury L.C. and Lord Esher M.R. referred specifically to only one
common-law authority. Their judgments had a declaratory quality;
they spoke as though they were simply confirming long-established
changes in judicial practice and popular opinion. Jackson was portrayed
as an anachronism and laughingly dismissed.

But if Edmund Jackson was an anachronism then it is difficult to
explain the reaction which the decision provoked. This will be discussed

in greater depth later. Suffice it to say at this stage that *R.* v. *Jackson* created a sensation.[9] In newspapers and popular journals, in legal journals and textbooks, in Clitheroe and in Parliament, 'the copiousness, variety and vivacity of the comments'[10] attested to the significance people attached to it. Opinion was naturally divided. Supporters of the decision hailed it as a 'charter of the personal liberty of married women';[11] opponents predicted 'chaos', 'social anarchy' and 'universal topsyturvydom'.[12] But love it or hate it, the commentators all agreed on one thing – that *Jackson* was *important*. They all thought that *Jackson* had changed things.

So, where did the truth lie? Was *Jackson* important primarily as a declaratory statement of the law from a distinguished superior court bench? Or did it reflect a fundamentally new understanding of the marital relationship? To answer this question we have to do what Lord Halsbury L.C. and Lord Esher M.R. failed to do and consider how much support there actually was for the proposition that a husband had the right to imprison, perhaps even to beat, his wife. Was it true that the existence of these rights rested on nothing more than 'quaint and absurd dicta'?

The Right to Beat

The Source of the Right

There is a story told about Thomas More. When he married Jane Colt, in about 1504, he decided to take her education in hand. He tried to interest her in books and music and would get her to repeat the substance of sermons she had heard. Jane did not respond well to this treatment; indeed, she did nothing but cry and wish herself dead. So More took her back to her country home and confided his troubles to his father-in-law. John Colt's advice was to make use of his rights and 'give her a good beating'. 'I know what my rights are,' the young lawyer responded, 'but I would rather you used your authority.' So Colt pretended to be so furiously angry with his daughter that she took refuge by falling at her husband's feet in a fit of penitence. They kissed and made up.[13]

One of the earliest clear authorities for the husband's power of chastisement dates from this period. In 1516 Sir Anthony Fitzherbert published a manual of procedure. It was designed as an updated version of two ancient texts, *The Register* and *The Natura Brevium*, which set out standard forms for writs. He called it *The New Natura Brevium* and it is its treatment of what is now known as 'binding over to keep the peace' which is of interest.

This is a power which magistrates, or Justices of the Peace, have possessed since at least the tenth century.[14] Someone who feared bodily harm from another could exhibit articles of the peace against that person, sometimes referred to as 'swearing' or 'praying the peace'. Alternatively, the Justices could grant the articles of their own motion. They would then take surety or security of the peace. The aggressor would be required to enter into a recognisance, that is, promise to pay a sum of money if he failed to keep the peace in the future. He might also be required to find sureties, that is, other people prepared to guarantee his future good behaviour. A refusal to be bound would lead to imprisonment.

An alternative route for the victim was to seek a writ of *securitate pacis* or *supplicavit*. This was available from the Court of Chancery and from the King's Bench and operated as an instruction to the Justices to take surety of the peace. It was not extensively used for it became clear in the seventeenth century that the superior courts had the power to take the recognisances themselves.[15]

In *Natura Brevium*, Fitzherbert said that the writ of *supplicavit* was available to wives whose husbands threatened to beat or kill them; however, it would be worded as follows:

A. the wife of B. has besought us that whereas she is grievously and manifestly threatened by the aforesaid B. of her Life, and maiming of her Members ... you will answer to us ... that he shall well and honestly treat and govern the aforesaid A. and that he shall not do, nor procure to be done any Damage or Evil to her of her Body, *otherwise than what reasonably belongs to her Husband, for the Sake of Government and Chastisement of his Wife lawfully* ...[16]

It seems that the surety would not have been liable for conduct which fell within the proviso.

This proviso in the writ of *supplicavit* was the main authority for the husband's right of correction. It was relied upon for support in *Eirenarcha*, Lambarde's 1581 handbook for Justices of the Peace, which explained that

some are allowed to have privately, a *natural*, and some a *civile* power (or authoritie) over others, so that they may excuse themselves if but (in reasonable manner) they correct and chastise them for their offences.

A parent's power over a child fell into the former category, a husband's over his wife into the latter, along with that of a master over his servants, a schoolmaster over his pupils, a gaoler over his unruly prisoners and a lord over his vassals. By a 'civile' as opposed to a 'natural' power, Lambarde presumably meant one created by law.[17]

The proviso was also decisive in *Sir Thomas Seymore's Case* in 1613.[18]

Sir Thomas threatened and beat his wife, with the result that she applied to an ecclesiastical court for a separation and maintenance on grounds of his cruelty. The powers of the church or ecclesiastical courts will be discussed later in the chapter; suffice it to say for the moment that, until 1857, they had exclusive jurisdiction in matrimonial matters. Any conflict about jurisdiction between the spiritual and the temporal courts was resolved by means of the royal writ of prohibition: the temporal courts could prohibit the ecclesiastical courts from acting if they felt that their jurisdiction was being usurped. Sir Thomas sought such a prohibition, arguing that his wife had a common-law remedy in the form of an action for assault and battery. A majority of the judges disagreed: a wife could have no remedy at common law against a husband who beat her for she was '*sub virga viri*', that is, under the rod of her husband.

The Extent of the Right

It is clear from Fitzherbert's proviso that the husband's right was not an absolute one. He could not beat his wife at will, but only as a punishment for misbehaviour, and that punishment, moreover, was not to be excessive. But how was reasonable chastisement to be measured? Initially, of course, the question was one for individual husbands and, in most cases, their judgement will never have been challenged. Some will have been capable of rationalising any amount of brutality as a justified response to the most trifling fault.

The law seems to have provided little guidance. The anonymous author of *The Lawes Resolutions of Womens Rights*, a handbook on women's rights published in 1632 (but probably written in the first few years of the century),[19] was unable to say how far the right extended.[20] However, Dalton, writing in 1618, said that an abused wife could only have sureties of the peace against her husband if he threatened 'to kill her, or outragiously to beate her';[21] and in *Bradley* v. *His Wife* in 1663 a court refused to bind a husband over to keep the peace unless the wife could prove that 'her life be in danger, because by the law he has power of castigation'. We are told that 'she used to provoke him'.[22] It seems, therefore, that a high degree of violence was considered acceptable.

It is possible that law imposed restrictions on the kind of instrument with which a wife could be chastised; this was certainly widely believed to have been the case. The nineteenth-century feminist, Frances Power Cobbe, wrote about a statute passed during the reign of Charles II (1660–85), 'which embodied the old Common Law, and authorized a man "to chastise his wife with any reasonable instrument" '.[23] She claimed that it was not repealed until 1829. This is inaccurate, which is strange, as Cobbe's writing was generally well-researched. Neither the seventeenth-century statute, nor the repealing legislation of 1829 can be found. With the exception of the Dobashes' *Violence Against Wives*,[24] none of the literature on wife-beating makes any mention of a statutory right to beat; and the Dobashes appear to have lifted the information straight from Cobbe's article.

Nevertheless, this phantom Caroline statute is interesting. It calls to mind another, more famous but equally elusive, legal authority – the 'rule of thumb'. It is said that, in 1782, 'a pedantic judge tried to revive the ancient doctrine that it was lawful for a husband to beat a wife, provided that the stick were no thicker than his thumb'.[25] In three cartoons which appeared in November of 1782, Sir Francis Buller is portrayed as 'Judge Thumb'. One of them is by the famous satirist, Gilray, and is entitled *Judge Thumb – or – Patent Sticks for Family Correction: Warranted Lawful*. It portrays a woman shrieking 'Murder!', and trying to escape from her husband who is beating her with a stick. The husband responds, 'Murder, hay? its Law you Bitch! its not bigger than my thumb.' In the background Judge Thumb is selling rods to the public.[26] In another of the prints, a document lying on the ground is inscribed, 'A Husband may Chastise his Wife with a stick the Size of his thumb. Coke.'

This is not necessarily a true story. Buller's famous pronouncement is not to be found in the law reports and, indeed, none of the cases which came before the King's Bench in Michaelmas Term of 1782 was likely to have provoked such a remark.[27] Nothing has been found in contemporary newspapers. It seems unlikely then that the statement was made in an official capacity. William Townsend suggested in his biography of Buller that it was 'an unguarded saying, which escaped from him unpremeditatedly'.[28] Another biographer, Edward Foss, refused to believe that he *had* expressed 'so ungallant an opinion'.[29] It is hard to know where the truth lies. Buller was an unpopular judge, known for his arrogance and inflexibility; 'in criminal cases he was sometimes considered prejudiced, severe and even cruel.'[30] However, in his *Nisi Prius*,[31] he deleted a reference to husbands and wives when he quoted Hawkins on the subject of special power relationships (such as master and servant), within which a certain amount of violence was considered justifiable.[32] Whatever the truth of the matter, his nickname stuck. Five years later, when he was vying (unsuccessfully) with Kenyon for the Chief Justiceship of the King's Bench, a cartoonist depicted him belabouring his rival with his 'Thumbstick'.[33]

It is said that under ancient Welsh law, a husband who beat a disrespectful wife was restricted to a maximum of 'three strokes with a rod the length of his forearm and the thickness of his middle finger'.[34] And Townsend tells of a Dr Marmaduke Coghill, a judge of the Prerogative Court for Ireland in the seventeenth century, who displayed a switch in court during a separation hearing and pronounced that moderate chastisement with an instrument of that size was 'within a husband's matrimonial privilege'.[35] But, beyond this, no legal corroboration for the rule of thumb can be found. And yet, the popular belief that some legal significance attached to the dimensions of the instrument used to beat a wife was a pervasive and persistent one.[36] In spite of the paucity of authoritative legal support, the 'reasonable instrument rule' had an air of legality about it. The fact that it survived for so long in popular mythology may have testified to the strength of the conviction that not only should wife-beating be legal, but that the question of reasonable severity should be one for the individual husband. A rule of thumb would, after all, have permitted the largest men with the largest thumbs to have used the biggest sticks and, therefore, inflict the severest beatings! The rule of thumb was, perhaps, a euphemism for no rule at all.

Challenges to the Right

All this is not to say that the existence of the husband's right to beat was never challenged. In fact, in *Sir Thomas Seymore's Case*,[37] one of the earliest authorities, Chief Justice Coke dissented from the majority view and denied that a husband possessed any right to give correction to his wife. *Lord Leigh's Case* in 1674[38] represented a more serious challenge. Lord Leigh and his wife quarrelled about a property settlement; she complained of 'severe usage, and of her *confinement*, and that she was in danger of her life'. A writ of *habeas corpus* was granted, obliging Lord Leigh to bring her into court, where she prayed the peace against him. Chief Justice Hale granted her security of the peace and held that the reasonable chastisement allowed for in *The Register* (a precursor of the *New Natura Brevium*) had not been intended as a licence to beat, but meant only 'admonition and confinement to the house, in case of her extravagance'.

This decision was in step with the times. Wife-beating was increasingly frowned upon in the seventeenth century for it jarred with the Protestant conception of the marital relationship. For the Puritans in particular, the inseparability of worldly and religious duties put the family at the centre of religious life; and the result was the sanctification of marriage and married love. The relationship between husband and wife was seen as a reflection of that between Christ and His Church. This meant that the husband was dominant, but it also imposed standards of behaviour on him. Also, the Puritans respected women as moral and religious personalities and this had implications for their status within the family. So Puritan doctrine imposed duties on husbands as well as on wives; husbands were expected to love their wives and be faithful to them and to treat them with consideration and respect.[39] These views were disseminated in sermons, conduct books and marriage manuals, and Matthew Hale, who was a religious man with strong Puritan sympathies, would certainly have been influenced by them.[40]

Clergy and moralists who advised husbands against wife-beating usually acknowledged that they were technically within their rights. The *Homily on Marriage* provides an example. One of a series published by the authority of Elizabeth I, it promised husbands great spiritual rewards if 'where thou mightst beat her, and yet for the fear of God thou wilt abstain and bear patiently her great offences'.[41]

Thomas Fuller thought that women were 'of a servile nature such as may be bettered by beating,' but nevertheless advised against it.[42] The preacher, William Whately, accepted that it was lawful for a husband to correct and punish his wife, but felt that only 'the utmost extremities of unwifelike carriage' ever justified violence.[43]

William Gouge, the author of the marriage manual *Domesticall Duties*, strongly disapproved of wife-beating, finding no authority for it in Scripture and considering it inappropriate that a man's

perpetuall bed-fellow, who hath power over his body, who is a ioynt parent of the children, a ioynt governor of the family, should be beaten by his hands. ... What if children or servants should know of it? ... can they respect her as a mother, or a mistresse who is under correction as well as they?

Nevertheless, it is clear that he did not regard wife-beating as illegal, for he suggested that

[i]f the case so stand as a wife must needs be beaten, it is fitter for an husband to referre the matter to a publike Magistrate ... and not to doe it with his owne hands.

On the whole, though, he preferred alternative forms of punishment: 'she may be restrained of libertie, denied such things as she most affecteth, be kept up, as it were, in hold'.[44]

There were some who went further and questioned the legality of the chastisement of wives. When the question was debated at Oxford University in 1608,[45] the arguments in support of the husband's right provoked a spirited response from William Heale, the chaplain of Exeter College. In a book entitled *An Apologie for Women*, he argued that, although husbands were undoubtedly superior to their wives, 'neither is the one so predominant, nor the other so servile, as that from them should proceede any other fruits, but of a roial protection, and loial subjection'. He said that there was no evidence that it was legal to beat a wife, and concluded that she might be admonished and reprehended, but never 'dealt withal with violent hands'.[46]

Although Hale C.J.'s rejection of violence was unequivocal, it is not at all clear that *Leigh* marked the demise of legal wife-beating. Many important legal writers ignored the decision. In Hawkins' 1716 *Pleas of the Crown*[47] and Burns' 1755 *Justice of the Peace*[48] the right of reasonable chastisement was maintained (albeit with a hint of uncertainty). As late as 1822, an edition of Comyns' *Digest of the Laws of England* claimed that 'in all proper cases [a husband] may use necessary coercion'.[49] But it was probably Bacon's *New Abridgment of the Law* which was most influential. Published in 1736, and described by Maine as 'our classical English Digest',[50] it contained the following passage:

The husband hath, by law, power and dominion over his wife, and may keep her by force within the bounds of duty, and may beat her, but not in a violent or cruel manner; for, in such case, or if he but threaten to beat her outrageously, or use her barbarously, she may bind him to the peace by suing a writ of *supplicavit* out of chancery.[51]

These words remained unchanged, right through to the seventh and final edition in 1832. They were to be frequently quoted;[52] to the extent, indeed, that one twentieth-century legal commentator thought that Bacon's *Abridgment* was the original source of the husband's right of chastisement.[53]

So, in spite of *Leigh*, the picture which legal and lay commentators painted of the law changed little; some questioned the legality of wife-beating but few denied it. It is not surprising, therefore, to find Sir William Blackstone reporting in 1765 that 'the lower rank of people who were always fond of the old common law, still claim, and exert their antient privilege'.[54] Daniel Defoe agreed that 'every vagabond thinks that he may cripple his wife at pleasure';[55] whilst Richard Steele wrote in the *Spectator*:

I can not deny but there are Perverse Jades that fall to Men's Lots, with whom it requires more than common Proficiency in Philosophy to be able to live, when these are joined to men of warm spirits, without Temper or Learning, they are frequently corrected with stripes; but one of our famous Lawyers is of opinion, That this ought to be used sparingly.[56]

Eighteenth-Century Judicial Practice

But what was actually happening in the courts? Practice probably varied; the uncertainty about the true state of the law would have left judges and magistrates free to impose their personal marital ideology upon those who came before them. The doctrine of moderate chastisement had not disappeared; Samuel Richardson recalled hearing Charles Talbot, when he was Solicitor-General (1726–33), arguing in the House of Lords that the 'law of England ... allows a man to give his wife *moderate correction*'.[57] The case concerned Sir Cleave Moore whose wife had left him on account of his cruelty. One day in 1716 he 'met with her in a Coach and took Possession of her'. He took her home, threatened her with life imprisonment and physically forced her to sign an agreement making over much of her wealth. She later tried to have the agreement set aside but it was held to be binding. The appeal to the House of Lords was unsuccessful.[58]

On the whole, though, there did seem to have been a change. It became extremely common in the eighteenth century for abused wives to swear the peace against their husbands. In addition to the numerous reported cases (mainly involving titled couples), King's Bench records reveal three or four instances a year of wives being granted security of the peace;[59] and there was probably a much greater number of women seeking help from the more accessible Justices of the Peace.

It seems that the remedy was available almost as a matter of course. I have not found a single instance, after *Bradley*, of an application being refused. It was standard form for women to claim that they went in 'fear of death or receiving some great bodily harm', which was, of course, consistent with the idea that chastisement was permissable if it stayed within the bounds of reasonableness. However, the court did not investigate the truth of women's claims, nor why their husbands had beaten them. Consider *Lord Vane's Case* in 1744. In 1737 Lady Vane went to the ecclesiastical courts, seeking a separation from her husband on grounds of his cruelty; but she was persuaded to abandon the suit in return for a private agreement permitting her to live apart from Lord Vane if she wished. They made another attempt at living together but he continued to abuse her and so she left him. In 1742, at Christmas time, he had her seized by five of his servants and brought to his house. She escaped after eleven days of confinement but subsequently heard that he had ordered a servant to seize her again and 'bring her home dead or alive'. She exhibited articles of the peace against him. Lord Vane went into court and demanded that the articles be discharged. He said that he had acted entirely within his rights:

[t]hat the husband has a right to seize his wife, to carry her home, and even to confine her if he thought proper. That by the common law he had power to govern, rule, and chastise her reasonably: and although she may sue a supplicavit in Chancery against her husband for cruelty, and to find sureties that he do not beat her or evil intreat her; yet even in that case there is a proviso, [covering reasonable chastisement].

The court was not interested. It held that

every person was entitled to exhibit articles of the peace for the security of his person, and to allow them was the constant course of the Court as a security against immediate danger. That it was not usual to inquire into the truth or circumstances of the facts charged in the articles but that the same must be received as true till the contrary appears upon a proper prosecution.[60]

So, if the wife was lying, she could be proceeded against on indictment for perjury but, provided that the allegations of abuse were considered sufficient to justify a fear of personal danger, articles of the peace would be granted. The husband's only hope was to argue that, on the face of the articles, a sufficient case had not been made out.[61]

Articles of the Peace

It has been emphasised that this free availability of articles of the peace did not mean that wife-beating was being treated as unlawful. Apart from anything else, breach of the peace is not in itself a criminal offence; a bind over is not a conviction.[62] Nevertheless, it clearly provided abused wives with a useful remedy.

It offered them a choice of courts. Working-class women could apply to the local magistrate or to the quarter sessions, while the better-off went to the King's Bench or the Court of Chancery. Women who could not face confronting their husbands in court might sue for a writ of *supplicavit*.[63]

Articles of the peace had at least the potential effectively to deter further abuse. The courts attempted to set the amount of the security demanded at a level that was meaningful for the individual husband; they considered both the severity of the abuse complained of, and the husband's occupation and financial means. As a result of this the figures varied widely, but the average recognisance was probably far in excess of the average fine for assault. An ordinary middle-class husband might be required to give security for the peace himself to the amount of £100, and find two sureties of £50 each.[64] For wealthier husbands, security of £1,000 and sureties of £500 were not unusual.[65] Some titled husband were required to find phenomenally large amounts. Lord Ilay was required to give a recognisance of £8,000 and find four sureties of £4,000 each;[66] while, in *The Countess of Strathmore's Case*, the recognisance was set at £10,000 and the two sureties at £5,000.

The Countess of Strathmore's Case[67] was heard in 1787 and concerned a wife who had come into court to exhibit articles of the peace for the second time. Shortly after the expiration of the previous articles, her husband, Andrew Robinson Bowes, had told her that a warrant had been issued against her. Under the pretence of taking her to Lord Mansfield's home at Caen Wood, he and a number of armed companions had carried her off to Strickland Castle in County Durham. Here she was detained and ill-treated until released by a writ of *habeas corpus*. Counsel for Bowes mustered a large number of precedents in an attempt to demonstrate that the amount of security demanded was excessive, but the court was unimpressed. He was guilty of 'as daring an outrage as ever was committed in a civilised country' and, in light of his station in life and the fact that articles were being exhibited for the second time, the most that the court was prepared to do was to substitute four sureties of £2,500 for the two sureties of £5,000.

Another wife who was obliged to return to court more than once was Countess Ferrers. Earl Ferrers was a 'homicidal maniac'[68] who subjected his wife and servants to constant violence and abuse. He told Mary Ferrers that 'he would rather Murder her than suffer her to be taken from him';[69] on one occasion he attempted to set fire to her bedroom and, on another, he had to be prevented from strangling her.[70] He held her prisoner in his house at Staunton Harold in Leicestershire and it was only with great difficulty that her brothers secured her release to enable her to swear the peace. Articles of the peace were granted in 1757 but, in 1758, Earl Ferrers broke his recognisance by drawing a pistol on her. (Her brother, William Meridith, had been threatened in similar fashion when attempting to serve a writ of *habeas corpus*.)[71] The Earl was brought before Lord Mansfield and commanded to give security himself of £5,000 and to find two sureties of £2,500 each. His consistently offensive behaviour had clearly tried the patience of the court; hints were dropped to the effect that 'it was necessary for [him] to give bail at the present, and not to pray time to do so, as the giving of it now was the only method he could take, if he expected to remain at liberty'. However, the court agreed to let his peruke-maker be bound for him until he could find a more acceptable alternative. The other surety was given by his mother.[72] Two years later he murdered his steward, lost an insanity defence and was executed and dissected at Tyburn.[73]

Another factor which was relevant to the effectiveness of the remedy was the term for which security was required. The courts were quite willing to tailor this term to the circumstances of the individual case. The general rule was that the security would be discharged at the end of one year if the offender had conducted himself peaceably during that period,[74] but the courts were not bound by this. Andrew Robinson Bowes was originally required to give security of the peace for fourteen years, for it was held that

this Court which has a general authority to preserve the peace, has a right to require such bail and for such a length of time as will best answer the ends of public justice.

It was eventually agreed that the period would be reduced to two years, but this was only done because criminal charges had been laid against Bowes in relation to the same events and his case was expected to be tried within that period. The judges emphasised their conviction that the original period would otherwise have been reasonable, and did not appear moved by Bowes' observation that the impossibility of procuring sureties for so long a period would have resulted in his lying in gaol for fourteen years.[75]

Before discharging articles the courts considered the likelihood of renewed abuse. In *Ex Parte King* a wife opposed her husband's request that a writ of *supplicavit* obtained against him twelve months earlier be discharged. Her husband had originally begun to abuse her as a result of a property dispute; her father had bequeathed her a large estate in Antigua and she was insistent that it had been intended for her separate use. This question had not yet been settled in court and she expressed

her great fears and apprehensions, if the *supplicavit* was discharged, her husband would compel her to give up her separate interest, or use her ill and carry her to Antigua, where, by means of his connections and estate, she would have no protection for her person.

King had neither struck nor threatened her during the preceding year, but the court refused to discharge the writ for 'here the wife is under the authority of the husband who has made a bad use of it, and the original cause of his ill-usage still subsists...'.[76] Finally, articles would rarely be discharged before the expiration of the prescribed term, even if the wife consented.[77]

The remedy had its disadvantages as well. A dependent wife who swore the peace against her husband took a certain risk. If he was imprisoned for failure to find sureties, or if he forfeited his recognisance as a result of breaking the articles, she might well suffer as much as he. In Daniel Defoe's words, it was 'revenging herself on herself'.[78] A more fundamental problem was that articles of the peace did not entitle a woman to live separately from her husband.[79] After accusing him of abuse in court, she was required to return home to him and, as the anonymous woman author of *The Hardships of the English Law in Relation to Wives* pointed out, a husband 'may revenge himself a thousand Ways not cognizable by the Law'.[80]

An abused husband could pray the peace in the same way as a wife.[81] In the 1655 edition of Dalton's *Countrey Justice*, this piece of information was followed by a few words of law-french: '*Et si el ne poit trouve Sureties, el serra commit ... and issint home poet est rid dun Shrew*',[82] that is, 'and if she cannot find sureties she will be imprisoned, and thus a man can get rid of a shrew'. As wives had no property of their own (something which is discussed at greater length later), they could not enter into personal recognisances. They had to find others to be bound on their behalf.[83] The author of *The Lawes Resolutions* suggested a way in which Dalton's ploy could be made to backfire. The abused wife was there advised to beat her husband back until he was driven to exhibit articles of the peace against her. As she had no property, the husband would be forced to give security for her himself. The wife should, thereupon, attack him once again and 'Let him known the price of it on God's name.'[84] The idea of the batterer being battered back and losing his money to boot is an attractive, albeit risky, one. However, it was a product of wishful thinking; a husband would never have been required to give security for his wife, when it was he who had exhibited articles against her.

Conclusion

To summarise, the *Leigh* decision did not eradicate the doctrine of reasonable chastisement. In the eighteenth and even the nineteenth century, legal abridgments proclaimed the continued existence of the right and there were almost certainly judges and magistrates who continued to countenance its exercise. But the situation had gradually begun to change; by the 1880s, legal textbook writers seemed agreed that the power of correction was a thing of the past. In the words of Montague Lush, the old doctrine 'scarcely require[d] notice'.[85]

The Right to Confine

The Cochrane Decision

The doctrine of reasonable confinement lasted a lot longer. In 1840 the Queen's Bench upheld 'the *general* right of the husband to the controul and custody of his wife'. The case was *Re Cochrane*. Cecilia Maria Cochrane had left her husband in 1836 and had spent the next four years living abroad. Alexander Cochrane applied for restitution of conjugal rights but she failed to respond to the ecclesisatical court's order. In 1840 Cecilia was induced to return to her old home by a communication from a Mr Warwick, an American who claimed to have owed her father money which he now wished to repay. When she arrived at her husband's lodgings, there was no Mr Warwick. Her husband locked the doors, nailed down the windows and refused to let her leave again. A writ of *habeas corpus* was brought on her behalf and the case was heard before Coleridge J.

Cecilia Cochrane was not guilty of any matrimonial misconduct. There was no lover in the picture. Since leaving her husband she had lived with her mother, and she had always behaved 'with the greatest propriety and prudence'. Coleridge J. began his judgment by acknowledging this. He did express unease about some Parisian masked balls she reputedly had attended but, in general, he accepted that she was not a threat to her husband's honour or property. However, this was irrelevant. Cecilia Cochrane had left her husband and had made it clear that she would do so again as soon as she got the chance. This could not be permitted.

Citing Bacon's *Abridgment* and Fitzherbert's *Natura Brevium*, Coleridge J. said that there could be

no doubt of the general dominion which the law of England attributes to the husband over the wife.... [I]t places the wife under the guardianship of the husband, and entitles him, for the sake of both, to protect her from the danger of unrestrained intercourse with the world, by enforcing cohabitation and a common residence.

He accepted that, by refusing to grant a writ of *habeas corpus*, he might be sentencing Mrs Cochrane to perpetual imprisonment, but said that '[c]ases of hardship will arise under any general rule'. He advised her to resolve cheerfully and frankly to perform the contract she had entered into, thereby making further confinement unnecessary.[86]

Cochrane was the main authority relied on by the Queen's Bench judges in *Jackson*, and by the counsel for the husband before the Court of Appeal. It was, of course, overruled by *Jackson*. Commentators writing after 1891 have tended to treat *Cochrane* as anachronistic ruling, a decision 'against the whole current of authority' and 'a retrograde step'.[87] It was labelled as the case which was 'responsible for the misapprehensions which have clouded the subject'.[88] But was this true?

The General Versus the Qualified Right

The *Cochrane* doctrine was not new. In 1718, in *Atwood* v. *Atwood*, a wife was refused a writ *de homine replegiando* (a remedy which was similar in effect to *habeas corpus*), on the ground that her husband had 'by law a right to the custody of her, and may, if he think fit, confine her; but he must not imprison her....'.[89]

In *R.* v. *Mary Mead* in 1758 Lord Mansfield C.J. declared that a husband had 'a right to the custody of his wife; and whoever detains her from him, violates that right; and he has a right to seize her wherever he finds her'.[90]

But other cases seemed to support a narrower doctrine. We have seen that, in *Lord Leigh's Case*, Hale C.J. sanctioned 'admonition and confinement to the house', but not at the husband's discretion; a wife might be confined 'in case of her extravagance'. There are two possible interpretations of this. One is that confinement was permissible only as a preventive measure; the other is that it could also be used as a punishment for extravagance. Whichever interpretation is the true one, it seems that the right of confinement envisaged by Hale C.J. arose only in the event of actual or probable misbehaviour.

This position was supported by the 1721 decision of *R.* v. *Lister*, sometimes known as *Lady Rawlinson's Case*.[91] Lady Rawlinson and her husband had lived apart for a number of years when he made up his mind to take her back. Apparently his aim was to make her part with some of her separate wealth. He seized her one day as she was coming out of church, forced her into his coach, and carried her off to the Mint. This was an area of Southwark which had long provided sanctuary for debtors. Although its legal status as a sanctuary had been removed in 1697, it continued as an effective debtors' sanctuary until the 1720s because its inhabitants, by sheer force of numbers, were able to intimidate officers and prevent arrests.[92] Here Lady Rawlinson was kept 'in custody under a strict confinement', until her relations discovered her whereabouts and applied for a writ of *habeas corpus*.

The court set her at liberty. It held that

the coercive power which the husband has over his wife ... is not a power to confine her; for by the law of England she is intitled to all reasonable liberty if her behaviour is not very bad.

In another report of the case, Chief Justice Pratt elaborated on the meaning of 'bad behaviour':

where the wife will make an undue use of her liberty; either, by squandering away the husband's estate, or going into lewd company; it is lawful for the husband, in order to preserve his honour and estate, to lay such a wife under a restraint. But where nothing of that appears, he cannot justify the depriving her of her liberty.[93]

So what was the true extent of the husband's power? Did he possess a general right to the custody of his wife, or a limited right to confine her as means of preventing or punishing misbehaviour? Doubtless many found the latter version more palatable. In *Jackson* itself there were hints that an adulterous wife might legitimately be restrained. If it was the more limited doctrine which predominated in the eighteenth century then *Cochrane*, in which Coleridge J. unequivocally denied that the right was restricted to cases of misconduct, was indeed a retrograde decision.

(1) Private Separation Agreements

However, there was a complicating factor; and that was the emergence, in the 1650s, of private articles of separation.[94] At this date marriages were literally indissoluble; assuming that the union had been validly contracted, there was no escape. Between 1690 and 1857, when judicial divorce was finally introduced, a marriage could be formally terminated by a personal Act of Parliament, but this was a hugely expensive procedure and was only available to someone whose spouse had committed adultery. The ecclesiastical courts could grant a separation 'from bed and board' (divorce *a mensa et thoro*), but not an absolute divorce; and even these separations were difficult to come by; proof of adultery or extreme cruelty was required. Thus, many couples were thrown upon their own devices; and the result of this was the private separation deed.

The function of such a deed was to enable the couple to avoid the legal consequences of marriage. These consequences are discussed at greater length later. Suffice it to say for the moment that, for the wife, they were extensive: the common law decreed that her property passed to her husband; she could not sue or be sued independently of her husband; she could not enter into contracts in her own name. As a result, she could not own even the bare necessities of life; nor could she enter into a binding agreement to buy them. At common law her husband had a duty to maintain her but, as she could not sue, she could not enforce this duty by action if he failed to fulfil it.

However, she could enter into contracts as her husband's agent. When she pledged her husband's credit for 'necessaries' — mainly household goods and services — it was presumed that she had her husband's authority to do so. If it could be shown that the goods or services were, indeed, necessary then the husband was obliged to pay the resultant bills. He could only escape if he could demonstrate that he had forbidden his wife to pledge his credit or that he had forbidden tradespeople to give her credit. However, if he was failing in his duty to maintain his wife, this escape route would be closed to him; in this situation the presumption that she was acting as his agent became irrebuttable. Of course, from the wife's point of view, this was a woefully inadequate remedy; it depended entirely on the willingness of vendors to advance credit and a husband who refused to fulfil his obligations towards his wife was hardly likely to be regarded as a satisfactory debtor.[95]

However, from an early date, equity, specifically the device of the trust, had provided a way of avoiding the wife's common-law disabilities. Although a wife could not hold property personally, it could be settled on her, that is, held for her benefit by a trustee. Subject to the terms of the settlement, a wife could enjoy and control this 'separate property' in much the same way as a *feme sole* or single woman.[96]

A separation deed was a contract between the husband and (usually) trustees for the wife. In it the husband agreed to provide the wife with an annual maintenance allowance and, in return, the trustees agreed, on behalf of the wife, to indemnify him from any future responsibility for her debts. This took the equitable developments described above a step further, and gave the wife not only the rights but also the responsibilities of property. It sought to remove the husband's obligation to pay debts that she contracted in his name and to make her maintenance allowance liable instead.

As time went on, these agreements became more and more detailed until, ultimately, they purported to provide comprehensive protection from the duties and obligations of marriage. Eighteenth-century articles of separation commonly contained the following provisions:

that [the husband] shall not nor will compel [his wife] to cohabit or live with him by any ecclesiastical censure or proceedings or otherwise howsoever; and that she ... shall be absolutely, and to all intents and purposes whatsoever, freed and discharged from the power, command, will, restraint, authority, and government of [the husband] and that he shall not nor will at any time hereafter, by any cause or under any pretense whatsoever, sue or prosecute any person or persons for receiving, harbouring, protecting, or assisting [her], or ill-treat or use, or offer any violence, force, or restraint to [her] person ... or molest, interrupt, or disturb her in her way of living, or in her liberty or freedom of going to, or staying in, or returning from such place or places as she shall think fit.[97]

As separation deeds permitted things which the law did not permit, the courts were understandably dubious about them. The ecclesiastical courts never recognised their validity. This meant that a husband could change his mind about the separation at any time and sue for restitution of conjugal rights. Alternatively, he might wait until his wife had been tempted into adultery and then seek a separation *a mensa et thoro*. This would relieve him of the obligation of maintaining her, for adulterous wives were not entitled to any alimony. In contrast, the Chancery and common-law judges would often enforce separation agreements; but it was always a controversial area and they were constantly changing their minds about the validity of particular provisions. There were times, for example, when the secular courts would grant an injunction to prevent breach of a promise not to litigate in the ecclesiastical courts; at other times they would not.

R. v. *Lister* involved a deed of separation. Lady Rawlinson had come to the marriage with a substantial separate estate but had eventually agreed to make a large part of it over to Lister in return for an annual maintenance allowance and his agreement that they would live separately. The court's decision to set her free after he seized and confined her had a great deal to do with the existence of this agreement. There was 'no colour for what he did in this case, there being a separation by consent'. The court held that '[a]n agreement between husband and wife to live separate, and that she shall have a separate maintenance, shall bind them both until they both agree to cohabit again. . . .'.[98]

However, the common-law courts had great difficulty accepting that a wife could be financially independent and, in particular, that she could be liable for her own debts. There was no guarantee during much of the eighteenth century that these provisions in separation agreements would be enforced. A wife might fritter away her separate maintenance and then, if she could find tradespeople who were ignorant of the separation, revert to pledging her husband's credit for goods. The husband might well have been forced to pay up. Similarly, if she became a pauper, he might have found himself forced by the parish to maintain her. Hence the proviso in *Lister*, permitting a husband to confine his estranged wife if she misused her liberty by squandering away his estate.

A wife who kept 'lewd company' was also liable to lose her negotiated freedom. It was very common for separation agreements to include provisions which apparently granted the parties freedom to commit adultery, but the courts repeatedly denied their validity. Regardless of what he had agreed to at the time of separation, a cuckolded husband would usually be permitted to seek a parliamentary divorce and to sue his wife's lover for damages (a criminal conversation action). Alternatively, it seems, he could preserve his honour by seizing her and locking her up.

Lady Vane (the same Lady Vane who had sworn the peace against her husband in 1744) committed both of the cardinal sins. She 'grew very expensive, and kept bad company at Fernhall in Essex'. Her husband responded by taking 'forcible possession' of her home. She attempted to have him prosecuted under the criminal law, on the basis that he had broken both the peace and their 1737 articles of separation, but the court refused to let her lay an information.[99]

There was a period in the second half of the eighteenth century when the common-law courts were much more accepting of private separation agreements. This was largely due to the influence of Lord Mansfield, who was Lord Chief Justice from 1756 to 1788, and who 'never liked law so well as when it [was] like equity'.[100] This attitude was reflected in the language used in confinement cases. In 1758 John Wilkes, later to make his name as a radical politician, sued out a writ of *habeas corpus* against his mother-in-law. He hoped to force her to hand over his wife, Mary Mcad, who had lived with her since the couple separated. Mary and Wilkes had not been well-suited and, in 1756, 'in consideration of a great sum which she gave him out of her separate estate', he had agreed that she should live separately, have an annual allowance and occasionally be allowed to see her daughter. In attempting to get her back, he was doubtless hoping to benefit from some money which she was due to inherit. When the case was heard, Lord Mansfield began, as we have already seen, by proclaiming the husband's right to the custody of his wife. He said that a husband had a right to seize his wife wherever he found her. But then he continued: 'But he may waive this right, as he has done here, by the articles of separation, which are a renunciation of his marital right to seize her...'. Mary Mead was told that she was 'at full liberty to go where, and to whom she pleased'.[101]

Another separated couple were Anne and Alexander Edgar. Anne's father had left his property in trust for her, 'not having any confidence in her husband, who treated her with great severity'. Eventually, articles of separation were drawn up, providing that Edgar would get £3,000 and, in return, would abandon all claims to her property. But, later, he seized and confined her, 'alleging that she was a lunatick, and using her as no man can by law use his wife'. A writ of *habeas corpus* was applied for on Anne's behalf. Lord Kenyon held that

[t]he husband has no claim after the articles of separation.... Unless she has done something notorious to destroy the articles, it is settled that the husband has renounced all right to the wife.

To Anne, he said, 'you are now a free woman; you may go where you please'.[102]

What these cases tell us is that the husband's 'general dominion' over his wife survived the eighteenth century intact. If a wife was abused by her husband, she could be brought into court on a writ of *habeas corpus* to enable her to swear the peace against him. However, she could not be permitted to leave him; the husband might be bound over to keep the peace, but he was entitled to take his wife home with him. However, a husband who had entered into a separation agreement was in quite a different position. Depending on the terms of the agreement and on the willingness of the courts to enforce them, his marital authority might be severely reduced, even non-existent. If he retained a right to seize and confine his wife, it could only be exercised to prevent or punish misbehaviour.

(2) Unreasonable Confinement

There were some circumstances in which, even in the absence of articles of separation, the courts baulked at enforcing the wife's duty of cohabitation. Gabriel D'Vebre had his wife, Deborah, committed to a private madhouse. In 1761 her relatives sued out a writ of *habeas corpus* against Turlington, the keeper of this institution and, as a result, the court ordered an independent medical inspection. The doctor found 'no sort of reason to suspect that she was or had been disordered in her mind: on the contrary, he found her to be very sensible and very cool and dispassionate.' She was brought into court and given her freedom, albeit temporarily: 'She desired not to go back to the madhouse: and the Court would not permit her husband to take her, under the present circumstances of danger apprehended by her from him.'[103]

In 1744 Sir Francis Head attempted to lock his wife in a madhouse. Lady Head obtained a writ of *supplicavit*, but this did not put a stop to his threats. Lord Chancellor Hardwicke emphasised that the writ did not entitle her to leave her husband, but admitted that it was 'an excuse at least for keeping from him for some time, till their passions might be supposed to subside...'.[104]

These men had clearly gone beyond the bounds of acceptable behaviour. It will be remembered that, in *Atwood*, a distinction was drawn between confinement of a wife and imprisonment; the one was permissible, the other not. Counsel in *Jackson* attempted to argue that the distinction turned on whether the wife was shut up in a single room, or whether she was given 'the free run of the house', but the judges poured scorn on him. This refinement was too great for their intellects, they said. Lord Esher M.R. and Lord Halsbury L.C. both considered that Mrs Jackson had suffered imprisonment, in spite of her absolute freedom to roam her husband's apartments.[105]

However, there *was* a real difference between being locked in one's house or bedroom and being chained to the floor in a madhouse. In 1728 a wife was allowed to bring criminal charges against a husband who had put her into a madhouse without cause. This was not the first such occurrence; she had previously been released by *habeas corpus* from another mental institution. Counsel for the husband said that, as the wife had been guilty of adultery,

> it was certain the husband might justify confining her in his own house, and for the same reason in another person's house, if it was not a mad-house; and they said, they could not see, how its being a mad-house could make such difference.

However, the court could. They said that

> it would be a thing of dangerous consequences to let such a matter as this pass without taking notice of it in a pretty severe manner ... a man might confine his wife in his own house for proper reasons; but they ... would never allow of such things as this.[106]

Clearly, disposing of wives in madhouses was very much in vogue in the eighteenth century. The *Gentleman's Magazine* told of husbands who did not even pretend that their wives were insane; one 'frankly declared that he considered the house as a kind of bridewell, or house of correction'.[107] The practice was possible because, until the 1770s, private madhouses were unregulated. Basically, they were

> squalid private prisons which, as long as the fees were paid, would accept anyone and keep them indefinitely behind bars, regardless of their mental condition or the motives of the persons who order their confinement.[108]

Legislation in 1774 introduced licensing, record-keeping and inspection systems and ensured that, henceforth, patients could only be admitted on the order of a doctor.

So the picture that emerges is that of a man whose right to the custody of his wife was absolute, unless he forfeited it in one of two ways. First, he might enter into a formal separation agreement. Once done, this prevented him from exercising his right of confinement except in the context of certain kinds of misbehaviour. Blackstone created the impression in his *Commentaries* that this limitation applied generally; he said that 'the courts of law [would] still permit a husband to restrain a wife of her liberty, in case of any gross misbehaviour'[109] and made no mention of articles of separation. However, the reported cases suggested otherwise. Secondly, a husband might exercise his powers unwisely and create a public scandal. In *Cochrane, Lister* was distinguished on the basis that it involved violence and actual imprisonment, and because Lady Rawlinson had been seized for an improper purpose.[110] A husband who was discreet and kept his marital disputes within the four walls of his own home could probably do pretty much what he wanted.

The difference between a general and a limited right of confinement should not be exaggerated. The idea of reasonable confinement, like that of reasonable chastisement, presented measurement and policing problems. A woman who believed that she was being unreasonably confined was at her husband's mercy unless she could get herself into court to have the question adjudged. A lot depended, therefore, on the effectiveness of *habeas corpus*. At common law the remedy was plagued by procedural defects. There was uncertainty, for example, about whether a writ could be issued in vacation, and there were considerable problems with enforcement. These difficulties had been addressed by the Habeas Corpus Act of 1679, but that Act only applied to people who had been imprisoned for alleged criminal offences.[111]

In 1758 a Bill was proposed which would have extended the benefits of the 1679 Act to civil cases; but it was rejected. There were many reasons for this, but one of them is of particular interest:

It is highly expedient ... in many cases, more especially for the sake of family government, that persons in subordinate capacities should be subject to reasonable confinement, by the authority of those to whom they are under immediate subjection, as wives to their husbands, children to their parents, and servants to their masters.

If the provisions of the Habeas Corpus Act are indiscriminately extended to all cases whatever, it may happen that a wife, under just restraint lest she should violate the honour of her family, may by means of this writ, procure her enlargement, and throw herself into the arms of a profligate adulterer.[112]

Lord Hardwicke grumbled that the proposed changes

would put it into the power of a great number of people ... to force husbands to bring up their wives ... from the remotest parts of his majesty's dominions at their own expence, without the least satisfaction from the persons who make such application, though there should be found not the least grievance in the case.[113]

Apparently parliamentarians were prepared to trust husbands to exercise their powers justly.

The 1758 proposals were not enacted until 1816 and, even then, they faced considerable opposition.[114] Serjeant Onslow, the promoter of the 1816 Bill, was obliged to hammer home the inadequacies of the common law:

The learned sergeant then adverted to the conduct of Earl Ferrers, who had disobeyed a writ of Habeas Corpus, returnable in vacation, which was sued out for the purpose of procuring the liberty of his lady. When they considered the paroxisms of passion to which that unfortunate nobleman was subject, they must conclude, that the care of Providence, and not the perfection of the law, had saved her. Another case was that of Lady Strathmore. Here, too, the writ was returnable in vacation. The consequence was, that a long period had elapsed before Mr Bowes was compelled to give up her ladyship.[115]

Notice how the examples he chooses are of husbands who were generally acknowledged to have overstepped the mark.

(3) The Proper Use of the *Habeas Corpus* Writ

Another way in which critics tried to diminish the significance of *Cochrane* was to say that its authority had been weakened by *R.* v. *Leggatt*. This was an 1852 decision and it concerned a woman called Anne Sandilands. Anne was not on good terms with her husband and so had chosen to live with Mr Leggatt, her son. In an attempt to get her back, her husband sued out a writ of *habeas corpus* against Leggatt. It will be immediately apparent that this was very different from most of the cases we have considered up to now. This man was attempting to use the *habeas corpus* writ to take someone into custody rather than release them from it; Anne was residing with Leggatt voluntarily. However, *habeas corpus* was frequently used in child custody disputes and, in that context, the presence or absence of restraint was regarded as irrelevant. The courts were not interested in where the child wanted to be, but in who ought to have the care of it.[116] Alfred Sandilands hoped that the same principle might be applied here:

It is admitted that there is no coercion. But to the statement that the wife is living with her son of her own free will the answer is that she cannot be considered to have a will apart from that of her husband, any more than a child of tender years can have a will apart from that of its parent.

The court rejected this analogy. Lord Campbell C.J. did not criticise *Cochrane*. He said that the question of whether a husband had a right to the custody of his wife was not one for that court. But, if he did have such a right, it differed from the right that a parent had over his child. A husband did not have a right to the custody of his wife in the way that a parent had a right to the custody of his child. *Habeas corpus* was not available, therefore, unless Anne Sandilands was being unjustly deprived of her liberty; and that was not the case.[117]

This was completely in line with authority. Husbands had attempted this manoeuvre in the past and it had always failed. The reasons given for the failure varied. In *Mary Mead*, as we have seen, the court focused on the articles of separation. In *Anne Gregory's Case*[118] the focus was on the husband's extreme violence. Anne and Abraham Gregory had run off together when she was just fourteen. Her mother was opposed to the match, but the fear of illegitimate offspring quickly made her relent. She consented to their marriage and even set her son-in-law up in business. But Gregory was a drunkard and quickly ran into debt. He began to beat Anne. She lost her first baby because he kicked her in the stomach and the second was born dead because he gave her venereal disease during the pregnancy. He forced her to beg money from her mother for him, threatening to kick her about the streets if she refused. She fled to her mother, who arranged for her to be spirited away to France. Gregory sought a writ of *habeas corpus*, claiming that his wife had been seduced away from him by 'Art and Management', but the court refused to order her relatives to deliver her up. Rather, she was granted articles of the peace and was told that 'she was at liberty to go where she thought proper.' An officer of the court was despatched to ensure her safe return from Westminster Hall.

However, in other cases, the court simply explained that it did not have the power to do what it was being asked to do. In 1721, in *R. v. Clarkson*, it refused to order a woman's guardians to deliver her up to a man claiming to be her husband:

We have nothing to do to order her to go with [the man], but only to see that she is under no illegal restraint: all we can do is, to declare that she is at her liberty to go where she pleases.[119]

Similarly, in *Frances Harford's Case*[120] and *R. v. Wiseman, Ex Parte Newton*,[121] the court's sole concern was to discover whether the wife was being kept away from her husband against her will.

The only case in which the court seemed at all inclined to grant the husband's application was *R. v. James Winton*. Winton was Margaret Greygoose's lover, and the two had lived together adulterously for some time. However, by 1792, the date of the court action, their relationship had changed. Margaret had resumed cohabitation with her husband for a short period, but Winton had induced her to return to him by threatening to publish an account of her conduct. Her husband believed that she was being detained against her will. This, then, was an illegal imprisonment situation to which the *habeas corpus* remedy could be straightforwardly applied.[122]

It may seem hard to reconcile these cases with *Cochrane* and its antecedents. If a wife escaped from her husband, the common law courts would not return her; but if he seized her again, they would not set her free. How is this to be interpreted?

On a practical level, the *habeas corpus* writ did not lend itself to the business of restoring runaway wives. Although the requirement for actual restraint was dispensed with in child custody cases, the remedy still notionally rested on the idea of relieving an improper detention.[123] A child who was happy to stay where it was could be ignored on the basis of its deficient understanding. With adult women, this was more difficult.

And, of course, the gaps in the common law were filled by the ecclesiastical law; as Lord Campbell remarked several times in *Leggatt*, the abandoned husband had the writ for restitution of conjugal rights at his disposal. Until 1884, these writs were enforced by attachment: the wife was imprisoned until she agreed to return to cohabitation.[124] We can only guess at husbands' reasons for attempting to use *habeas corpus* instead. The most likely one is that they were afraid of sparking off prolonged litigation in the ecclesiastical courts, as their wives made (perhaps well-founded) counter-allegations of adultery and cruelty. Another possibility is that the temporal authorities were unenthusiastic about enforcement; Mrs Cochrane, for example, had succeeded in remaining at liberty until her husband decided to take matters into his own hands. Finally, many husbands who seized their wives had an ulterior motive. The plan was to bully her into parting with her separate estate and a prison was perhaps not the best environment for this. A man could bring his powers of persuasion to bear much more effectively in the privacy of his own home.

The end result of the common law position was a practice of non-intervention in marital disputes. Wives were left to their fleeing and husbands to their seizing without the help or the hindrance of the law. This may, on the surface, appear evenhanded, but the effect, of course, was to hand power to the physically and psychologically dominant partner – usually the husband.

(4) THE PRICE DECISION

A final reason for questioning the popular portrayal of *Cochrane* as a maverick ruling is the fact that it was strongly confirmed twenty years later in the little-discussed case of *In Re Price*.

Price tells just one part of the fascinating story of the Nottidge sisters and their involvement with a bizarre religious group, the Agapemonites.[125] The founder of the 'Agapemone' was one Henry James Prince, a Church of England clergyman who had become acquainted with Harriet Nottidge (later Mrs Price) and her unmarried sisters, Agnes, Clara and Louisa, when he took up a curacy close to their home in Suffolk in 1842. Prince, who believed that God had appointed him to make His nature more perfectly known to men, proceeded to acquire a great influence over these women and, for a number of years, the family followed him around the country in order to benefit from his religious teaching.

In 1845 in Brighton, he summoned Harriet, Agnes and Clara and told them that they could give great glory to God by marrying themselves to three of his followers, Price, Thomas and Cobbe. This they did, without the knowledge of their mother, and dressed all in black at Prince's request. None of the sisters had their (considerable) property settled on themselves before the group-marriage, and most of it ended up in Prince's pockets. It seems that Agnes, at least, was aware of the importance of securing a separate estate. She discussed the subject with Thomas, who assured her that the idea was 'very agreeable to [his] own feelings', but said that

God will not have it so; He shows me that the principle is entirely contrary to God's word, and altogether at variance with that confidence which is to exist between us, who are 'one spirit'.

Prince began professing the belief that Judgement Day had passed: 'Jesus had now left the mercy-seat, the door of mercy was shut.' Sinners who had not already been saved, could now never be saved. All private and public prayer had, therefore, become useless. He instructed the sisters that there was no longer any occasion for their reading the Bible, 'as their husbands were now their Bibles, and that through their husbands only they would know the will of God, as made known to them by Prince'.

The sisters, their husbands and Prince lived together in variety of places and, in 1847, they settled in a large building in Bridgewater, which they called the *Agapemone*. Beneath a flag inscribed with the words 'Oh Hail, Holy Love', bloodhounds prowled, guarding the institution against intruders. Followers of both sexes regularly engaged in athletics in the grounds, a fact which judges made much of when the organisation came to their attention.

By this time Agnes had left. She had quickly become disillusioned and had come into conflict with Prince when she tried to persuade her husband to leave him. She had been alarmed to discover that her younger sister, Louisa, was also falling under Prince's spell. The tension became worse when Prince discovered that Agnes was pregnant; he seems to have envisaged 'purely spiritual' marriages between the sisters and his followers. Thomas informed her that the pregnancy was the result of her rebelliousness and the community ostracised her. She went home to her relatives.

Some years later, Thomas attempted to kidnap her child and a custody battle ensued. A father at this time had the sole right to the custody of his children; the common law courts recognised no rights in the mother, even when the father was dead, or of bad character. However, the courts of equity proceeded on the principle that the primary consideration was the welfare of the child and, in some cases, would refuse the father custody.[126] In this case the court decided that a man holding opinions which were

noxious to society, adverse to civilisation, opposed to the usages of Christianity, contrary (in the case of prayer at least) to the express commands of the New Testament, and finally, pernicious in the highest degree to the young person unhappy enough to be imbued with them

was disqualified for the guardianship of an English child. They instructed that the boy be left in his mother's custody until some other proper person could be appointed as his guardian.

Agnes was right to have feared for her sister, Louisa. She soon became a follower and began to make Prince gifts of money. Her male relatives suspected that she was on the point of making over all her property to him and so they seized her and placed her in a madhouse where she was kept for eighteen months. She was then discharged by the order of the Lunacy Commissioners and later succeeded in obtaining civil damages. No sooner had she been released than she did, in fact, make over her entire fortune to Prince. However, ten years later, after her death, her family succeeded in persuading the courts that the gift had been made under an undue influence, and it was set aside.

Harriet, like Louisa, remained faithful, but her husband did not. By 1860, Price had seceded from the *Agapemone* and wanted Harriet to accompany him. When she refused, he 'removed her by stratagem and detained her by force in his own house'. A writ of *habeas corpus* was applied for on her behalf. Baron Wilde's judgment was short but emphatic. He said that if Harriet were in improper custody, then she would certainly be entitled to her liberty

but *prima facie*, the proper residence of a wife is with her husband.... This is not an application by the husband to obtain the custody of his wife. He has it: and as ... the conjugal rights remain unaffected, he is entitled to it. And if he believes, as is assigned, that she intends to leave him to reside in an improper place, he has a right to restrain her. She must, therefore, return to her husband.[127]

So, Harriet was handed over to Price, a man whom she had only agreed to marry because Prince had commanded it.

The Nottidge sisters' real enemy was their legal status as women and wives. The Agapemonites and their male relatives both used it to deprive them of self-determination.

The Abused Wife's Options

Up to this point, a small number of legal remedies have been examined in considerable detail. It is now appropriate to recap, and also to fill the picture out a little more. What were the abused wife's options?

One 'option', of course, was just to put up with it, and this is probably what the majority of wives did. Many others will have relied on non-legal help, the intervention of family and neighbours, for example. However, we are concerned mainly with the law, for the kinds of legal remedies that existed, their availability and their effectiveness, indicate how seriously society took the problem.

The remedy most commonly sought by the abused wife was security of the peace. Its advantages were obvious. It was accessible: it was available from Justices of the Peace as well as in the King's Bench and in the Court of Chancery; a wife who had been imprisoned could use *habeas corpus* to get herself into court. It was freely granted: from the eighteenth century onwards it seems never to have been refused. It was also affordable: if a husband made it necessary for his wife to exhibit articles of peace against him, she could pledge his credit for the cost of it; it was he who would have to pay the lawyer's bill.[128] On the other hand, it was rarely of assistance to the woman who felt that she had to get away from her husband. Unless her husband had agreed to a separation or had been guilty of some excess, such as locking her in a madhouse, the court would expect her to accompany him home after she had prayed the peace against him.

Wives also pursued criminal prosecutions, particularly after 1828, when summary jurisdiction was extended to common assault and battery.[129] Henceforth, abusers could be convicted and sentenced by the magistrates, without the need for a possibly lengthy jury trial. Before long, the magistrates' courts were inundated by, mainly working-class, abused wives.[130]

However, the higher courts seemed to exude an aura of disapproval when wives asked for more than the customary security of the peace. In 1836 Mary Godmond indicted her husband for assaulting and imprisoning her. He was convicted and sentenced to twelve months imprisonment and a fine of £50. The attorney she hired had refused to carry on with the prosecution unless money was advanced, but she had managed to persuade her brother to pay him. The brother subsequently sued her husband for reimbursement, but was unsuccessful. The court found it

impossible to say that, under any circumstances, a prosecution of the husband is necessary for the wife.... If she apprehends ill-treatment from him, she has another mode of proceeding open to her, by exhibiting articles of the peace.[131]

So articles of the peace counted as 'necessaries', but criminal prosecutions did not. This meant that wives had to find the money themselves and the figures involved could be substantial. Mary Godmond's attorney's bill was £115, an amount which a dependent wife might have difficulty mustering even today. A man whose wife had no separate wealth effectively had nothing to fear beyond the very minor penalties which could be inflicted summarily.[132] It seems that protecting abused wives was one thing, but punishing abusive husbands was another. The courts may no longer have recognised a husband's right to beat his wife, but they had not advanced so far as to recognise *the wife's right not to be beaten.*

What of the wife set on permanent escape? One possibility was a private separation agreement. But this, of course, required the husband's agreement and, as we have seen, the freedom it provided was always precarious. Divorce was not really an option. Judicial divorce did not exist until 1857[133] and, for a woman, a parliamentary divorce was virtually unattainable. Only four women ever succeeded in having their Bills passed. Two were based on incestuous adultery, and two on bigamous adultery. A Bill based on adultery and cruelty was rejected, even though plain adultery frequently sufficed when the petitioner was a man.[134]

A wife's only real hope was to petition the ecclesiastical courts for a separation *a mensa et thoro* on grounds of cruelty. This was by no means an ideal solution: the bond of matrimony remained undissolved; she could not remarry; all the common law disabilities attendant on wifehood continued to apply. On the other hand, it enabled her to live apart in the face of her husband's objections, and entitled her to regular alimony payments.[135]

However, 'cruelty' was strictly interpreted. Until the late eighteenth century, the courts required severe and repeated physical violence which posed a threat to life or limb. In *Holmes* v. *Holmes* in 1755, a wife failed to establish cruelty, even though her husband had once come to her with two male friends

and swore he would lie with her in presence of said men; and they said he was her husband, and had a right to do so, and they would hold her for him to lie with her; whereupon she got out of the window, over a palisade, and over to the next house, whither he and the said two men followed her, and he there pulled off her cap, and dragged her by the hair of her head, and attempted to drag her home, but was prevented.

In the judges' opinion, nothing had been charged here

but words, except the single fact of his dragging her by the hair ... it was not suggested that he had ever beat her or put her in any danger while they lived together.'[36]

In addition, the violence had to be unjustified. A wife who provoked her husband, by nagging him or by neglecting her wifely duties, would be left to seek her remedy 'in the change of her own manners'.[37]

The definition of cruelty was only very gradually relaxed. By the beginning of the nineteenth century, threats of violence would sometimes suffice; and, in the middle of that century, the idea of mental cruelty began to develop.

For many wives, there was no legal avenue of escape. Such a wife either stayed with her abusive husband or, if she had the courage and the opportunity, she took matters into her own hands and fled. If she succeeded in making her escape, the common law courts would not assist her husband in recovering her. However, he could seek restitution of conjugal rights in the ecclesiastical courts; or, alternatively, he could take her back by force.

A wife's chances of escaping abuse by any of the means discussed above were significantly reduced if she lacked money, helpful friends and relatives or legal awareness. The latter, at least, seems to have been fairly widespread. People were interested in the law; legal pamphlets circulated widely and newspapers contained regular and detailed coverage of court actions. Londoners, in particular, were well-informed,[138] but they did not have a monopoly on legal *savoir-faire*. A 1775 affidavit describes an imprisoned Mildred Fenton, peering through the barred window of her husband's Yorkshire home, and issuing instructions to her relatives: '[F]or God's sake go immediately to London and apply to Lord Mansfield for I am confined here and my life is in danger.'[139]

Conclusion

What this chapter attempts to demonstrate is that the *Jackson* judgments were misleading. They created the impression that the outcome of the case was a foregone conclusion. It was not. There was clear, strong and reasonably current authority for Edmund Jackson's position. On the strength of this authority, legal textbook writers had been assuring their readers, right up until 1891, that a husband was entitled to 'coerc[e] his wife into domestic habits'.[140] *Cochrane* may have represented a tightening up, but it was not an anachronistic decision; or, at least, not as regards its substance. What *was* new in *Cochrane* was the tone and the language. It was the rhetoric in Coleridge J.'s judgment, the inflexible attachment to principle, which set it apart from the eighteenth-century case law. But, on the other hand, these things made it consistent with developments elsewhere in nineteenth-century family law. The Mansfield period had been followed by an extremely conservative reaction; Jamil Zainaldin, writing about child custody law, has said that the 'nineteenth-century English judges adopted a patriarchal paradigm of family relations',[141] and Susan Staves has observed the same phenomenon in the area of private separation agreements.[142] We are faced, then with two questions. First, what produced this shift? And, secondly, what happened in the second half of the nineteenth century to produce the much more radical shift represented by *Jackson*? These questions will be addressed in Chapters 3 and 4 respectively. First, however, we must consider the basis of the husband's right to beat and confine in more depth.

2

Wife-Beating, Coverture and the Power Principle

Introduction

In his influential eighteenth-century *Commentaries on the Law of England*, Sir William Blackstone explained that the husband's right of chastisement and confinement arose as a consequence of coverture:

For, as [the husband] is to answer for [his wife's] misbehaviour, the law thought it reasonable to intrust him with this power of restraining her, by domestic chastisement, in the same moderation that a man is allowed to correct his apprentices or children; for whom the master or parent is also liable in some cases to answer.[1]

'Coverture' is used here as a collective label for the legal disabilities attendant on wifehood. Some of these have already been touched upon and they will be examined in closer detail in the course of this chapter. Suffice it to say at this stage that the wife's disabilities could have serious legal implications for the husband. In outline: he was bound by contracts which she made in his name; he was liable jointly with her for her torts; and he could be held criminally responsible for crimes which she committed in his presence. As he was liable to be held legally responsible for his wife's conduct it was right, in Blackstone's view, that he should have the power to control that conduct.

This view persisted into the twentieth century. The editor of the 1933 edition of *Lush on the Law of Husband and Wife* explained that confinement was

not the wife's punishment, but the husband's protection against her involving him by her improper conduct in excessive and unreasonable liability to third parties.[2]

In 1946 the American feminist, Mary Beard, wrote:

To the enlightened conscience of modern times, several of the discriminations against women, such as the right of the husband to inflict punishment on his wife, are barbaric; but even as to that it must be remembered that the husband was at law responsible for his wife's behaviour.[3]

Just as the right to chastise and confine is treated as a consequence of coverture, coverture, in its turn, is treated by Blackstone as a consequence of the fiction of marital unity:

> By marriage, the husband and wife are one person in law: that is, the very being or legal existence of the woman is suspended during the marriage, or at least is incorporated and consolidated into that of her husband: under whose wing, protection, and *cover*, she performs everything; and is therefore called in our law-French a *feme-covert*; ... and her condition during the marriage is called her *coverture*. Upon this principle of an union of person in husband and wife depend almost all the legal rights duties and disabilities, that either of them acquire by the marriage.[4]

For Blackstone, then, it was the fiction of marital unity which was fundamental. It lay at the heart of the doctrine of coverture which, in its turn, explained the husband's right to beat and imprison his wife. In this chapter I shall be challenging this analysis, for my thesis is that it was not the fiction of unity but the husband's right to beat and imprison which was fundamental. Coverture embodied the patriarchal assumptions that women should be subordinate to men and that men were entitled to use their power coercively. It was an acceptance of the husband's right to physical control of his wife which lay at the heart of the legal construction of the marital relationship. Far from being a *consequence* of coverture, the husband's right of control was its very *essence*.

The Fiction of Marital Unity

Blackstone was not alone in his views. In the nineteenth century most family lawyers agreed that it was the fiction of unity which best captured the essential nature of the marital relationship. Montague Lush said of the fiction that

> [f]rom the earliest times it has been laid down as a fundamental principle of law, a principle upon which the whole law relating to husband and wife has hitherto depended....[5]

R. S. D. Roper admitted that modern times had introduced exceptions to the doctrine but insisted that 'the general rule still continues, and its wisdom is proved from the inconveniences that have been felt by a departure from it'.[6] In short, on questions relating to the marriage relationship, the fiction of marital unity represented 'the fountain of all reasoning'.[7]

The paragraph from Blackstone's *Commentaries* cited above became famous.[8] Blackstone's rendition of the fiction was short, clear and elegantly phrased and was consequently seized upon and endlessly reproduced. It was common for both standard family law texts and scholarly treatises on the laws affecting women to open with a quote from it.[9]

While these kinds of pronouncements must have been influential, they were, at least, made in the context of extensive and detailed studies of the law on marriage. Read in their entirety, these studies revealed a reality which was much more complex. This was not always the case with the student manuals and do-it-yourself legal guides which were popular at the time. In this kind of literature and in popular books and magazines, works which naturally enjoyed a much wider reading public than Lush or Roper on the law of husband and wife, the principle of unity was often described, without qualification or explanation, as the basis of the marital relationship.[10]

Coverture in the Nineteenth Century

What I wish to do now is to examine the reality of the marital relationship at the beginning of the nineteenth century.[11] In what sense and to what extent could the various aspects of coverture be regarded as deriving from the fiction of unity? What did legal writers understand the fiction of unity to mean? Did they really regard it as the sole, or even the main principle underlying the husband and wife relationship? Or was it simply a convenient rhetorical device?

Property Rights

It is appropriate to begin with property rights. According to the author of *The Lawes Resolution of Womens Rights*, the effect of marriage on a woman's property rights was the best illustration of the husband's prerogative. In this area, he said, 'practice everywhere agree[d] with the Theoricke of Law'.[12]

Changes occurred even before the marriage was solemnised. Merely becoming engaged affected a woman's property rights. An engaged woman could not dispose of any of her property without the knowledge and consent of her intended husband, for this would be to deprive him of property which he had expected to acquire when he proposed. Any such disposition could be set aside as a legal fraud.

On marriage the husband acquired the right to manage his wife's freehold and copyhold lands and to receive and use any rents and profits. He did not become the absolute owner of this land: both husband and wife were seised of it in right of the wife. This meant that he did not acquire her inheritance: if he alienated the land without her consent or devised it by will it could be recovered back after his death. However, if the wife predeceased him and a child had been born to the marriage then, by the 'curtesy of England', he was granted a life-interest in her lands. This interest he was free to dispose of.

If the wife survived the husband she similarly enjoyed an interest in his lands, but it was not nearly as generous as that conveyed by the curtesy. A widow's rights of dower and free-bench entitled her to a life estate in a third of the husband's lands. The husband could deprive her of any share in his copyhold lands by alienating them during his lifetime. As regards freehold lands, the wife could agree before marriage to give up her rights in exchange for a jointure. This involved the settlement of land on husband and wife jointly for the life of the survivor. She could also effectively bar her right to dower by consenting to a conveyance of the land to a third party.

A husband was free to dispose of his wife's leasehold lands during his lifetime. If she predeceased him, they became his absolute property. However, he could not devise them by will while she was still alive. If he died first, they reverted back to her absolute possession and control.

All the personal possessions that a woman owned on marriage or afterwards acquired became the absolute property of her husband. He could give them away, sell them or devise them by will without her consent. Only her 'paraphernalia' – her clothes and personal ornaments – were treated differently. The husband could dispose of these during his lifetime, and they could be taken by his creditors in settlement of his debts on his death but, if neither of these things happened, they reverted to his widow or her heirs.

The early nineteenth-century husband was free to bequeath all of his personal property, including that obtained from his wife, to whomever he liked. Neither his wife nor his children had any claim to a share. They were in a better position if he died intestate. The widow of an intestate was entitled to a half of his personal property – a third if there were children. In the first case, the remainder went to the husband's relatives, in the second, to the children.

He had the right, finally, to reduce his wife's choses in action into possession. This covered things like: debts owing to her; a right to damages for injuries sustained due to a breach of contract or tort; and shares and bonds of joint-stock companies. Once they were converted into personal property he owned them absolutely; he could dispose of them during his lifetime and bequeath them in his will. However, if he died without reducing them into possession, they reverted to the wife's ownership and control.

As was mentioned in Chapter 1, equity had long provided ways of avoiding the common-law incidents of marriage.[13] It did this primarily through the device of the trust: the courts of equity recognised property held in trust for a wife as her 'separate estate'. These trusts were typically established in marriage settlements, most often by the woman's father. In addition, when a husband applied to the courts of equity to enforce a right of property acquired through marriage, they would insist on settling a portion of the property on the wife. This was known as her equity to a settlement.

It was possible, in theory, for a wife to be in almost the same position as a *feme sole* or single woman. However, in practice, this was rarely the case. Marriage settlements rarely gave control of the separate estate to the wife herself. Normally, her father or her husband would be empowered to act as her trustee. In addition, there would often be a 'restraint on anticipation'. This was a condition inserted in the settlement which prevented the wife or her trustees from alienating or charging the capital during the marriage. In effect, the wife's absolute property was postponed until widowhood.

However, the most serious obstacle on this equitable escape route was the high cost of the proceedings. In reality, it was impracticable to tie up any but substantial sums of money in trust settlements. A lawyer's fee for drawing up a marriage settlement could, alone, amount to over £100. As a result, only those possessing both wealth and skilled legal advice, perhaps one-tenth of married women in England, could make use of these equitable devices.[14] It is for this reason that I concentrate on the common law.

At common law, as we have seen, a woman effectively had nothing during marriage. Although some kinds of property remained distinguishable as hers, she had no property at her disposal or in her control. With the exception of a well-nigh unenforceable common-law right to be maintained, she had no rights over any of her husband's property. It was not even possible for the husband to make her a gift.

How, then, did the common lawyers explain these things? It appears to have been Edward Coke, in his commentary on Littleton, who first attributed the inability of spouses to make gifts to each other to the fiction of unity.[15] His sparse explanation was frequently repeated,[16] and was elaborated upon by Blackstone in the next century:

a man cannot grant anything to his wife, or enter into covenant with her, for the grant would be to suppose her separate existence: and to covenant with her, would be only to covenant with himself.[17]

Some, including A. V. Dicey,[18] treated the fiction of unity as a sufficient explanation of *all* the wife's property disabilities; others felt it necessary to elaborate. Matthew Bacon, writing some 30 years before Blackstone, explained that, as a result of the fictional unity of husband and wife, the law

allows of but one will between them, which is placed in the husband, as the fittest and ablest to provide for, and govern the family; and for this reason, the law gives the husband an absolute power of disposing of her personal property....[19]

Some nineteenth-century commentators on the law went further. Thomas Barrett-Lennard, in his 1883 treatise on women and the law, said that a wife had no disposing power as regards her property, because 'she was regarded as being so much under the coercion of her husband as to be unable to exercise any such power'.[20] It is unclear whether he regarded this as a consequence of the spouses' fictional unity. Arthur Rackham Cleveland, on the other hand, was quite decided on this point. In his view, the fiction of marital unity was of limited use only. It was sufficient to explain things like spouses' inability to make gifts to each other but, in many circumstances, it was clear that the law treated husband and wife as separate entities. The wife had limited property rights, not because the law identified her with her husband, but because it held her 'in considerable subjection to her husband'.[21]

Testamentary Capacity

Matrimony also affected a wife's testamentary capacity. The ceremony served to revoke the prior wills of both husband and wife but, thereafter, the law departed from this equality of treatment. A husband was free to devise his real property after marriage, subject to his wife's rights of dower and free-bench. A wife was specifically barred from willing her real property. She could make a will bequeathing her personal property but only with her husband's consent, and this consent could be withdrawn at any time before the will was proved. If her husband predeceased her it had the effect of revoking the will. If she died before making another she was held to have died intestate.

A husband could never bequeath his wife's real property. However, he was free to bequeath her personal property, both before and after her death. Her paraphernalia represented the only exception to this. If he survived his wife and she had failed to make a will, perhaps because he refused to give his consent, then he became absolute owner of her paraphernalia, her leasehold lands and her choses in action. He was then free to bequeath these things by will also.

Why was a wife's testamentary capacity so much more limited than her husband's? Why, in particular, was she unable to devise her real property? In the eighteenth century Richard Burn argued that the inability derived not from any lack of capacity but simply from her lack of devisable property.[22] Tapping Reeve, an American jurist, made the same argument at the beginning of the nineteenth century,[23] and the position has been endorsed by eminent historians.[24] As we have seen, the wife was not technically deprived of ownership of her real property. However, until the sixteenth century *no one* could devise real property. The legislative changes in the reign of Henry VIII which enabled landowners to dispose of nearly the whole of their real property by will, specifically denied that right to a wife.[25] As regards the rest of her property, the law gave the husband absolute rights to it if she predeceased him. She did not lack the *capacity* to devise it but her husband's consent was necessary because it involved an infringement of his legal rights.

The problem with this line of argument is it does not tell us anything about the motivation behind the statutory injunction on a wife's devise of land. Matthew Bacon explained it thus:

> as the law will not allow a woman under coverture to make a will, lest she should be influenced by her husband in the disposition of her estate; so, for the same reasons, a will made by a feme sole is revoked by the marriage, lest she should be influenced by her husband (if it continued after the coverture) to revoke it, or let it stand, as it best answered his interest.[26]

In Bacon's view, the law acted against the husband's interest, on the assumption that he would have influence over his spouse and would use it to his advantage.

Other writers used stronger terms. Coke, for example, said that a wife was prevented from devising land to her husband

> because at the time of making her will she had no power, being *sub potestate viri*,[27] to devise the same; and the law intendeth it should be done by coertion of her husband.[28]

It is interesting to note that Blackstone gave the same explanation. As we have seen, Blackstone was one of the most influential proponents of the notion that almost all the legal rights, duties and disabilities incident on marriage resulted from the wife's fictional unity with her husband. However, it seems that this was not one of them: 'there are some instances in which she is separately considered; as inferior to him, and acting by his compulsion...'.[29]

Some writers went further and suggested that marriage deprived a woman of her understanding and volition:

A wife by generall rule hath no will but her Husbands, and all Testaments of a feme-covert to devise any Manors, Lands, Tenements and Hereditaments are ineffectuall....[30]

Contractual Capacity

At common law a married woman could not enter into contracts in her own name. She could make contracts in her husband's name but had no inherent authority to do so: she had to have her husband's express or implied consent to act as his agent. As we have seen, if she pledged her husband's credit for necessary household goods and services, she was presumed to have the authority to do so. The vendor could recover the money from her husband as long as it could be shown that the goods really were 'necessaries'. However, if the husband could demonstrate that he had given his wife sufficient money to pay for necessaries without pledging his credit, or that the goods or services in question were not suited to their station in life, then the claim would fail. It was also open to the husband to rebut the presumption of agency by proving that he had forbidden his wife to pledge his credit or that he had forbidden tradespeople to advance her credit.

A wife had a common law right to be maintained by her husband and the doctrine of agency could be used to enforce this right; if a husband failed to supply his wife with necessaries then the presumption that she had his authority to pledge his credit in order to buy these things was irrebuttable. However, this was of no use whatsoever unless the wife could find people prepared to advance her credit. Cooperative tradespeople took a considerable risk: the husband might not have been creditworthy; the goods might have been adjudged unsuitable to the wife's station in life; she might have forfeited any right to be maintained by committing adultery or by leaving her husband without what a court would have regarded as good reason. Few shop-keepers can have been sufficiently well-informed to have felt sure of recovering the debt.

A husband and wife could not make a contract with one another; contracts which they had made with one another before marriage became unenforceable. Legal writers suggested different explanations of this. Some explained it in terms of the now familiar Blackstonian doctrine of unity: husband and wife were one person − a man could not enter into a contract with himself.[31] Others explained it in terms of the wife's incapacity to contract with *anyone*.[32] But why should a wife have been thus incapable? Some simply pointed to the fiction of unity.[33] However, in 1897, J. De Montmorency strongly denied that this could be the basis of the rule for, if it were, a husband and wife should logically have been capable of binding each other simply by virtue of their marriage. Instead, 'the wife, in so far as binding her husband went, was no wife, but merely his business agent or nothing at all'.[34] Others held that the incapacity to contract was simply a consequence of the wife's proprietary disabilities: she had nothing to sell and nothing with which to buy and, therefore, her contracts were void.[35]

Thomas Barrett-Lennard appeared to think that a wife was incapable of contracting because she could not sue or be sued upon her contracts. This, in its turn, was explained by the fact that her contracts were void![36] Another intriguing suggestion came from Tapping Reeve, who explained that if a wife could bind herself by her contracts

she would be liable to be arrested, taken in execution, and confined in a prison; and then the husband would be deprived of the company of his wife, which the law will not suffer.[37]

However, most commentators were of the 'power' school of thought. For them, the explanation lay in the husband's control of his wife. Blackstone, for example, regarded this as another area in which the wife was deemed to be acting under her husband's compulsion.[38] James Kent, the nineteenth-century author of one of the most influential American commentaries on the law, was insistent that no 'want of discretion' should be imputed to the wife.[39] However, others appeared to disagree. Their choice of language implied a belief that a wife's very mind was somehow under control, so that she 'want[ed] Free-will'.[40] This was reflected most strongly perhaps in the 1659 case of *Manby* v. *Scott*, which established that a wife who left her husband without his consent lost the right to be maintained and to pledge his credit for necessaries. Hyde J. said in the course of his judgment that, for a contract between two people to be valid, it was necessary that there be

a mutual assent of their minds, which mutual assent is agreement ... but a feme covert cannot give a mutual assent of her mind, nor do any act without her husband; for her will and mind, as also herself, is under, and subject to the will or mind of her husband; and consequently she cannot make any bargain or contract, of herself, to bind her husband.[41]

Some commentators thought that this power relationship had been deliberately created by the law. Others thought that it arose as an inevitable consequence of women's nature and that the law was forced to recognise it. John Bright was an example of the former. With unapologetic frankness, he announced that

[w]ith a view to the safety of the husband, the law disables the wife from

making any personal contract, or incurring any debt to bind him, without his express or implied authority.[42]

Those who favoured the latter approach argued that the wife was rendered incapable of binding herself by contract for her *own* protection.[43] As she was controlled by her husband and, thereby, deprived of freedom of volition, it would be unfair if she could be bound by contracts entered into with him. On this view, the law embodied the assumption that, left to himself, the husband would use his superior power to his own advantage. Bacon and Coke, it will be remembered, explained the wife's limited testamentary capacity in this same way. It also provides a plausible explanation of the 'fine', a device which was used when a wife's freehold lands were being alienated. This could only be done with the wife's consent and, as an extra precaution, she would be examined separately, out of her husband's presence, to ensure that the consent was freely given.[44]

Civil Liability

(1) CONTRACT AND DEBT
It was impossible for a woman to incur contractual liability at common law while she was married. A wife could not make a valid contract: she could not, therefore, be liable for breach of contract. She could enter into contracts as her husband's agent but the sole responsibility for these lay with him.

A single woman was responsible for her debts and contracts, and this responsibility did not end on marriage: if an action was brought against her as a *feme sole* she could be taken in execution and imprisoned, even though she married before judgment was given against her; pleading her coverture would not have obtained her discharge.[45] However, if she were sued after marriage her husband would be joined as a party. He became liable for her antenuptial obligations to the full extent of his property, whether or not he knew of them beforehand, and they could both be imprisoned if they ignored a judgment against them. However, as a matter of indulgence, the court would order the wife's release if she could show that she had no separate property from which the judgment could be satisfied. The husband's liability was a joint one only: it ceased when his wife died and only attached to his executors on *his* death if judgment had already been obtained.

Just as a wife could not be sued alone, neither could she sue alone. Any action in contract or debt had to be brought jointly with her husband and, as we have seen, once a wife's choses in action had been reduced into possession, the money recovered became the husband's absolutely.

A husband and wife could never sue one other. As the wife could not sue or be sued without her husband, this was clearly an impossibility.

These rules have been explained in terms of the fiction of unity.[46] Alternatively, they have been attributed to the wife's dearth of property. However, Courtney Stanhope Kenny thought that the proponents of the latter view might have reversed the true order of events: the wife's limited property rights might have been a consequence of her inability to sue alone, without her husband effectively acting as her representative. Except as regards land, married women were never seen to assert their property rights in court, and this could gradually have given rise to the supposition that they had no rights.[47]

Others suggested that '[i]t is only fair ... that the husband who takes the benefit should bear the liability'.[48] However, this 'fair exchange' approach was a little hard to sustain: a husband was liable for his wife's antenuptial debts whether or not he had obtained property from her; a widow became liable again, even though her husband may have left her little or none of the property she brought to the marriage. The anonymous female author of a 1735 book entitled *The Hardships of the English Laws in Relation to Wives, With an Explanation of the Original Curse of Subjection Passed upon the Woman*, pointed out that a husband was free to devote the property he acquired from his wife to the payment of *his* antenuptial debts. Moreover, he was in a better position to conceal his debts and entrap a wealthy spouse.

According to this eighteenth-century writer, the rule against suing a wife alone was best explained by the fact that 'a woman's lying in Jail will pay no Man his Money'.[49] It might be thought that most husbands would have paid up in order to gain the recovery of their wives, but Tapping Reeve thought otherwise. Reeve who, as we have seen, was a strong proponent of the notion that wives needed protection from their husbands, suspected that many would have left their wives lying in gaol forever if the penalty had not affected them also.[50] The author of *Hardships* doubted this. She thought that as husbands regarded their wives as their property they would feel bound to guard against 'the Hazard of having their Chastity attempted in such Confinement'.[51]

(2) Tort Law

The position in relation to torts was roughly similar. A wife could not sue or be sued alone. If a husband and wife were successfully sued for the wife's tort, the husband was liable for the damages to the full extent of his property. If a husband and wife sued successfully for a tort committed against the wife, the money recovered belonged absolutely to the husband. However, tort law was different in that these rules applied not just to antenuptial torts but to postnuptial torts also. It seems that a married woman, although incapable of making a valid contract, was perfectly capable of committing a tort and of having a tort inflicted upon her.[52]

The difference was attributed to the element of moral turpitude involved in some torts.[53] It was argued that the law could not deny a married women's capacity to do wrong, even though her procedural and proprietary disabilities effectively protected her from any penalty. Modern scholars have suggested that the principle governing the relationship of husband and wife in this respect was a variant on the common-law principle of representation. This was a familiar concept in feudal times; it was the basis, for example, of an abbot's responsibility for his monks.[54]

A husband and wife could not sue each other in tort which meant, of course, that an abused wife could not obtain damages for personal injuries.[55] This rule could not have been based on the wife's procedural and proprietary disabilities alone, for these would not have precluded a suit after the termination of the marriage. For a long time, of course, the majority of marriages were terminated by the death of one of the spouses; civil divorce only became possible in 1857. Thus, it was not until the middle of the nineteenth century that the problem of the post-marital tort action was properly addressed. It was rapidly disposed of. It was revealed that acts committed by one spouse against the other during marriage were prevented from being tortious by the fiction of unity: 'The reason ... why the wife cannot sue the husband for beating her must be because they are one and the same person ...'.[56]

Criminal Law

(1) The Wife as the Victim of Crime

Turning now to criminal offences: the fact that the victim was a married woman did not normally affect liability; except, that is, when the perpetrator was the woman's husband. For a number of reasons husbands were rarely convicted of crimes against their wives.

(a) The Marital Immunity in Rape Law

First, there were some actions which, although normally criminal, were legal when performed by a husband. A husband could no longer beat his wife with impunity in the early nineteenth century: a claim of lawful chastisement was unlikely to be accepted. However, he could force sexual intercourse upon her without being guilty of rape, a situation which persisted until the House of Lords decision in *R.* v *R.* in 1991.[57]

The authority invariably cited for the existence of the marital immunity in rape law[58] was Sir Matthew Hale's *History of the Pleas of the Crown*. Whether the immunity predated Hale is unclear.[59] What does seem clear is that it was he who identified the basis of the immunity as an irrevocable consent to intercourse embodied in the marriage contract:[60]

> But the husband cannot be guilty of a rape committed by himself upon his lawful wife, for by their mutual matrimonial consent and contract the wife has given up herself in this kind unto her husband, which she cannot retract.[61]

For John Stuart Mill, this was one of the best illustrations of the lowliness of a wife's legal status:

> a female slave has (in Christian countries) an admitted right, and is considered under a moral obligation, to refuse to her master the last familiarity. Not so the wife: however brutal a tyrant she may unfortunately be chained to ... he can claim from her and enforce the lowest degradation of a human being, that of being made the instrument of an animal function contrary to her inclinations.[62]

(b) Prosecution of a Spouse

Even when a husband's conduct was capable of constituting a criminal offence it may not have been possible to prosecute: the prohibition on civil proceedings between spouses may have been mirrored in the criminal law. According to *R.* v. *Lord Mayor of London*, prosecutions between husband and wife were only possible in cases of actual or threatened personal violence.[63] However, the judge failed to cite any authority. Nor did he clarify the scope of this supposed rule. Was it possible, for example, for a third party to bring a prosecution?

(c) Evidence – The Prohibition on Spousal Testimony

Even if prosecutions between spouses were technically possible, the rules of evidence made it unlikely that many would succeed. Until well into the nineteenth century there was a general common-law rule that spouses were incompetent to testify for or against one other. This incompetence applied to both criminal and civil proceedings; it applied to events occurring before as well as during the marriage and it endured after the marriage had ended.[64]

The prohibition dated back to the seventeenth century. One of the earliest clear authorities on the subject was Coke,[65] who explained that

a wife cannot be produced either against or for her husband, *quia sunt duae animae in carne una* [because they are two souls in one body]; and it might be a cause of implacable discord and dissention between the husband and the wife, and a mean of great inconvenience.[66]

Hawkins, in the next century, repeated Coke's reasons for the rule, but then went on to talk of 'the great Danger of Perjury from taking the Oath of Persons under so great a Biass, and the extreme Hardship of the Case'.[67]

In Blackstone's view, husband and wife were

not allowed to be evidence for, or against, each other: partly because it is impossible their testimony should be indifferent; but principally because of the union of person.[68]

Buller, finally, summarised thus:

Husband and wife cannot be admitted to be witness for each other, because their interests are absolutely the same; nor against each other, because contrary to the legal policy of marriage.[69]

The eminent American academic, John Henry Wigmore, was unimpressed by these reasons.[70] Arguments based on the fiction of marital unity he dismissed out of hand: these were entirely 'void of force'.[71] Nor could he accept the view that the law acted to avoid family discord.[72] This argument presupposed a husband who expected his wife to perjure herself on his behalf and who would make her suffer if she did not. Rules of evidence could not protect such a wife from tyranny. And why should the law protect the marital peace of such a husband? The argument that a spouse's evidence would be unreliable because of the ties of affection or because of marital identity of interest was more plausible. At this time a party to a civil case and the defendant in a criminal case was prohibited from giving evidence on his own behalf; as he was interested in the outcome he could not be relied on to tell the truth. His spouse would often share his interest in the outcome. But not always. As Wigmore pointed out, the prohibition applied even when the spouses' interests were divergent. Further, the abolition of incompetence through interest by the Evidence Act 1843, and the extension of its provisions to the parties in civil cases by the Evidence Act 1851, did not have the effect of making the spouse of a party into a competent witness.[73]

The abridgment writers, with the exception of Coke,[74] dealt with the prohibition in predominantly gender-neutral terms: 'the husband regularly is not allowed to be a witness for or against the wife, or *e converso*'.[75] However, the early case law dealt exclusively with wives' testimony and Wigmore was of the view that the rule had developed with wives rather than spouses in mind. For Wigmore, the true explanation of the prohibition lay in what the House of Lords in a modern case described as 'the natural repugnance of the public at the prospect of a wife giving evidence against her husband...'.[76]

This repugnance, in its turn, had its roots in the history of the marital relationship. It reflected the view that a man should not be condemned

by admitting to the witness stand against him those who lived under his roof, shared the secrets of his domestic life, depended on him for sustenance and were almost numbered among his chattels. In a day when the offense of petit treason by a wife or a servant – violence to the head of the household – was still recognized, it would seem unconscionable that the law itself should abet (as it were) a testimonial betrayal which came close enough to petit treason, and should virtually permit a wife to cause her husband's death.[77]

The rule against spousal testimony was subject to a number of exceptions.[78] So, for example, a wife was competent to give evidence against her husband if he was charged with an offence involving personal violence against her; or if he was charged with abducting and marrying her against her will.[79] According to Hullock J. in *R.* v. *Wakefield* in 1827,

[a] wife is competent against her husband in all cases affecting her liberty and person.... It would be unreasonable to exclude the only person capable of giving evidence in certain cases of injury: our law recognises witnesses *ex necessitate*, and it would be strange, indeed, that the husband should be allowed to exercise every atrocity against the wife, and her evidence not be admitted.[80]

However, this assertion that the law recognised a *general* exception based on necessity was not supported by the case law; the exception did not extend to all cases of wrongs done to a wife, even when she was the only one in a position to testify regarding them.[81] In Lord Mansfield's words:

[the] necessity is not a general necessity, as where no other witness can be had, but a particular necessity, as where, for instance, the wife would otherwise be exposed without remedy to personal injury.[82]

The earliest known instance[83] of one spouse giving evidence against the other in a criminal case was in *Lord Audley's Case* in 1631. Lord Audley held his wife down while his servant raped her; it was held that, in a case like this, she could be a witness against her husband 'for she was the party wronged; otherwise she might be abused'.[84]

The exception extended to all cases in which a husband was accused of actual or attempted personal violence towards his wife.[85] If he threatened her with violence she could swear the peace against him, and her evidence would be admitted for this purpose also, for it was 'a matter concerning her person'.[86]

A wife may also have been competent to give evidence against a husband accused of treason. However, the authorities on this were inconsistent. Hale, for example, initially appeared undecided:

> the great obligation of duty she owes to the safety of the king and kingdom, the horridness of the offence of treason, and the great danger that may ensue by concealing it, seems to render her guilty of misprision of treason, if she should not detect it; on the other side, it may be said, she is *sub potestate viri*, she cannot by law be a witness against her husband, and therefore cannot accuse him: *ideo quaere*.

But later, he said: '[a] feme covert is not a lawful witness against her husband in case of treason'.[87]

Francis Buller, on the other hand, reported that

> in case the [*sic*] of high treason it has been said, that a wife shall be admitted as a witness against her husband, because the tie of allegiance is more obligatory than any other.[88]

The question seems never to have been settled.[89] Cohen collected all the authorities for and against the existence of a treason exception in his *Spouse-Witnesses in Criminal Cases*, and found the latter to be overwhelmingly predominant.[90]

We have seen that Wigmore attributed the general prohibition on spousal testimony to the feudal nature of the marital relationship. Historically, a wife had been akin to a chattel or a domestic servant: she could not be permitted to bear witness against her lord and master for that would have been tantamount to treason. The possibility that her testimony was inadmissible even against a traitor lends strong support to the thesis that a wife's primary allegiance was thought to be to her husband rather than to the state.

(2) THE WIFE AS CRIMINAL – THE DISADVANTAGES OF WIFEHOOD

(a) Petit Treason

Wigmore was not describing the Middle Ages: the offence of petit treason to which he referred was not abolished until 1828.[91] Petit treason was committed when a servant killed his or her master or mistress, when an ecclesiastic killed his or her religious superior and when a wife killed her husband.[92] What these relationships had in common, according to Blackstone, was that they embodied 'obligations of duty, subjection and allegiance' similar to those characterising the relation of citizen and sovereign.[93] Thus,

[a] wife killing her husband is petit treason; but a husband killing his wife is only murder; because of the obedience which in relation of law is due from the wife to the husband.[94]

Until the end of the eighteenth century,[95] the punishment for women guilty of petit treason differed from that imposed upon murderers; it also differed from that imposed upon male petit traitors. Whilst wife-murderers and male petit traitors were hung, female petit traitors were sentenced to burning alive.[96] In practice, many women were garrotted or strangled before the flames reached them, but this was not invariably the case. It seems that much depended on the mood of the crowd: if the woman's crime had aroused particular hostility the executioner might have been prevented from disposing of her mercifully.[97]

A letter which appeared in the *Gentleman's Magazine* in 1749 set out the stories of two spouse-murderers who had been executed on the same day.[98] One of them, Amy Hutchinson, had poisoned her jealous and abusive husband after her lover threatened to murder her if she did not. She was strangled and burned for her crime after writing a confession in which she urged young married people to take heed of her plight and allow no cause for jealousy or discord 'between two who should be one'. The other, John Vicars, killed Mary Hainsworth shortly after their marriage. He stabbed her in the throat with the words, ''tis now too late, you should have been ruled in time', and went to his death insisting that 'he should do the same again on such provocation'. He asked to be executed after Amy so that he could watch her being burned. When this was over Vicars was hanged 'and expired in a few minutes'. These kind of events, and the lurid accounts which appeared in contemporary periodicals, must have conveyed powerful messages to the public about the nature of the marriage relationship.[99]

(b) Adultery as Provocation

The differential sentencing of male and the female spouse-murderers was abolished by statute in 1790. Thereafter, both were hanged. However, there was one situation in which women who killed their spouses continued to be treated more harshly. A man who killed his wife upon detecting her in the act of adultery would be guilty of manslaughter rather than murder.[100] A wife who acted under similar provocation had no such defence. Bray J., explaining in 1913 why the law distinguished in this regard between married and cohabiting couples, incidentally revealed the probable reason for its differential treatment of husbands and wives:

> It is a gross offence against a husband that his wife should commit adultery, but there is no such offence against a man if a woman not his wife, although he may be living with her, chooses to commit such an act. In the latter case, the man has no such right to control the woman as a husband has to control his wife.[101]

In the nineteenth century a wife's *confession* of adultery was considered sufficient provocation to reduce murder to manslaughter.[102] However, the *suspicion* of an illicit intrigue was never enough to justify the killing of a woman, 'even your own wife'.[103]

(3) The Wife as Criminal – The Advantages of Wifehood

There were situations, therefore, in which a woman criminal was treated more harshly as a consequence of her status as a wife. Usually, however, it operated to her benefit.

(a) Conspiracy and Larceny

First, some activities which would normally have been criminal, did not constitute crimes where the marital relationship was involved. A husband and wife, for example, could not be guilty of conspiring with one another. Nor was it a larceny for a wife to take her husband's property without his consent. (A husband could not steal from his wife because marriage left her with nothing capable of being stolen.) Both rules were frequently explained in terms of the fiction of unity.[104]

(b) Aiding a Felon-Husband

A wife could protect a felon-husband from justice without becoming an accessory after the fact. The scope of this rule had expanded gradually with the passage of time. Bracton said only that a wife was not bound to accuse or betray her husband.[105] However, subsequent authorities made it clear that she could *receive* him without incurring liability.[106] There were some mid-nineteenth century cases which went further: *R. v. Good* established that a wife could not be found guilty of 'comforting, harbouring *and assisting*' her husband;[107] and, according to *R. v. McClarens*, concealing evidence of the husband's crime counted as comforting, harbouring and assisting, as long as it was done with the intention of protecting him from the consequences of his actions and not with the aim of profiting from the crime.[108] *R.* v. *Manning* went even further and suggested that a wife could *never* be an accessory after the fact to her husband's felony.[109]

The rule was commonly represented as a concession to the dictates of wifely duty and natural conjugal affection. Consider Hawkins, for example:

> It seems agreed. That the Law hath such a Regard to that Duty, Love and Tenderness, which a Wife owes to her Husband, as not to make her an Accessary to Felony by any Receipt whatsoever given to her Husband.[110]

Strangely, this concern for the dilemma of the loving spouse was restricted to the wife: a husband who aided a felon-wife was not exempted from liability as an accessory.[111] Were husbands not expected to reciprocate their wives' affection?

Bracton and Hale probably came closer to the mark: Bracton explained the rule by saying that a wife had no power over herself;[112] Hale said

> [i]f the husband commit a felony or treason, and the wife knowingly receive him, she shall neither be accessary after as to the felony, nor principal as to the treason, for such bare reception of her husband; for she is *sub potestate viri*, and she is bound to receive her husband; but otherwise it is, of the husband's receiving the wife knowingly after an offence of this nature committed by her.[113]

(c) The Defence of Marital Coercion

Secondly, and more significantly, many criminal wives could rely on the defence of marital coercion. This defence was related to the rule about aiding a felon-husband but could assist a wife who would otherwise be liable as the principal offender.

The exact scope of the defence is difficult to establish. Legal commentators disagreed about the kinds of crimes to which it applied. It seems to have extended to the majority of ordinary felonies, such as burglary, larceny, housebreaking, receiving stolen goods, arson and forgery. It also seems to have applied to robbery,[114] although Hawkins said that it did not.[115] Hale thought that manslaughter was excluded,[116] while Ling-Mallison believed that it was unavailable in cases of witchcraft.[117] The only thing on which they all agreed was that murder and treason were definitely excluded.[118]

The authorities on misdemeanors were also inconsistent. In the 1837 case of *R.* v. *Price* it was said that 'the same rule which applies in cases of felony should apply also to cases of misdemeanor'.[119] However, this was flatly contradicted in *R.* v. *Cruse* in 1838.[120] C. S. Kenny and James Fitzjames Stephen were both of the opinion that the defence probably applied to some misdemeanours.[121]

Finally, Ling-Mallison 'assert[ed] with confidence that [the defence] never applied to non-indictable offences'. Glanville Williams, on the other hand, suggests that it may have done.[122]

For the defence to be available the crime had to be committed in the husband's presence; it was useless for a wife to argue that her absent husband had bullied her into acting or that he had threatened to abuse her if she disobeyed him.[123] However, if the requirement of physical presence was satisfied, coercion was *presumed*: she did not have to prove actual coercion in order to escape liability.[124]

For a long time there was uncertainty about the status of this presumption. Was it conclusive or rebuttable?[125] By the nineteenth century it was clearly established that it was open to the prosecution to rebut the presumption of coercion.[126] However, it seems that it was not enough simply to demonstrate an absence of coercion.[127] It had to be shown that the wife was 'principally instrumental' in the commission of the crime or, at least, that she had played an 'active and independent part'.[128] According to J. M. Beattie, common practice in the eighteenth century was for the wife to be convicted only where the husband was acquitted.[129]

What, finally, was meant by coercion? What kinds of behaviour were husbands presumed to have indulged in when their wives committed crimes in their company? In 1925 the presumption was finally abolished and replaced by a statutory defence based on *actual* coercion by the husband.[130] In the parliamentary debate Thomas Inskip, the Solicitor-General, expressed the opinion that the term extended to 'coercion in the moral, possibly even in the spiritual realm'.[131] However, it is difficult to reconcile this view with the 1838 decision in *R. v. Pollard*.[132] In that case the presumption of coercion was held to be rebutted by the fact that the husband, although present at the scene of the crime, was a bedridden cripple and, therefore, incapable of coercing his wife. The defence amounted, in short, to a legal presumption of domestic violence.

Legal commentators often expressed the view that the defence originated to compensate women criminals for their inability to claim 'benefit of clergy'.[133] Clergymen had once been permitted to plead their religious affiliation as a defence to crimes punishable by death. They would then be turned over to the ecclesiastical courts where they usually managed to escape serious punishment. Gradually, in an effort to soften the rigours of the English penal system, benefit of clergy was extended to every man who could read the first verse of Psalm 51 – or the 'neck verse', as it came to be known. As women could not be clergy the defence was originally not available to them. This meant that a wife could be hanged while her husband was saved, although they had both committed the same offence.[134] This injustice was avoided, according to C. S. Kenny, 'by the establishment of ... [an] artificial presumption of conjugal subjection'.[135]

A possible objection to this proposition is that the origins of the defence of coercion appear to have predated *Pro Clero*, the 1350 statute which created the defence of benefit of clergy.[136] An early instance of wives being exempted from criminal sanctions by virtue of their marital subordination is to be found in the seventh-century laws of King Ine. Section 57 of those laws imposed forfeiture of property on any man found to be concealing a stolen beast in his home:

his wife only being exempt, since she must obey her lord. If she declare with an oath, that she has not tasted the stolen (meat) she shall retain her third of the (household) Property.[137]

Another example is to be found in the laws of King Canute in the eleventh century. Wives were relieved of liability regarding stolen goods found in their homes

unless the goods had been put under the wife's lock and key ... But it is her duty to guard the keys of the following – her storeroom and her chest and her cupboard. If the goods have been put in any of these, she shall be held guilty ... But no wife can forbid her husband to deposit anything that he desires in his cottage.[138]

The substance of this law was repeated by Bracton in the twelfth century,[139] and its influence can be discerned in Dalton's *Countrey Justice*, where it is said that a wife will be guilty of larceny if she 'receive stolne goods into her house knowing them so to be, or shall locke them up in her Chest or chambers, her husband not knowing thereof'.[140]

Clearly, therefore, an embryonic but recognisable version of the defence of marital coercion existed before the defence of benefit of clergy was created. And there are other examples of a 'lack of fit' between the two defences. Benefit of clergy was available on a manslaughter charge while the defence of marital coercion was probably not. Conversely, benefit of clergy never applied to misdemeanours but the defence of marital coercion probably did.[141] And, finally, the defence of marital coercion continued to thrive long after benefit of clergy was extended to women in 1691.[142] All this tends to cast doubt on the argument that the defence originated in the judiciary's desire to give wives a rough equivalent of a defence available to their husbands.

On the other hand, however, the mainstream version of the defence of marital coercion appears to have emerged in the sixteenth and seventeenth centuries[143] – the period when the generalised lay use of benefit of clergy was rapidly developing. Before this time it was not clearly established that coercion could be *presumed*; this and other extensions of the defence may well have derived from judicial reluctance to impose statutory death sentences on women. By the time benefit of clergy became available to women the new rules would have become fossilised within the precedental system; it is not surprising, therefore, that they continued in being after 1691.

The development of benefit of clergy probably played a part then, but this was not the whole story. As we have seen, the earliest authorities explained the defence of marital coercion in terms of a husband's power over his wife and her duty to obey him; and legal commentators throughout the centuries endorsed this rationale. Neither Blackstone nor Matthew Bacon, for example, made any reference to benefit of clergy.[144]

Some believed that the law had simply responded to the reality of women's lives; that the presumption of coercion was 'based on a knowledge and understanding of the relations that usually exist[ed] between husband and wife'.[145] It was thought that in crime, as in other spheres of life, the husband *would* inevitably be the dominant partner and that it would be wrong to punish the wife for behaviour over which she had no effective control.[146] Others found this hard to stomach, at least where the lower classes were concerned:

The law supposes that everything is in the property of the husband and that the wife is under his control. But in point of fact, in the lower positions of life that possibly may not be the case at all.[147]

Such evidence as is available about female criminality in past centuries tends to support the former view.[148] Then, as now, the vast majority of crime was committed by men. Women who broke the law were usually acting in the company of others, commonly male family members; and their role tended to be a subsidiary, dependent one. They would often act as decoys, for example, or receive and conceal property that had been stolen by others. Women who operated independently tended to commit less serious crimes; and, in addition, there were a number of crimes which were regarded as distinctively female – infanticide, witchcraft and prostitution are all good examples. Whether acting as principals or accomplices, women criminals were less likely than men to be confrontational and to exhibit daring and initiative. In particular, they were much less likely in engage in violence.

All this suggests that the presumption of coercion may have been an entirely justified one, and that it was right for men to bear the bulk of the responsibility for criminal activity. But is the picture which emerges from the criminal statistics an accurate reflection of reality? There is a distinct possibility that the existence of the defence of coercion *obscured* the real dimensions of female criminality.[149] When spouses were indicted together for serious offences the judge would often have directed the jury to acquit the wife unless there was some evidence that she had been acting independently. Moreover, it is likely that many such wives were not indicted at all. This is particularly likely to have been the case in the sixteenth and seventeenth centuries when the defence was in a state of evolution and judges were unsure whether the presumption of coercion was rebuttable.[150]

Similarly, some of the areas in which women *did* feature prominently were those to which the defence of coercion may not have extended. There was doubt, for example, about whether it applied to misdemeanours and to summary offences – the kind of less serious crimes for which women were commonly convicted. Again, under the early law, wives were liable in respect of possession of stolen property if it was found in areas of the home – such as chests, storerooms and cupboards – which were assumed to be under their control. The defence may not have applied to witchcraft and it seems that it did not apply to the offence of

keeping a Bawdy-House; for this is an Offence as to the Government of the House, in which the wife has a principal Share: and also such an Offence as may generally be presumed to be managed by the Intrigues of her Sex.[151]

Just as the operation of the defence of coercion may have hidden female activity in certain areas, the limitations on the defence may have played a part in the emergence of 'peculiarly female'[152] crimes.

There is a further, and more difficult, question that needs to be considered. Did the defence of coercion do more than simply *obscure* the true extent of female criminality? Is it possible that it played a part in *creating* women's subordinate role in crime? It is certainly arguable that it did. Through the medium of the presumption of coercion, particular kinds of roles were represented as appropriate for husbands and wives,[153] and spouses in criminal partnerships were provided with a powerful incentive to conform to those roles. The incentive for the wife was obvious. As late as the 1820s there were over 200 offences which were punishable by death;[154] a wife who took herself outside the scope of the defence by behaving ' "mannishly", aggressively, or without due deference'[155] might literally have been risking her neck. There were incentives for the husband too. By conforming to the model of male behaviour woven into the defence of coercion he could protect his spouse-partner from conviction and possible execution in the event of their arrest. There are a number of reasons why he might have wanted to do this. Apart from the obvious considerations of affection and attachment, he might have been concerned that his affairs be taken care of in his absence, that his children be cared for, or simply that there be someone to arrange for his defence or to petition for mercy on his behalf.

This presupposes, of course, that criminals were familiar with the existence of the defence of coercion. Valerie Edwards thinks that

women were probably as aware of the possibilities of the defence of marital coercion as men were of their much wider right of benefit of clergy. They perhaps pleaded it habitually and automatically as a last straw, whether entitled or not, just as illiterates prayed benefit of clergy in the hope of being able to recite the 'neck verse' with sufficient accuracy to convince the court.[156]

It seems, then, that the presumption of coercion may have been *prescriptive* rather than descriptive of reality. On this view, it was not designed to protect the victims of physical abuse: its primary function was ideological rather than material. It served to communicate and enforce establishment views about women's role within marriage. In Francis Bacon's words:

where baron and feme commit a felony, the feme can neither be principal nor accessary; because the law intends her to have no will, in regard of the subjection and obedience she oweth to her husband.[157]

This approach accords with the fact that no proof of actual coercion was required in order for the defence to apply.

(4) SPOUSES AND THE CRIMINAL LAW – CONCLUSION

The picture that emerges from an examination of the criminal law principles relevant to spouses is of a relationship which, in the nineteenth century, was still essentially feudal in nature. For a husband, the home represented a sphere of autonomy. Although in his public life he was subject to the laws of the state, within his marriage he was all-powerful: 'every mans house is (to himselfe, his family, and his goods) as his castle, as well for his defence against iniurie and violence, as also for his repose and rest'.[158]

A husband was free to control his wife's behaviour. He could imprison her or force intercourse upon her with impunity. If she committed adultery she signed her own death warrant: the law recognised that he was partially justified in killing her by reducing the charge to manslaughter. A wife who killed her husband was regarded as a traitor.

A husband was not simply *permitted* to control his wife's behaviour – he was *expected* to control it. In return for the power over her which the state allowed him, he was required to answer for her conduct. If he permitted her to break the law he could expect to be held responsible.

The state surrendered most of its power over the wife. As she was subject to her husband, she could be exempted from state control. Even if the husband was a criminal her primary bond of allegiance was to him rather than to the state or to her fellow-citizens: she was not required to bear witness against him; she could protect him from justice with impunity; she could even assist him in his wrongdoing without incurring criminal liability. The rule about aiding a felon-husband and the defence of marital coercion operated to free her from the necessity of judging right and wrong for herself. The husband's authority was allowed to supersede all other forms of authority.

It was possible for the husband to forfeit his authority. If he committed treason his wife may have been permitted to give evidence against him; and, similarly, the defence of marital coercion did not extend to treason. In return for the grant of autonomy within the home, the state expected loyal service outside of it. In Blackstone's words:

the husband, having broken through the most sacred tie of social community by rebellion against the state, has no right to that obedience from a wife, which he himself as a subject has forgotten to pay.[159]

And in the words of the author of *The Hardships of the English Laws*:

it is for the Interest of the community as a Body Politick, that Wives should be punish'd as free agents for Treason, but that, in Respect to the private Royalties of Husbands, in other cases they are not expected to judge of Right and of Wrong; 'tis sufficient for them, if their actions confess they accede to the jurisdiction of their Husbands.

But if they will tell us, that this Exemption from Punishment, was designed as a Favour to the Weakness of the Sex, we must take upon ourselves to say, that, that Sophistry is vain; we understand better, and know that it is a fine compliment to the Authority of our domestick Lords and Masters: Had they a real care for the Sex, they would not grant such an Impunity, which might be a Temptation to commit such Facts upon which everlasting Damnation is denounced. But they teach us whom to fear. What are their Judgements, if their Mercies are thus Cruel![160]

The Theoretical Basis of the Marital Relationship – Competing Approaches in Law

Contrary to Blackstone's confident assertion, it does not seem to have been true that almost all of the wife's disabilities depended on the fiction of unity. Confusingly, the disabilities were presented by legal writers in a variety of different relationships and were often explained in terms of each other. Thus, for example, a wife's inability to make a contract or a will and to be sued alone for a tort or breach of an antenuptial contract were all attributed to her lack of property. Conversely, it was suggested that her lack of property rights may have resulted from her inability to defend them through litigation; while her exemption from contractual liability during marriage was due, it was said, to her personal incapacity to bind herself by contract.

Clearly, the fiction of unity was *not* the sole principle underlying the legal relationship between husband and wife. It is true that it recurs in the abridgment and treatise literature with regularity, but then so do a mixture of other ideas.

Five basic theoretical approaches can, I think, be identified.[161] First, there was the 'contract' or 'fair exchange' approach – the husband's protection and financial support was given in return for the wife's goods and services.[162] The implication, of course, was that there was a balance between the benefits and burdens accruing to each party. However, as we have seen, the law did not provide for any such balance.

Secondly, there was the notion that the husband represented his wife in the outside world.[163] This idea probably emerged in feudal times when landholding involved military duties which could not be performed by women, but it is not made clear why nineteenth-century wives should have required this kind of representation.

Thirdly, there was what was considered by its proponents to be a 'practical' explanation. This approach emphasised the necessity of one person having ultimate decision-making power within a family if peace were to be preserved.[164] While this may or may not have been simply a question of practical necessity, the choice of the decision-maker depended on the writer's general theory of marital relations. The proponents of the 'practical' approach justified the monopolisation of the role by the husband in terms of one or other of the two variants of the fourth basic theory – the 'power principle'.

While this principle emphasised a husband's power over his wife, it encompassed two attitudes towards that power which are sufficiently distinct to be remarked upon. The first, I will call the 'coercion principle' and the second, the 'authority principle'. The coercion principle embodied the idea that a wife's vulnerability to coercion by her husband was the inevitable and unpreventable consequence of his greater physical power. The authority principle, on the other hand, portrayed the husband's power as legitimate, in the sense of being recognised by state power, reflected in legal rules and, indeed, maintained by them. This approach is summarised well by John Bunyon:

the English law ... recognises the authority of the husband, and decrees that the wife shall be subject to him. It constitutes him her ruler, protector and guide, gives him within certain limits the control of her person, and subject to large and increasing qualifications, makes him master of her pecuniary resources, and save in his name, withdraws from her civil rights and remedies. . . .[165]

The difference between these two approaches may have been more apparent than real. It should certainly not be assumed that the former was less conducive to the subordination of wives than the latter. It is true that supporters of the authority principle saw the husband as genuinely superior and argued that the wife was duty-bound by the laws of God or Nature to obey him.[166] The coercion principle, on the other hand, was ostensibly a benign one; as we have seen, it was used to justify certain laws as providing wives with a necessary protection from male power. However, there are a number of points which should be made. First, the insistence on the inevitability of male power hinted at a belief in the naturalness of that phenomenon. Thus we see, following closely behind recognition of the fact that the male is generally stronger, the idea that his *will* is stronger. Also, women were seen not only as more liable to be influenced by their partners, but as more open to imposition generally.[167]

Secondly, representing the problem in this way imposed limitations on the possible solutions. Implicit in the coercion principle was the tactic of using 'the wife's helplessness as a means to an end'.[168] Thus, her common-law disabilities could be justified because they made it impossible for her husband to force her into acts advantageous to himself. But the wife's disabilities had other consequences. They deprived her of the power to use the law to her *own* advantage – as *she* perceived it. For some proponents of the coercion principle this was not an unintended consequence: they clearly regarded wives as being as much in need of protection from their own natures as from their husbands. Also, the wife's disabilities could operate to protect the *husband* from the *wife*, in that he could not be made liable for acts to which he had not consented.[169]

A further problem with the coercion principle concerns the ideological and psychological power of language and images. Is there much difference, in this respect, between saying that a married woman has no will, and saying that she is deemed in law to have no will because she ought not to be held responsible for her actions during marriage?

The fifth basic principle or theory of the marriage relationship was, of course, the fiction of unity.

Conclusion

Coverture was based, not on the fiction of unity, but on the power principle. It was the power principle – the acceptance of the husband's right to physical control of his wife – which lay at the heart of the legal construction of the marital relationship. This is particularly evident when one examines the criminal law principles relevant to spouses.

But what, then, was the function of the fiction of marital unity? Our study, so far, does not seem to have brought us any closer to an understanding of this concept. Was it really a principle in its own right, or was it simply a kind of shorthand expression of other principles or policies? And if it had no substantive meaning of its own, why was it regarded in the nineteenth century as 'a fundamental maxim of the common law'.[170] These are the questions which we must consider next.

3
Wife-Beating and the Fiction of Marital Unity: History of an Idea

Introduction

Throughout the nineteenth century, and well into the twentieth, family law textbook writers continued to refer to the fiction of marital unity. Increasingly, however, they questioned whether it could really be the key to the intricacies of coverture.[1] According to Joel Bishop, for example, the common-law rules affecting wives could be explained in terms of a variety of principles, including the fiction of unity; it might, in fact, have been immaterial which principle was chosen.[2] The 1933 edition of *Lush on the Law of Husband and Wife* went further and denied that the fiction *was* a principle: in reality, it had been introduced as an 'umbrella, to shelter or to conceal the anomalous character of certain rules of law'.[3] Writers began to admit the possibility that judicial decision-making in this area might depend 'rather upon considerations of social policy and convenience than upon any abstract principle of law'.[4]

Nevertheless, the enduring popularity of the fiction of marital unity[5] needs to be explained. Why was it for so long considered to be of such central importance? What *was* it? Where did it originate? If it was not, in fact, the principle upon which coverture was based, then what *was* its role? What, in short, was the fiction of marital unity *for*?

The Fiction of Marital Unity in Modern Scholarship

There is very little scholarly writing devoted specifically to the fiction of marital unity. The most significant analyses that have appeared during the last century issue from just three academics, Frederic Maitland, Mary Beard and Glanville Williams. The thinking of each of these writers will be considered in turn, to see what light, if any, it throws upon the role of the fiction. Later, I will be considering and, I hope, developing the ideas of Norma Basch in this area.

Frederic Maitland

In 1895 Frederic Maitland dismissed the fiction of unity as a useless and meaningless abstraction.[6] It was completely at odds with the legal realities: in Charles Donahue's words, '[the] fundamental characteristic of the ... common law of marital property ... was not the unity of husband and wife but their separation'.[7] Nor was it true that the law treated the wife 'as a thing or as somewhat that is neither thing nor person'. Maitland accepted that a married woman's activities were greatly circumscribed, but emphasised the fact that her rights were not totally subsumed within her husband's. She retained ownership of her land and it could not be alienated without her consent. On termination of the marriage it returned to her heirs, just as the husband's land returned to his in the time before the power of testamentary disposition was enlarged.

Maitland proposed a new and influential principle.[8] Drawing on a phrase of Bracton's,[9] he described the legal relationship between husband and wife in terms of 'an exaggerated guardianship'. This is clearly more useful than the fiction of unity. It helps to explain the husband's responsibilities as well as his rights and it accords with the fact that the wife continued to be treated as a person with certain rights and powers of her own.[10] Moreover, Maitland accepted that this guardianship was a profitable right: like feudal wardship, it was more beneficial to the guardian than the ward. No matter what the underlying principle was, the reality for most women was that they had no power to possess, enjoy or convey their property during marriage.

However, as John Johnston has pointed out:

> no one has convincingly explained how every single woman, who was a fully competent legal entity the instant before her marriage, suddenly came to *require* a guardian immediately after saying her vows. In the case of infants or legal incompetents, the need is clear; but the notion that every married woman needs a guardian – and that every husband is fit to act as his wife's guardian – is simply absurd.[11]

Nor did Maitland suggest any alternative role for the maligned fiction of unity.

Glanville Williams

In an article published in 1947, Glanville Williams reviewed those legal rules that were said to have had their origins in the fiction of marital unity. He concluded that, in reality, few of them were based entirely on the fiction; they could usually be better explained and, indeed, justified, in other ways. If they could not, they were probably bad law and should be abandoned. Thus, for example, people's natural repugnance at the idea of a man being condemned by someone with whom he was intimately connected was a more likely explanation of the rule preventing spouses giving evidence against one another. Again, the rule which protected a woman who shielded her felon-husband could not be a deduction from the principle of unified personality; if it were, it would have applied equally to husbands. It was better explained in terms of a husband's power over his wife.[12]

Like the nineteenth-century legal commentators, Williams complained of the inadequacy of the fiction of unity, but failed to investigate its nature. He did not ask why an obviously impractical concept like the legal unity of husband and wife should ever have been developed, nor why it was used with such frequency. He did not ask what fictions are *for*. He treated the fiction as similar in nature to other possible explanations of the common-law rules under investigation, although a less convincing one. When discussing the rule which prevented a husband or wife who took the other's property from being guilty of theft, for example, he remarked that the legislature, having considered and confirmed it in the Married Women's Property Act of 1882, 'must have regarded it as supportable on grounds of policy, apart from the doctrine of unity'.[13] Although he made no attempt to identify the substantive meaning, if any, of the fiction, he rejected it on the grounds that it was not the 'real' reason for many of the rules comprising coverture. It seems to me harsh to criticise a fiction for not being real!

Williams concluded with the proposition that the fiction of marital unity could still legitimately be used to bolster up decisions arrived at on other grounds: 'a doctrine that enables the Judges to mould other rules of law in accordance with public policy or humanitarianism is not lightly to be cast aside'.[14] This is interesting. If the fiction had no substantive content – and Williams did not demonstrate that it had – then what was to be gained by making it an additional basis for new rules of law? It is unfortunate that Williams did not elaborate on the role which he envisaged for the fiction.

Mary Beard

By far the most interesting writing on the fiction of marital unity is to be found in the work of the American, Mary Ritter Beard. Beard, who died in 1958, was a feminist, an historian and an author. She was married to Charles Beard, who helped to found Ruskin Hall, a working-man's school in Oxford, and the couple collaborated on numerous publications. Beard's own work was devoted to an analysis of women's role in history; her most famous book, *Woman as Force in History*, was published in 1946.

Beard's message to women was that they represented a powerful force in the creation of civilisation and culture; they had a vital historic past and possessed the power to shape the future. She rejected the image of the female as the eternal victim, oppressed since the dawn of history; according to Beard, women's historic subjection was a myth.[15]

This myth that women were a subject sex had begun its life in the pages of legal textbooks, in Coke's *Institutes* and Blackstone's *Commentaries* in particular. These works represented the climax of a lengthy process of simplification and rationalisation of the common law which had commenced in the fifteenth century. The royal judges, in the interests of a strong, centralised state, had sought to create a coherent and uniform body of law, and the great textbook writers had been instrumental in bringing this about. They had given the common law a rigid form and enabled it to be uniformly applied.

Before this time, regional customs and usages had allowed some wives a much greater share in community life.[16] Among those with wealth in land the classification of women as married or single was important because on it depended the legitimacy of children and, therefore, inheritance, rights to dower and property rights generally. However, poorer women were sometimes allowed to avoid the legal consequences of marriage.[17] For example, with the growth of commerce in the sixteenth and seventeenth centuries, and as women's importance as buyers and sellers began to be recognised, the special laws of the City of London and some borough customs had enabled wives to trade as single women. However, as the common law developed, these regional customs and usages were increasingly threatened. Gradually, the law became 'more severe and discriminative towards women'.[18]

Coke and Blackstone were both notable for their rigid adherence to common law principles. The former was a supporter of greater parliamentary power; he fought to protect the common law from the encroachments of equity because it issued from a prerogative court and also because, in its wide sense, it represented the notion that judges should have discretion to modify the law in the interests of justice and reason.[19] Blackstone too was hostile to equity and, in Beard's view, dealt with it 'in such a brief, cursory, and inadequate manner as to give his readers the impression and induce the conviction that they need pay little serious attention to [it]'.[20] Beard was unsure about the reasons for this:

Generosity may well plead his ignorance as a sufficient explanation. Devotees of the common law may seek to account for his operations by referring to his overweening fondness for the common law. Technologists of the law may, with justice, point out his affection for the precision and certainty of common-law doctrines and his fear of the vagaries, variety, and uncertainty in the practices of men and women allowed and enforced by equity.[21]

Personally, she suspected that the seeds of his hostility to equity and to everything which resembled it, had been sown when Oxford University rejected his application for a professorship in Roman Civil law!

Whatever the reasons for Blackstone's predilections, the consequences were calamitous. In Beard's view, the *Commentaries* were the source of a seriously distorted conception of wives' legal status. The passage which opened with the words, '[b]y marriage, the husband and wife are one person in law', was hugely influential. It was written in 'the sparkling fashion which intrigues readers who detest "dry facts"'[22] and, consequently, it was seized upon and popularised in non-legal literature. But it was grossly misleading. What laypeople and, indeed, many lawyers failed to appreciate was that Blackstone's account dealt only with the common law. It could not serve as a comprehensive assessment of the wife's legal position for other sources of relevant law and custom, such as legislation, private contracts and equity, were virtually ignored. In particular, Blackstone failed to deal adequately with trusts, which were 'so important in correcting, even obliterating, the property "disabilities" of the married woman'.[23]

According to Beard, it was actually nineteenth-century feminists who were chiefly to blame for the spread of Blackstone's 'great dogma'. It was in feminist writing and speech-making that the notion of women as a subject sex was 'first given its most complete and categorical form'; and the authority invariably used as a focus was 'the inevitable passage from Blackstone, forever ringing like a bell to summon women to a wailing wall or to gird themselves for battle'. The passage became the

main support, indeed the very basis, of a great fiction – the fiction that women were, historically, members of a subject sex – 'civilly dead', their very being suspended during marriage and their property, along with their bodies, placed under the dominion of their respective 'lords' or 'barons'.[24]

Beard was primarily concerned with Blackstone's influence in the United States and with the way he was used by American feminists. However, her criticisms extended to the English feminists. She considered the work of John Stuart Mill, for example, to have been infected with the flawed American approach. That 'veritable bible' of the women's movement, *The Subjection of Women,*

followed the American example in taking Blackstone's creed without qualifications and in making it a dogma of history to be accepted by everybody,
everywhere, as if established by irrefutable knowledge.[25]

She thought that this was probably due to the influence of Mill's wife,
Harriet Taylor, who had been intellectually involved with American
feminism.

Beard was critical of the nineteenth-century feminists because she
believed that, in demanding equality rights, they were buying into an
essentially male dialogue on male terms. Instead of settling for an equal
share in the *status quo*, they ought to have devoted their energies to the
creation of a better and more humane society. Their slogan ought to
have been equity rather than equality, for the system of protection for
women's property operated by the courts of equity reflected a true
understanding of the realities of women's lives. Women's lives would
always be inexorably bound up with the lives of husbands and children,
and it was right that the law should recognise this.

Charlotte Stopes and Matilda Fenberg

Beard was not alone in taking this kind of extreme 'human agency'
approach to women's history. In 1894 Charlotte Stopes accused Coke
of bearing much of the responsibility for women's inferior status.[26] She
was particularly concerned about the effect that his pronouncements
had had on women's right to vote. In 1947, a year after the appearance
of *Woman as Force in History*, Matilda Fenberg published an article
entitled 'Blame Coke and Blackstone'. She, like Stopes, cast Coke as
chief villain, and dedicated much of the article to an account of his
stormy family life, particularly with his proudly independent second
wife, Elizabeth Cecil Hatton. According to Fenberg, 'Coke read the
law in order to find in it a means to controlling Lady Hatton that he
did not have under the law as it actually was'.[27]

Critique of Beard[28]

Beard's achievement should not be underestimated. *Woman as Force in
History* was 'provocative, imaginative, scholarly and enormously bold
for its time. It projected a model for women's history when there was
little on which to draw'.[29] It also served as a much-needed corrective
to the popular notion that 'from the age of savagery until the present
day every change in marital law has been favourable to the wife'.[30] On
the other hand, however, it would be unwise to dismiss as a myth the

fact that women have generally occupied a lower status than men. It is simply not true that women's legal disabilities were invented by Blackstone or by nineteenth-century feminists. The law *did* treat men and women unequally and, in parts of her book, Beard acknowledged this.

Beard believed that equity operated as a counterbalance to the common-law rules on married women's property. However, she greatly exaggerated its ameliorating effects. She represented it as an 'independent legal system, equal in weight and antithetical in direction to the common law'; in reality, 'it was ancillary, filling in gaps left by the rigidity of the common law'.[31] In some respects, its principles were as patriarchal as those of the common law; it originated in the concept of the King as *parens patriae*, the father of the country, to whom people under disabilities could make special appeals. Moreover, the married woman's separate estate had not been developed to enhance the independence of wives; it was largely designed to assist the rich father who feared that property transferred to his daughter would come to grief in the hands of a spendthrift son-in-law. As I pointed out in the previous chapter, marriage settlements rarely gave control of the separate estate to the wife herself. Often the father would retain control himself. Alternatively, there might be a restraint on anticipation, preventing the daughter or her trustees from alienating or charging the capital during marriage. Without this, there was the danger that her husband would 'kiss or kick'[32] her out of her rights. A final practical limitation on the usefulness of equity was the expense involved; equitable relief was a reality only for women from wealthy families.

There is a further problem with Beard's analysis. As Peggy Rabkin has pointed out, there was a contradiction in her treatment of the role of nineteenth-century feminists. On the one hand, she claimed that they mistook Blackstone's writings on the law of husband and wife for an accurate and comprehensive statement of the law. Lacking legal training, they were unaware that equity even existed. At the same time, however, she seemed to accuse them of deliberately exploiting Blackstone's dogma. They used him as 'the warrant for adopting a theory of total subjection on which to base a demand for freedom and equality'.[33] Thus, a dual image of the nineteenth-century feminist emerges: on the one hand, she was a well-meaning but misguided amateur; on the other, she was a cynical tactician. Which of these images, if either, was closer to the reality?

It cannot be denied that Blackstone oversimplified the law relating to married women. Although he *did* address the position in equity, he did not deal with it in any depth. It is undoubtedly true that there were some feminists who were familiar with only the one famous passage and who did not appreciate the true position. It is equally certain that there were others with considerable legal knowledge. Rabkin cites Elizabeth Stanton and Lucy Stone as American examples. Stanton was the daughter of a judge, the wife of a lawyer and was known to have read far beyond Blackstone. Stone was responsible for drafting an alternative marriage contract, the terms of which reflected an understanding of both common law and equity. The position in England was no different. The women who, in the second half of the nineteenth century, were actively involved in the battle for women's rights were clearly conversant with the relevant law.

However, this does not mean that their use of Blackstone was purely tactical. Unlike Beard, these feminists recognised that, for the vast majority of women, equity was irrelevant; the common law continued to apply in all its rigour to those who lacked wealth and skilled legal advice. The *Commentaries* were not, unfortunately, out of date. It may be true that the feminists were attracted to Blackstone's description of the common-law position because of its dramatic absolutism and the opportunities which it offered for oratory. However, it may also have been the case that they perceived the enormous psychological power of Blackstone's images and that, for this reason, they regarded them as a worthy object of attack. Ironically, however, by helping to popularise Blackstone's imagery, they may have extended its influence even further. In this respect, Beard's analysis may have been correct and this is one of the reasons why it continues to be important. These are issues which are returned to later in the chapter.

Finally, Beard grossly overstated the role played by Blackstone himself. She regarded him as the source of the fiction of unity, or 'the Blackstone fiction' as she subsequently called it.[34] He was also treated as responsible for the notion that the wife's legal existence was suspended during the marriage; that, in the eyes of the law, her personality merged with her husband's. One section is introduced by the uncompromising heading: 'BLACKSTONE EXTINGUISHED THE MARRIED WOMAN'S PER-SONALITY'.[35] This is inaccurate. The fiction of unity did not originate in Blackstone's eighteenth-century *Commentaries*; it predated both Blackstone and his partner-in-crime, Coke. It dates, in fact, from the twelfth century. It is true that Alfred Dewes thought that the idea of the wife's legal existence being suspended or incorporated into her husband's had originated with Blackstone.[36] However, Holdsworth mentions a medieval tendency to analogise wives with people who had taken religious orders and were, therefore, deemed dead in law;[37] and in *The Hardships of the English Laws*, published in 1735, the expressions 'Dead in Law' and 'Law of Annihilation' are used in relation to wives.[38] Nevertheless, I believe that there was more than a germ of truth in Beard's assertions. Although she was wrong about the *origins* of the fiction, she may well have identified a centrally important period in its *history*. It will be argued below that Coke and Blackstone were, indeed, influential; not because they invented the fiction, but because they recorded and facilitated a transformation in its nature.

Norma Basch

In her excellent 1982 study of married women's property rights in nineteenth-century New York, Norma Basch had this to say of the fiction of marital unity:

> The concept functioned in a diversity of historical contexts. Its religious origins lay in the one-flesh doctrine of Christianity, its empirical roots in the customs of medieval Normandy. Its introduction into English law after the Norman conquest signalled a decline in the status of English wives which reached a nadir in the early capitalism of the sixteenth and seventeenth centuries. It was part of the baggage that English colonists carried to the New World. But what is most striking about the long course of the concept of marital unity is its ability to serve the needs of three shifting social structures: the kin-oriented family of the late Middle Ages, the patriarchal nuclear family of early capitalism, and even the more companionate nuclear family of the late eighteenth century.[39]

In the remainder of this chapter I adopt and seek to build on this intriguing analysis. Like Basch, I believe that the fiction of marital unity was a chameleon concept; its role changed over time in response to changing circumstances. However, Basch did not have time to elaborate fully on this relationship. She did not specify the demands that were made of the fiction at different periods, and the adaptations which it underwent in order to meet those demands. This is the task which I now undertake. My conclusions are based primarily on an examination of the way in which the fiction was treated in the writings of legal and lay commentators at different periods; they are necessarily highly speculative.

The Origins of the Fiction of Marital Unity

The image of husband and wife as one person or one flesh has featured in legal literature since the time of the Norman Conquest.[40] It appears in the earliest English law book, the twelfth-century *Dialogus de Scaccario*, and in the work of every leading common-law writer since.[41] Glanvil mentions it in the twelfth century; Bracton makes frequent use of it in the thirteenth. It is used by Littleton in the fifteenth century;[42] and by Fitzherbert in the sixteenth.[43] We are told that '[h]usband and wife are one flesh';[44] they are described as 'one blood and one flesh and one body[45] ... although different souls'.[46]

The emergence of the fiction coincided with a marked deterioration in women's legal status. It is generally accepted that, in the Anglo-Saxon period, women enjoyed a greater degree of independence and influence than they would for many centuries to come. However, from the time of the Conquest, rights which they had previously possessed were gradually withdrawn.[47] The end result was 'a society in which the role of women was very sharply differentiated from that in the pre-1066 era'.[48]

The Wife in Anglo-Saxon Times

It is difficult to generalise about this period; as Christine Fell rightly cautions, one cannot

assume that all pre-Conquest Anglo-Saxon society is the same society and that the laws of one century and region reflect attitudes common to the whole of Anglo-Saxon England from the sixth century to the eleventh.[49]

It must also be remembered that the law afforded women differential treatment according to class. Bearing these things in mind, the picture which emerges from the law-codes is of a wife whose independence was safeguarded and whose interests were protected.[50]

It seems clear that on marriage a certain amount of the husband's property, part of which was called the morning-gift, was nominated as the wife's. The wife's share was customarily a third but, later, could be increased by agreement to a half. Although the husband had powers of personal enjoyment and administration over this property, it belonged absolutely to the wife; he could not permanently alienate it from her possession. The wife could certainly dispose of her morning-gift during her life and by will, and this may have been true of all her property. She also retained ownership of everything that came to her by inheritance or by gift. If a couple had children, the morning-gift was superseded by a principle of community: the wife became co-possessor with the husband of the family property. No distinction was made in Anglo-Saxon times between real and personal property.

It is true that the husband was the wife's guardian, and it is certain that she was expected to be obedient to him. However, if he mistreated her, she could expect assistance and support from her kin. Before agreeing to her marriage, her family would have stipulated on her behalf for her honourable treatment as wife and widow, and the law recognised their continuing interest in this.

The Wife in Anglo-Norman Times

After 1066 things changed.[51] The principle of community property was rejected and the system of marital property law described in the last chapter began to develop. The law acknowledged the wife's need to be maintained but turned its back on the notion that she was a working partner in her marriage who was, therefore, entitled to a share in its profits.

By the end of the twelfth century a wife had lost control over her real property during her lifetime. She could veto alienation, but that was all. When her husband died she acquired an interest in his property, but it was limited to a life-interest in a third of the real property. The amount could be reduced by agreement but could no longer be increased. She had no rights over this property during her lifetime. If her husband alienated it, she could claim it back later from the purchaser; however, if it could be shown that she had opposed her husband's disposal of her dower, she might be punished by losing her right to reclaim it. This was because she was considered to be 'in a legal sense under the absolute power of her Husband'.[52]

Her personal property passed absolutely to the husband. Until the fourteenth century, under the doctrine of 'reasonable parts', she was entitled to a half of her husband's personal property when he died; a third if there were children. However, she had no interest in these chattels while he was alive. Both Glanvil and Bracton thought that the husband should consent to her devise of the chattels that she would be entitled to as a widow; they regarded this as 'a mark of affection and highly creditable to the husband'.[53] However, if he refused this consent, she was unable to make a will.

There are a number of reasons why these changes occurred when they did. First, the Normans brought with them an extreme version of the Germanic notion of the *mundium*: the idea that the guardianship or legal control of the wife was vested in the husband. In some areas of France, contact with Roman law had gradually softened the customs of the Germanic settlers, but when the Northmen conquered Normandy they came fresh from their native country; the doctrine of the 'mundium' which they espoused retained all its Scandinavian simplicity.[54]

Moreover, Norman society was a society organised for war; the prime motive of its economy was the support of the warrior. This produced what was essentially a man's world. Those who were not expected to fight inevitably took second place to those who were, and the superiority of men over women became part of an unchallengeable order of ideas.[55]

But perhaps the most important factor was the growing influence of the Church. Of course, England had been Christian long before the eleventh century. However, before that time, the source of ecclesiastical influence was homiletic rather than legal; that is to say, it emanated from preaching and theological writing. In particular, the Anglo-Saxon clergy reached the people through manuals of offences and penances, called penetentials. These compilations had no legislative authority behind them but, like the influential seventh-century Penetentials of Archbishop Theodore of Canterbury, would often be held in great esteem. This home-grown kind of ecclesiastical law did not impose the Church's teachings in all their rigour. Rather, concessions were made to the customs of the land, particularly in the area of divorce and separation.[56]

However, during the eleventh and twelfth centuries, ecclesiastical authority became centralised in the pope in Rome. Theological teaching hardened into canon law and William I, who owed much to the help of the Church, assisted its introduction into England. A system of English ecclesiastical courts emerged, distinct from the temporal courts, and part of a transnational hierarchy of tribunals which had the pope at its apex. Gradually these Church courts gained control over many areas of law which affected women. Questions of matrimony and bastardy, probate of wills and testaments and succession to personal property all fell within their exclusive jurisdiction.[57] Through the medium of canon law, the Church's theories on the inferiority of women were brought to bear on Anglo-Norman wives.[58]

The early Church's thinking on the subject of women and marriage was characterised by contradiction; some would call it hypocrisy. On the one hand, there was the idea that a woman's soul was equal to a man's in the eyes of God. This was conducive to a principle of equality within marriage, and was even supported by some of the writings of Saint Paul.[59] However, an alternative view emphasised that woman had been created after man; indeed, she was a by-product of him. She had been created in response to his needs. Most significantly, she had been the agent of his downfall and the cause of his banishment from paradise. All of these things were taken as proofs of her inferiority.

It was the latter rather than the former set of ideas which was most enthusiastically embraced. An early and enduring systematisation of canon law announced that 'women should be subject to their men'.[60] This belief in the inferiority of women fed a clerical horror of sexuality.

Saint Paul had said that it was 'good for a man not to touch a woman' and he portrayed marriage as a poor but necessary alternative to perpetual virginity; after all, it was 'better to marry than to burn'.[61] Celibacy became a Christian ideal and itself contributed to anti-female sentiment.

The Fiction of Unity and the Power Principle in Anglo-Norman Times

As we have seen, the appearance of the fiction of unity coincided with these changes and it is tempting to posit a connection. Was the fiction used as an expression of the new attitude towards wives? It is contended here that it was not; that there was no direct connection at this time between the fiction of marital unity and the subjection of wives.

At a later period the fiction of marital unity would be used to explain and justify the law's subordination of wives. However, this was not how it was used in the Middle Ages. Early common lawyers who discussed the position of wives had recourse instead to the power principle. They were unabashed about this. They did not talk of 'unity' when they meant 'subjection'; when they thought that the wife was or ought to be in a subordinate position, they felt free to say so. Expressions of the coercion and the authority principles are found in medieval legal records and literature much more frequently than the fiction of unity.[62] The wife was described as being *sub virga viri*, literally, 'under the rod of the husband';[63] she was 'completely subject to his authority and could gainsay him in nothing',[64] nor 'contrary to his pleasure, look to her rights'.[65]

What did the common-law writers mean then when they talked of the fiction of unity? It must be remembered that the medieval lawyers and writers were clerics: it is my belief that they were simply referring to the canonical doctrines of the unity of flesh and of the indissolubility of marriage.[66] Saint Paul had said that 'a man [shall] leave his father and mother and cleave to his wife; and the twain shall become one flesh';[67] and this was thought to mean that marriage created a relationship between husband and wife which resembled that between brother and sister. Thus, divorce was

not so much an infraction of the divine law as an impotent pretence, an attempt to alter a fact of nature, and a denial of the existence of that which exists. It may be compared with a law which should purport to destroy the kinship of a brother and a sister, of a parent and a child.[68]

Henceforth, husband and wife counted as one for the purpose of computing relationship. The wife was assimilated to the husband with respect to his relations and, similarly, the husband was as one with his wife with respect to hers. The relations of either spouse were the *same* relations of the other; someone related to a wife by consanguinity, was related to the husband by affinity in the same degree. Marriage was forbidden by law with both sets of relatives to the same degree of relationship and in exactly the same way. Thus, the notion of the marital unity of flesh gave rise not only to the prohibition on divorce, but also to the prohibition on marrying, for example, one's deceased wife's sister.

The fiction does not appear before the time of the Conquest because Anglo-Saxon customs were resistant to these rules. In Anglo-Saxon society the larger kinship group dominated and a wife was not regarded as a member of her husband's family. Marriage did not change her status; although her children assumed their father's status, she kept that of her own father. Marriage occurred between both blood and affinal relatives within the degrees of relationship prohibited by the Church; and the attitude towards divorce was casual.[69]

The laxity in the divorce laws applied not only to men but, to some extent, to women also. Until the seventh century, divorce by mutual consent was available. The authorities disagree as to whether Archbishop Theodore permitted separation by mutual consent; however, it seems clear that separation at least was available in cases of adultery (although not necessarily on equal terms to both sexes), and that there were some grounds which even justified complete dissolution of the marriage.[70] After the Conquest, of course, dissolution of marriage, except by annulment, became impossible. Separation remained available on a number of grounds, but this was an unattractive option for women, as they remained subject to all the legal disabilities of wifehood.

In summary, then, the early common-law writers used the fiction of marital unity to refer to the canonical doctrines of unity of the flesh and indissolubility of marriage. These doctrines contributed to a wife's dependence but were not at the root of it. At the root of her subordination lay the power principle. The medieval common lawyers recognised and acknowledged this; they unashamedly called a spade a spade. In the Middle Ages, the fiction of unity had not been consciously adopted as a legal principle which explained or justified the law's subordination of women. This process began in the seventeenth century. Oliver J. notes in *Midland Bank Trust Co. Ltd.* v. *Green* (No. 3) that

[b]y the time of Coke ... the rationale of the rule seems to have shifted rather away from an axiomatic biblical principle of unity towards a consideration of the public policy which ought to guide the law in the extent to which it should interfere in the relationship between husband and wife.[71]

It was in the seventeenth century that lawyers began to use the fiction of unity frequently and to connect it explicitly with the wife's subordinate position. This was done in a fanciful and intriguing fashion by the author of *The Lawes Resolutions of Womens Rights*:

> It is true that Man and Wife are one person, but understand in what manner. When a small brooke or little river incorporateth with Rhodanus, Humber, or the Thames, the poore Rivolet loseth her name, it is carried and recarried with the new associate, it beareth no sway, it possesseth nothing during coverture. A woman as soon as she is married is called covert ... that is, vailed, as it were, clouded and overshadowed, ... she hath lost her streame, she is continually sub potestate viri [under the power of the husband].... her new Selfe is her superior, her companion, her master....[72]

The Functions of Legal Fictions

Why did the fiction of unity become important as a way of describing the marital relationship? And why did this happen when it did? These are the questions which need to be answered next. However, before we can proceed, we need to confront a wider issue. Why do legal fictions exist at all? What are legal fictions for?

Lon Fuller addressed this question in his 1967 book, *Legal Fictions*. He began by examining some specific examples and then went on to consider possible motives for the use of fictions generally.[73]

His comments on the fiction of marital unity were rather unsatisfactory. The statement that husband and wife are one person was treated as fictitious simply because it was an inadequate description of the legal situation of the parties. In reality, the courts did not always treat husband and wife as one person in law; if they had done, the statement would not have been a fiction. Fuller thought that the fiction of unity was simply an example of the shorthand way in which legal relations were commonly described. He did admit, though, that it seemed to involve 'an unnecessary and aberrational obscurity'.[74]

According to Fuller, fictions are generally used to reconcile legal results with some premise or postulate – either a specific, recognised rule of law, or an unexpressed principle of jurisprudence or morals. It can be an emotive or persuasive device, designed to induce the conviction that a given legal result is just and proper. It can do this by making it appear that the principle or rule of law mentioned above has not, in fact, been departed from. It can be used to introduce new law in the guise of old. Alternatively, it can serve as an 'apology' for a rule of law that has existed from the beginning of our legal system: in short, a way of obscuring an unpleasant truth.

Fuller did not consider whether any of these motives might have applied to the use of the fiction of unity. Had he done so, he might have found it less obscure.

Did the fiction of unity, like other fictions, serve to obscure the implications of some rule of law or principle of jurisprudence or morals? It is contended here that it did. As has been said, the fiction came to the fore in the seventeenth century – a time of enormous religious, economic and political change. Out of this upheaval, a new philosophical and political idea was emerging – an idea which stood at odds with the subordination of wives. It was only the fiction of marital unity which made the two appear to be compatible. The principle in question was individualism.

The Role of the Fiction of Marital Unity in the Seventeenth Century

The upheavals of the Stuart era had their roots in changes which had begun in the previous century. The modern state was emerging out of and replacing the large feudal households as the main organising institution of society. Mercantilism and the early forms of capitalism were replacing the feudal economy. The Protestant Reformation had transformed the English religious world.[75] These developments had profound implications for the old established order.

Religious and Political Individualism

Through its courts and its priesthood, the pre-Reformation Church had exercised a strong degree of social control. Absolution from sin was dispensed in return for penance. However, Protestantism situated the battle with sin within the individual conscience. The individual could learn God's will through the study of the scriptures without the mediation of priests or of sacraments. Outward penance and absolution were replaced by inward penitence. These were dangerous ideas[76]

[f]or if the individual can set up his conscience against priest and church, by the same token he can set himself up against the government with which the church is so intimately associated.[77]

However, initially, this danger was averted by the notion of 'the elect': only a minority of people were assured of salvation; the unregenerate mass were irretrievably damned. This ungodly majority had to be kept under control and the elect (who tended to be drawn from the propertied section of society) accepted that only a coercive state could perform this task effectively.

Among the radical Puritan sects that thrived during the Civil War and the Interregnum, the doctrine of predestination was challenged. The radicals asserted that all believers were spiritually equal; that 'Christ died for all men alike, the reprobate as well as the elect'.[78] They also denied the need for a preaching ministry to convey the content of the scriptures to the people. In fact, the role of the scriptures was downplayed and a greater emphasis was placed on personal revelation and the working of the spirit within the individual; the inner light was set above scripture as a source of authority. The revolutionary implications were clear. The principle that 'the Spirit bloweth where it listeth'[79] proved an extremely powerful solvent of the established order; it challenged the notion that the structure of society was divinely ordained in all its details.

The new emphasis on the individual in the religious sphere was mirrored by a similar development in political philosophy. Previously, patriarchal theorists had insisted that relationships of subordination and authority were God-given or natural. Thus the hierarchical social structures which had characterised the feudal age could be justified. However, these arrangements were no longer consistent with the needs of a changing economy. The growth of early capitalism created a need for individuals who were theoretically free and equal, for '[h]ow could [they] freely enter contracts, make equal exchanges, and pursue their interests in the market, if they were not so conceived?'[80]

As Carole Pateman has pointed out, this created a problem of political obligation. How could these free and equal individuals legitimately be governed?

The assumption that individuals were born free and equal to each other meant that none of the old arguments for subordination could be accepted. Arguments that rulers and masters exercised their power through God's will had to be rejected; might or force could no longer be translated into political right; appeals to custom and tradition were no longer sufficient; nor were the various arguments from nature, whether they looked to the generative power of a father, or to superior birth, strength, ability or rationality. All these familiar arguments became unacceptable because the doctrine of individual freedom and equality entailed that there was only one justification for subordination. A naturally free and equal individual must, necessarily, *agree* to be ruled by another.[81]

So, individuals possessing the qualities necessary for the maintenance of the market economy could only be bound to obey the laws on the basis of their own consent. But why should they give that consent?

This was the question which seventeenth-century political philosophers were required to answer. Why should free and equal individuals agree to submit themselves to the will of another?

Women in the Seventeenth Century

The significance of these new ideas was not lost on the women of the time. In almost every area of seventeenth-century life traces of a nascent feminist consciousness could be found. Women challenged their subordination in religion and in the home, their legal disabilities and their exclusion from the electorate.

Women were disproportionately represented in the radical Puritan sects.[82] The idea that '[t]he soul knows no difference of sex'[83] offered them greater scope for involvement and self-expression than was available elsewhere. Many of the small independent congregations which proliferated after 1642 allowed their women members to debate and to vote. In some they were even permitted to preach or, failing that, to prophesy. Women, like men, could claim to be in direct communication with God and to speak with His voice.

Few religious radicals advocated equality in any but the religious sphere. The women who became involved were seeking liberty of conscience and religion rather than freedom from male authority generally. Nevertheless, their beliefs could all too easily give rise to conflict with traditional expectations of their role within the family:

The spirit might move a woman to celibacy, or to challenge the husband's right to govern her conscience, or to tell her where to worship. The spirits had little regard for the respect due to worldly patriarchy, they recognised only the power of God.[84]

Some of the radical Puritan women had left the former family church without the consent of their husbands. Some even abandoned unregenerate spouses and chose new mates who shared their new-found faith.

The radicals were, of course, a small minority of the population. However, women were becoming more vocal within mainstream Protestantism as well.[85] When an authoritarian moralist, William Gouge, preached on 'Domesticall Duties' to his Blackfriars congregation, his female parishioners criticised him severely for his views on the extent of a husband's rightful authority. He was obliged to preface the 1622 published version with an apology, 'that I might not ever be judged (as some have censured me) an hater of women'.[86] The women objected, in particular, to being told that a wife could not dispose of the common goods of the family without her husband's consent.

Discussions about the position of women and the proper relations between husband and wife featured in the popular literature of the day and generated both interest and controversy. By about 1625 it had become a common journalistic and literary theme.[87]

Even among lawyers there was concern about the inequality between the sexes. Handbooks on women and the law were beginning to appear.[88] One of the earliest, *The Lawes Resolutions of Womens Rights*, seems to have been written around 1600. It was significant for a number of reasons. First, it constituted a sometimes biting critique of the legal position of married women. Secondly, although it was a complex and legalistic work, it was purportedly designed for a female readership.[89] And, finally, it advised wives to take political action to improve their position: 'Have patience (my Schollars) take not your opportunitie of revenge, rather move for redress by Parliament.'[90]

In the 1640s there were women who took this advice, petitioning Parliament and demonstrating.[91] During the first year of the Long Parliament some 400 working women, who were suffering severe financial hardship as a result of the decay of trade, petitioned the Lords and the Commons for a change in public policy. They based their claim on the fact that 'in the free enjoying of Christ in His own laws, and a flourishing estate of the Church and Commonwealth consisteth the happiness of women as well as men'.[92] This was followed by a number of similar events, culminating in a demand by female Levellers for equal participation with men in the political process. These women explicitly rejected the idea that wives were legally or politically represented by their husbands. However, the Leveller leadership never included women in their demands for a greatly enlarged suffrage and, after 1649, this women's liberation movement vanished.

There were also four instances of female intervention in parliamentary elections in the first half of the century. Surprisingly, the early judicial responses suggested that there was no reason in law why a propertied and unmarried woman could not vote. According to Beatrice and Mary Chapman and to Charlotte Stopes, women's political disability dated from an unsupported pronouncement in the fourth part of Coke's *Institutes* which was not published until 1644.[93]

It was inevitable that female subjection should come under scrutiny during this period for women were not blind to the implications of contemporary political theory. The social contract theorists denied that people were 'naturally bound together in a hierarchy of inequality and subordination';[94] authority relationships were grounded in convention only. Why then were wives still regarded as naturally inferior to and bound to obey their husbands? And if men were born free and equal and could not, therefore, be bound to obey the laws of government without having freely assumed that obligation for themselves, what of women? In the words of the seventeenth-century feminist, Mary Astell, '*If all men are born free,* how is it that all Women are born slaves?'[95]

The Political Philosopher's Solution – the Social and Sexual Contracts

Social contract theory developed as a challenge to patriarchal theory and, on the face of it, it embodied an emancipatory and therefore alarming doctrine. This was the notion that individuals must agree or contract to be governed. Conservatives were naturally anxious but, as Carole Pateman has pointed out, their fears were groundless. Social contract theory performed precisely the same function in the seventeenth century as patriarchal theory had performed in the feudal era which preceded it: it legitimised the power of the state. Far from undermining subordination, the contract theorists justified modern civil subjection:

The classic social contract theorists assumed that individual attributes and social conditions always made it reasonable for an individual to give an affirmative answer to the fundamental question whether a relationship of subordination should be created through contract. The point of the story of the social contract is that, in the state of nature, freedom is so insecure that it is reasonable for individuals to subordinate themselves to the civil law of the state....[96]

The point at which it became rational for men to enter the social contract was the point at which inequalities of wealth became so great that a limited, impartial government was necessary to secure protection of property rights.

The woman problem was dealt with just as adroitly. The way in which this was done is examined in detail in the works of Carole Pateman;[97] her important and fascinating analysis can only be briefly summarised here.

John Locke's solution to the woman problem was seemingly straightforward. Women were *not* free and equal individuals because they were subject to their husbands. The husband was 'the abler and the stronger' of the two and, thus, there was a 'Foundation in Nature' for his domination. When a man and woman were married it was necessary that one of them be the decision-maker; given his superiority, 'it naturally [fell] to the Man's share' to govern over their 'common Interest and Property'.[98] This was clearly at odds with the principle that authority relationships were conventional rather than natural. However, this principle was apparently only relevant in the political sphere; and family relationships were not political. Thus Locke solved the problem by distinguishing between political and paternal power. Natural subjection had no place in the new civil society but there was a private, politically irrelevant sphere in which it continued to exist.

Locke's women were not parties to the social contract. Rather, they were incorporated into civil society through their marriage contracts. Given their lack of natural freedom, it is hard to see how they could be capable of entering into this contract. However, it was essential that they did. As Pateman explains, the principle of civil society was universal freedom; and the way in which freedom was exhibited in civil society was through contract. If the principle of universal freedom was to be presented as a reality everyone had to enter into a contract.

Hobbes's women were not parties to the social contract either; as with Locke, the 'individuals' who entered the capitalist economy were heads of households. This is harder to understand in Hobbes's case, for he regarded men and women as equals in the state of nature. Seemingly, by the time the original contract was entered into, the men had managed to conquer the women and reduce them to the status of servants. Women were not 'wives' in Hobbes's state of nature; that only came with the creation of civil society, when their subjection was secured through the marriage contract. Hobbes never treated male domination as natural: in the state of nature it was acquired through force; in civil society it was conferred by the civil law which included the laws of matrimony. These laws were inevitably patriarchal 'because for the most part commonwealths have been erected by the fathers not the mothers of families'.[99] Thus, Hobbes recognised that conjugal right was *political* – it was created by the civil laws of matrimony and these, in their turn, were created through the original compact.

Pateman finds Hobbes's characteristically stark and honest account a good deal more illuminating than Locke's:

Hobbes's political theory makes clear what the other classic contract stories, and contemporary commentators on contract theory leave implicit: that the original contract is not only a *social* contract that constitutes the civil law and political right in the sense of (state) government; it is also a *sexual* contract that institutes political right in the form of patriarchal – masculine – power, or government by men.... Matrimonial law takes a patriarchal form because *men* have made the original contract. The fact that the law of matrimony is part of the civil law provides another reason for self-interested individual men to make a collective agreement. In addition to securing their natural liberty, *men as a sex* have an interest in a political mechanism which secures for them collectively the fruits of the conquest made severally by each man in the natural condition.[100]

Men had a two-fold reason then for agreeing to subject themselves to the power of the state. Not only did they gain civil security; they also acquired control over women. Just as the social contract legitimised the state's power over men, the sexual contract legitimised men's power over women. Pateman calls this 'male sex-right' or 'conjugal right'; I have called it the power principle.

The Lawyer's Solution – The Fiction of Marital Unity

The law also played a central role in the legitimisation of women's subjection. In theory, society was now built upon the principle of universal freedom; and yet one half of its members were not free. This was an embarrassing and dangerous contradiction, for how could women be obliged to obey the state's laws if they were incapable of being parties to the social contract? The political philosophers had used the marriage contract to incorporate women into civil society, but this was clearly unconvincing: if the marriage contract was one that women were capable of entering into then it could not have been a real contract. It fell to lawyers to persuade people that women's inferior status was compatible with the principle of individualism.

The persuasive device which they used was the fiction of marital unity. The fiction obviated the necessity of qualifying the principle that *every* individual was free and equal and, therefore, entitled to equal protection under the laws and to a voice in government. In the eyes of the law, a husband and wife constituted *not two individuals, but one.* The fiction became a means of obscuring the reality that wives were excluded from full legal personhood and from citizenship.

Thus Beard was right to have focused on the influence of Coke and Blackstone for they both helped to engineer this transformation in the fiction's role. What legal textbook writers managed to do, with the help of the fiction of unity, was to justify married women's exclusion from the franchise in purely legal terms. As the law did not recognise the possibility of separate interests within marriage, a wife could effectively be represented by her husband.

The great legal commentators created the first clear maps of the common law; their systems of classification affected the way in which people thought about the law. And they structured their treatment of coverture in such a way that connections between private law and public law – between a wife's legal status within the family and her status as a citizen of the state – were avoided.[101] When they discussed the general right to hold property they did not deny its connection with the right to vote. Property qualifications were designed, according to Blackstone, 'to exclude such persons as are in so mean a situation as to be esteemed to have no will of their own.'[102] The propertyless were regarded as dependent, without a real stake in society and, therefore, incapable of full citizenship. However, coverture, which entailed, among other things, a loss of control over property during marriage, was dealt with entirely separately. In legal textbooks, and in the minds of those who read them, coverture was in a different compartment.

Thus lawyers helped to contain the early impetus towards political emancipation, at least as regards married women, and, since the destruction of the convents had deprived women of the only alternative career which had stood as high in public esteem as marriage,[103] nearly all women eventually ended up in this category.

The Fiction of Marital Unity and the Protestant Conception of the Marital Relationship

In the nineteenth century Frances Power Cobbe identified 'sentiment' as the most powerful support of the fiction of unity. Men had formed in their minds a poetical vision of the wife's true relation to her husband and it involved 'the beautiful ideal of absolute union of heart, life and purse'. This was 'the feeling at the bottom of nearly all men's hearts, and of the hearts of thousands of women also'.[104] This was no less true in the seventeenth century; the fiction of unity emerged alongside the Protestant sanctification of marriage and married love[105] and the two ideas were mutually supportive.

The Catholic Church had regarded matrimony as a protection against the sin of fornication for the morally weak. However, Protestantism made of marriage 'a state in itself far more excellent than the condition of single life'.[106] In 1549 Archbishop Cranmer had officially added the desire for 'mutual society, help and comfort' to avoidance of fornication and production of children as legitimate motives for marriage. The Puritans in particular emphasised the values of family life and the mutuality of marital obligations. Conduct likely to jeopardise domestic security was deplored; sexual infidelity was regarded as much of a sin in husbands as in wives. Gradually

marriage came to be seen as a sanctified partnership, the relationship most conducive not only to productivity but to the fulfilment of all other spiritual and emotional needs. Especially in its radical puritan expression, this new conjugality came closest to the modern norm of companionate marriage.[107]

The significance of these developments must not be exaggerated. First, as John Gillis has pointed out,

[h]istorians of such differing perspectives as Lawrence Stone and Christopher Hill have been correct in locating the origins of the conjugal ideal in the revolutionary 1640s and 1650s, but wrong in assuming a linear, continuous progression from that time to our own. In fact the precocious conjugality of the 1640s and 1650s was utopian, a volatile ideal rather than a sustained reality.[108]

And, secondly, it was always clear that the primary Protestant message was one of wifely subjection. Men were enjoined not to beat their wives but reminded that their

Tenderness ought still to be so construed, as to retain a just decorum of superiority, that [their wives] may not think they can command, and subvert the Order of Obedience. They are made to be governed not to govern.[109]

In sermons, pamphlets, marriage manuals and conduct books, the wife's duty to obey was hammered home.[110] In the official *Homily on Marriage* − one of a series published by the authority of Elizabeth I from which every parson was obliged to read in church on Sundays[111] − she was told of her sacred duty to love her husband and submit to his will in everything. For the sake of a happy Christian marriage, she should 'endeavour in all ways to content her husband, do his pleasure and avoid what may offend him'.[112] Husbands were asked to remember that 'a woman is the weaker vessell, of a frail heart; inconstant, and with a word soon stirred to wrath',[113] and temper their rule over them accordingly.

However, these same sources contained images of an ideal relationship in which the husband's power to dominate was softened by the couple's perfect unity. As one early eighteenth-century commentator put it: 'It is possible there may be Persons so united together, that the Will of one, is the Will and Choice of the other.'[114]

William Gouge thought that the marital relationship was 'the nearest to equality that may be … wherein man and wife are after a sort even fellows and partners,'[115] while the *Homily on Matrimony* envisaged the ideal marriage as a yoke drawn 'in one accord of heart and mind' by spouses united by a 'pleasant and sweet love'.[116]

Seventeenth-century women were undoubtedly attracted by these images of an intense and special relationship and it cannot be denied that for some they represented reality. Consider, for example, the powerful words of Anne Fanshawe who led an adventurous life with her Royalist husband during the Civil War years: 'Glory be to God,' she wrote

We never had but one mind throughout our lives, our souls were wrapped up in each other, our aims and designs were one, and our resentments one. We so studied one the other that we knew each others mind by our looks; whatever was real happiness, God gave it me in him.[117]

For many women, the Protestant ideal of conjugality imbued the fiction of marital unity with a religious and romantic significance which helped to reconcile them to the harshness of the marriage laws.[118]

Individualism and the Feme Covert – Conclusion

In the words of Mona Caird, '[t]he Anglo-Saxon race is not naturally addicted to "ideas", but it prefers them, if the worst comes to the worst, to revolutionary changes'.[119]

The idea that emerged to deal with the alarming implications of individualism for the status of wives was the fiction of marital unity. It was the fiction of marital unity which turned the radical Leveller woman of the Civil War into the 'disappearing free and equal individual'[120] of liberal democracy. Its installation as the fundamental principle underlying the marital relationship was part of the process of turning the world the right way up again after the crises and upheavals of the seventeenth century.

The Role of the Fiction of Marital Unity in the Nineteenth Century

In the nineteenth century, as we have seen, the fiction of marital unity became a focus for feminist wrath. Women railed against the idea that their legal existence was suspended during marriage and, in the process, made the Blackstonian rendition of the fiction into common currency. The wife was described in feminist writing as 'non-existent',[121] as a 'non-entity' and a 'shadow';[122] she was reduced to 'very nothingness'.[123] Frances Power Cobbe likened husband and wife under English law to a pair of tarantula spiders: left to themselves, the larger would gobble the smaller one up 'making him thus, in a very literal manner, "bone of his bone" (supposing tarantulas to have any bones) and flesh of his flesh'.[124]

Mona Caird preferred the image of 'amiable vampire',[125] while Caroline Norton, on a darker note, recalled 'those ingenious twisted groups of animal death we sometimes see in sculpture; one creature wild to resist, and the other fierce to destroy'.

Caroline Norton was a society beauty, the granddaughter of Richard Sheridan and a successful writer herself. She did not regard herself as a feminist; indeed, she rejected the 'wild and stupid theories advanced by a few women of "equal rights" and "equal intelligence"'.[126] Nevertheless, she was destined, through her life and works, to provide the general public with an education in the less savoury aspects of the law of husband and wife.[127] Her marriage was an unhappy one; her husband physically abused her. When she left him he accused the prime minister, Lord Melbourne, of being her lover and sued him for criminal conversation. He exercised his legal rights to deny her access to her children and to deprive her of the money she earned through her writing. She 'learned the English law piecemeal by suffering under it',[128] and recorded her experiences and her humiliation at discovering her legal non-existence in lengthy publications.[129] Her image of husband and wife as creatures locked in deadly combat featured in an influential 1854 *Letter to the Queen on Lord Cranworth's Marriage and Divorce Bill.*[130]

The fiction of marital unity provided an ideal focus for polemical attacks; however, feminists saw it as more than a tactical device. In my view, they made it central to their case for reform because they perceived the vital role that it played in maintaining their oppression. And that role was no less significant in the nineteenth century than in the seventeenth. On the contrary, by the second half of the nineteenth century, the fiction of marital unity had undergone yet another metamorphosis. By meshing with and supporting important new concepts and trends it had consolidated and extended its influence.

Nineteenth-Century Challenges to the Establishment

Like the seventeenth century, the late eighteenth and early nineteenth centuries were times of social and political unrest. Class and gender distinctions were once more under attack.

The French Revolution of 1789 inspired 'an appalling sense of social disharmony and disintegration' in England.[131] It was felt that an alienated working class could threaten the whole structure of social hierarchy and political order; and 'Jacobin' demands for universal suffrage and the disturbances of the 1790s served to fuel these fears. During the same period, and inspired by the same events, Mary Wollstonecraft's *Vindication of the Rights of Women* appeared. This was a book that 'was to have ripples for generations'.[132] Wollstonecraft insisted that it was not for men to decide what was in women's best interests; all human beings needed the freedom to determine their own fate. She demanded educational, legal and political equality for women.[133]

Calls for an extended franchise persisted and they came from the 'middling people' as well as from the working class.[134] Men whose wealth had been garnered from trade and industry challenged the political and social domination of the landed gentry. This group was generally content with the idea that Parliament represented property rather than people; however, they wanted representation to be extended to the 'new wealth' of the merchants and the industrialists. These middle-class demands were met by the Reform Act of 1832; those of the working class were not. The result was the emergence of Chartist movement – 'the first concerted mass organisation of workers on a continuing national basis'.[135] Rioting, unrest and political agitation were to be common features of the next two decades.

In the early years at least, women played an active part in Chartism.[136] They attended meetings and marched at the head of the great processions and demonstrations. They formed radical associations which published addresses and manifestos and, in riots and violent clashes, they fought alongside the men. There was widespread support among the Chartists for the idea of women's votes. A letter in the *Northern Star* in 1838 proclaimed 'the right of every women to have a vote in the legislation of her country, and doubly more so now that we have got a woman at the head of the government'.[137] On the other hand, female suffrage was never a priority for the Chartists. The 'People's Charter' called only for universal *male* suffrage and many of those who regarded votes for women as an aspiration for the future confined their proposals to single women. John Watkins wrote in his 1841 *Address to the Women of England*:

So far from being excluded from taking part in politics, women ought to be allowed to vote; not wives – for they and their husband are one, or ought to be as one – but maids and widows....[138]

On the whole, Chartist women accepted that their husbands could represent them; they did not see their interests as being in opposition.

The Owenite socialists took a more radical stance.[139] Not only did they advocate equal rights for women but they attacked the institution of marriage. Their utimate aim was to replace competition by co-operation as the principle governing economic and social activity; in their view, marriage and the nuclear family were hindrances to the development of genuinely co-operative communities. Small isolated family units promoted individualism and competition; the Owenites wanted to extend the home and to break down the division between the contained family circle and the community as a whole. They also posited a connection between the subordination of wives and the sexual division of labour. In their experimental model communities they sought to combat marital subjection through communal forms of housework.

It was the Owenite, William Thompson, who challenged the seventeenth-century solution to the woman problem most directly.[140] In 1820 James Mill, John Stuart Mill's father, had published his famous 'Article on Government', in which he asserted that the interests of almost all women were included in those of their fathers or husbands; they could, therefore, be 'struck off (from political rights) without inconvenience'.[141] Thompson responded in a book entitled *The Appeall of one Half of the Human Race, Woman, against the Pretensions of the other Half, Men, to retain them in Political, and thence in Civil and Domestic Slavery,* published in 1825. He examined the proposition that husbands and wives enjoyed an identity of interest and, with vehement precision, tore it to shreds:

The very assumption of despotic power by the husbands over wives, is itself a demonstration that in the opinion of husbands, a contrariety, and not an involving, of interests, exists between them and their wives.[142]

As men and women clearly had separate and sometimes conflicting interests, it was

worthwhile to look a little more closely into this so mysteriously operating connexion in marriage, which unindividualizes the nature and interests of one of the parties, and operates the miracle ... of reducing two identities into one.[143]

The political philosophers explained that women signed away their individuality through their marriage contracts, but Thompson was unimpressed:

A Contract! where are any of the attributes of contracts, of equal and just contracts, to be found in this transaction? A contract implies the voluntary assent of both the contracting parties. Can even both the parties, man and woman, by agreement alter the terms, as to *indissolubility* and *inequality* of this pretended contract? No. Can any individual man divest himself, were he ever so inclined, of his powers of despotic control? He cannot. Have women been consulted as to the terms of this pretended contract?[144]

Thompson perceived the sexual contract which lurked beneath the marriage contract. Women's subject status was part of men's reward for entering the social contract and creating the state: wives were '[w]hite slaves – parcelled out amongst men (as if to compensate them for their own cowardly submission almost every where to the chains of political power)....'[145]

In reality, women's claim to political and legal equality was unanswerable. The only way in which it had been possible to evade it had been through the manufacture of a *fiction*: 'this romance of an *identity of interest* is the ingenious, say rather the vulgar, the audacious, fiction devised'.[146]

The Nineteenth-Century Solution

In 1825 it must have looked as if the game was up for the fiction of marital unity. However, it soon became clear that it was not. Once again, the fiction demonstrated its strength and adaptability in the face of adversity. In response to the nineteenth-century challenges to the established patriarchal order, new ideologies of sexual difference and sexual relations were emerging. The fiction of marital unity played a central part in these new developments. By meshing itself with the doctrine of separate sexual spheres and with the Victorian cult of domesticity and respectability, it guaranteed its continuing influence.

Evangelicalism, the Separate Sexual Spheres and the Cult of Domesticity

The new repressive ideas had a religious origin; it was Evangelicalism which was largely responsible for their dissemination and early influence.[147] From the 1780s onwards, the Evangelicals were a vitally important stabilising force in English society. They influenced not just religious but political, economic and social developments as well.

The Evangelical revival both began and remained within the Established Church. The Evangelicals were always staunchly Anglican; they had no interest in following the example of John Wesley who had effectively seceded from the Established Church in the 1780s to form the Methodist sect. Rather, they committed themselves to reforming Anglicanism from within. They criticised many aspects of Church policy and practice, rejecting 'nominal Christianity' in favour of 'real religion'.[148] Theirs was a conversionist and intensely active faith. They believed that the spirit could work through other means than the trappings of the Church, that the key to moral regeneration was individual faith. Like the Puritans, they sought to reinstitute religion as the mainspring of daily life.

While Methodism was always associated with the lower orders and the poor, Evangelicalism had very different social origins. Initially, much of its support was drawn from the lesser gentry, from families which had once had wealth and status but whose fortunes were in decline. The influence of the important Clapham sect was due, in part, to its aristocratic connections. However, as we shall see, the Evangelical leadership was far from uncritical of the old order and, increasingly, their support came from the middling ranks, from merchants, manufacturers, professionals and farmers. Evangelicalism came to play a vital role in the development of middle-class cultural practices and institutions and in the formation of a distinctive middle-class consciousness. The idea that it was virtue and respectability rather than rank which conferred honour gave the middle class a means of translating their growing economic power into moral and cultural authority. This, in its turn, provided a basis on which to challenge the aristocratic monopoly on political power.

The Evangelicals identified the licentiousness and the moral laxity which they saw all around them as the source of England's political difficulties:

The nation ... was suffering from moral degeneracy. Events in France were a warning of what was to come if individuals did not inspire a revolution in the manners and morals of the nation, a transformation which must begin with individual salvation.[149]

Initially they focused their attention on decadence in high places, seeing the dereliction of moral duty amongst the upper classes as the central problem. They wanted a political leadership that was informed by Christian principles. However, they gradually sought to extend their message. Particularly in the context of the political disturbances of the 1790s, 1830s and 1840s, it was the manners and morals of the working class which came to be of primary concern. The Evangelicals set themselves up in opposition to the Chartists and the Owenites and sought to reinterpret the political crises of the age in moral and religious terms. Where the political radicals talked of problems of wages and labour, the Evangelicals talked of neglect of piety, immorality, drunkenness and swearing. They were determined to encourage a new seriousness and respectability and to make labouring people 'sober, industrious, frugal, temperate, virtuous and happy';[150] and the upper classes supported them in this venture, at least while the memory of the French Revolution was still fresh in their minds.

The campaign for the reform of manners and morals reached its peak about mid-century. Its effect was to universalise Evangelical and, therefore, bourgeois values; and chief among those values was a commitment to home and family life. For the Evangelicals, like the Puritans before them, the home was at the centre of religious life. For them it was a naturally religious sphere; a properly-ordered home could confer a foretaste of the heavenly home above. It was a 'sacred refuge' where virtue could be inculcated and maintained more easily than in the turbulent world of competition and sinful distraction outside.[151] Thus it 'provided both the best context for salvation and the best hope for reformed manners and morals in the world at large'.[152]

This linking of the religious with the domestic created a sharp contrast between the public and the private spheres in Evangelical ideology. The outside world was portrayed as hostile and amoral, the home as a haven of love and moral purity. This split between the public and private worlds correlated with an exaggerated division in sexual roles. The Evangelicals believed that women and men were spiritually equal but that they were called by God to perform different, although complementary, tasks. Thus they were endowed with different qualities.

Women's calling was to the domestic sphere; the home was 'the proper scene of [their] actions and influence'.[153] The reasons the Evangelicals gave for this tended to be contradictory and circular. On the one hand, women were seen as possessing qualities which made them more susceptible to religion than men. They were naturally gentle, passive, simple and pure; they had a special aptitude for faith. As they were naturally more religious than men, they were suited to the domestic sphere which was naturally more religious than the public sphere. However, these same qualities of passivity and simplicity were also thought to make women more susceptible than men to immoral influences. On this view, women did not occupy the domestic sphere because they were naturally religious: they were religious because they naturally occupied the domestic sphere. Their confinement to the home protected them from temptations which they would not have been able to resist. Although the Evangelicals may have been unclear as to precisely how God had constructed women's superior religiosity, they were quite clear about His reasons for doing so: a woman's task was to create a godly and Christian home for her husband and to teach her children the precepts of Christian living.

Men were called primarily to the world of work for '[w]ork was not to be despised, rather it was to be seen as doing God's duty in the world'.[154] To equip them for the bustling world of political and business affairs, men were blessed with grandeur, dignity and force. However, the Evangelicals recognised that this might not be enough, given the many temptations and distractions in the worldly sphere. It was essential, therefore, that men recharged their spiritual batteries on a regular basis; and the best place to do this was in a godly and Christian home. The Evangelicals envisaged men 'emerg[ing] from the bosom of their families, carrying their Godliness with them and exercis[ing] their trust in the world with "manly determination and resolution" '.[155]

Evangelicalism and Capitalism

The Evangelical rule of life was undoubtedly grounded, at least until the 1820s, in sincere religious beliefs. However, we cannot ignore that, in a number of respects, these beliefs served the interests of industrial capitalism. First, Evangelicalism elevated work into a dignified, serious and godly pursuit. To the growing middle class, whose livelihood so often derived from 'the despised activities of commerce', this was a very necessary transformation.[156]

Secondly, the family model which the Evangelicals espoused, and which was to become the bourgeois norm, was well-suited to the capitalist context. It provided men with a 'haven in a heartless world' :[157] a psychological refuge from the cold and competitive values of the market-place and from the dehumanised mechanisation of the factory. In doing so, it undoubtedly fulfilled a real need.

It also provided middle-class women who, for the first time, could afford to leave paid employment in large numbers, with a clearly-defined social role. Because the Evangelical writers defined their ideal way of life with this kind of woman in mind, the domesticity they advocated was of a distinctly genteel variety. The envisaged occupation of wives was actually domestic management – the supervision of servants and the keeping of regular accounts – not household tasks themselves. There was an absolute assumption that servants would be available.

However, through the campaign for the reform of manners and morals, these middle-class notions of domesticity and respectability, and the middle-class family model, came to be imposed on the working class. Again, economic as well as religious interests were being served.[158] The bourgeois family model, with its bread-winning husband and non-working, dependent wife and children, was thought to encourage the male work ethic. Underlying the exercise was the assumption that the working class, particularly the men, was naturally given to idleness. However, for the same reason, the ideal of the non-working wife was not imposed quite as rigorously here. There was always the danger that the husband would succumb to his natural fecklessness and fail in his obligations to maintain his dependants. Then, on balance, it was considered preferable for the wife to go out and earn, than for the whole family to become chargeable to the Poor Law.

Compensatory Definitions of Self-Worth for Wives

In many ways this was the worst of times for women. By the middle of the nineteenth century, their lives were more confined than they had ever been before. They had been consigned to a relative and dependent role within the private sphere and their social subordination was absolute. And yet the doctrine of separate sexual spheres and the cult of domesticity offered significant compensations:

[S]ubordinate did not mean inferior. Subordination in marriage did not imply that women were less important than men, but only that they were operating 'in a different department and sphere of action'. Men and women were in separate spheres and those spheres were not hierarchical; the contribution of women in the home and family was quite as vital as that of men in the world outside.[159]

The cult of domesticity elevated and empowered women within their own special sphere.[160] The importance of the role of mistress of the house was widely acclaimed:

As mistress of the house, the middle class woman gained a new position in society. Her personal influence grew greatly, as overnight she became an important decision-maker in her realm of home and family. Instead of obeying orders, the middle class women now gave directions to servants and tradesmen. For the first time in her life she was responsible for very important sums of money.[161]

In Margaret Oliphant's words, the 'merest girl' was transformed by marriage into a 'lawmaker, supreme and absolute' in her new household.[162]

As the century progressed, the cult of domesticity changed somewhat. A high infant mortality rate, and the implications this was feared to have for the health and welfare of an imperial nation, generated a shift in emphasis from 'genteel domesticity' to 'mothercraft domesticity'.[163] Motherhood came to be seen as woman's 'noblest function'.[164] The rhetoric of maternalism that developed was applied to women of all classes; middle-class women were expected to be more personally involved in housework and child-rearing than had previously been considered compatible with cultured, ladylike behaviour. As 'giver of life, ... maintainer of life, teacher to her children, confidant and disciplinarian',[165] the Victorian middle-class woman could earn a considerable measure of respect.

Evangelical beliefs imbued the woman's role as wife and mother with further layers of significance. In fact, Evangelicalism offered women a key position in its struggle to reform the nation. The only way to save the nation was to reform from the bottom up and a godly home provided the only sure foundation. Women played a central role in nurturing morality in an amoral world; although they were denied any *power* in that outer world, they could assert themselves through their moral *influence*. The Evangelicals cast women in the role of moral regenerators – 'faithful repositories of the religious principle'[166] for the benefit of their families. Although they could not be like men, they could be *more*: they could be 'the *makers* of men'.[167] Men could only operate in the moral world of the market if they could be rescued by women's moral vigilance at home; they relied on their wives to do some of their spiritual work for them. Women also took on much of the spiritual responsibility of parenthood and their moral influence as mothers was seen as the linchpin of religious regeneration. In short, the woman's sphere, although apparently narrow, could exercise an unbounded influence in the world at large.

Dorothy Thompson rightly warns us against treating these nine-teenth-century ideologies purely 'as a confidence trick, designed to delay the achievement of women's right to a full place in society'.[168] First, they were not developed entirely by men: some of the most influential writing on Evangelicalism and domesticity was produced by women. Hannah More, Ann Taylor and Sarah Ellis were just a few of the women who played a prominent part in developing and popularising the nineteenth-century view of women's proper sphere. And, secondly, the compensations which it offered were very real: nineteenth-century religion provided women with a 'vital individual space, a place for self-fulfilment at a time when that was not generally highly valued for the female sex';[169] the cult of domesticity gave women power and authority within their homes and ensured a degree of public recognition of the importance of the work they did there.

If it did nothing else, the new perception of women's role created an impetus for improved female education, for 'how could they fulfil such important work without proper preparation?'[170] Admittedly, the typical education envisaged for middle-class women was directed, first and foremost, towards producing moral excellence. However, it did, at least, eschew the previous emphasis on 'accomplishments'. It was no longer deemed sufficient for women to be able to dress well, dance and play the piano.

The education advocated for working-class women always had a more practical orientation.[171] The daughters of the poor were trained to be good housewives and mothers. However, they were not completely excluded from the perception of women as superior moral beings; middle-class commentators frequently expressed the opinion that work-ing-class women were less given to fecklessness than their husbands and that they were unlikely to neglect their children if it was at all within their power to provide for them.

Although the nineteenth-century ideologies conferred real benefits, they could also impose intolerable burdens:

Victorian society, in terms of its official culture, was very demanding of its women. It expected them to be perfect ladies, perfect wives and perfect mothers. The Victorian woman was to have an observing eye, a calculating head, a skilful hand, concise speech, a gentle step, external tidiness and internal purity. She was expected to exercise constant patience and forbearance, in spite of narrow means, inconvenient houses, crying children and preoccupied husbands.[72]

Middle-class women had to run their households, often on limited budgets and with few servants, and simultaneously live up to their popular image as 'angels', 'goddesses' and 'dolls'. For many, it must have been virtually impossible.[73]

Inevitably, though, it was working-class women, to whom the bourgeois family ideal was extended through the campaign for the reform of manners and morals, who were put under the greatest pressure. They were expected to achieve higher and higher standards in housekeeping and child-care without having the means to do so. Whitened doorsteps, net curtains, and a struggle to keep children in clean clothes became symbols of an often hopeless effort to conform.[74]

Scientific Theories of Sexual Difference

Women's will to resist their banishment to the private sphere was undermined, not only by compensatory definitions of self-worth, but by scientific theories of sexual difference.[75] These theories, which were usually of an evolutionary nature, abounded in the nineteenth century. Often they were based on circular reasoning; scientists took their own society as the model from which they formulated their ideas and then used those ideas to justify the *status quo*. Women were prevented by their confinement to the private sphere from acquiring certain capacities, and then that confinement was sanctioned by science on the grounds that those capacities were 'naturally' absent. Nevertheless, science spoke in the nineteenth century 'with the imperious tone of a discipline newly claiming, and in large measure being granted, decisive authority in matters social as well as strictly scientific'.[76]

There was an overwhelming consensus among nineteenth-century scientists that women were inherently different from men in their anatomy, physiology, temperament and intellect. Even as adults, women remained childlike in mind and body. This was regarded as a product of mankind's successful adaptation to social survival; women's development was arrested earlier than men's to permit the conservation of their energies for reproduction. The more highly developed the society, the greater the differentiation in sex roles; and the more able women would be to produce superior offspring. Women lost out but the race gained. Science, then, linked women's inferior position within marriage to human progress.

On this basis, doctors advised against 'unfeminine' activities such as advanced education, as liable to damage the development of women's reproductive systems. An attachment to the domestic sphere and a manifestation of moral virtue were treated as indications of health in women.[177]

The Fiction of Marital Unity in the Nineteenth Century

The fiction of marital unity needed help in the nineteenth century but, unfortunately, help was available from all sides. When buttressed by scientific, social and religious theories about femininity and women's place in society, it could still serve as a plausible justification for the exclusion of married women from political rights. In the words of Margaret Oliphant:

The constitution of the household is more entirely representative than even that glorious constitution which keeps our ship of state afloat. The man is the natural representative of his wife in one set of duties – the wife is the natural representative of the husband in another; and if any one will tell us that the nursery is less important than the Exchange, or that it is a more dignified business to vote for a county member than to regulate a Christian household, we will grant that the woman has an inferior range of duty. Otherwise, there is a perfect balance between the two members of this one person.[178]

In its revitalised form, the fiction of unity was more than capable of meeting the nineteenth-century challenges to the Establishment. Patriarchal values were reasserted with a vengeance.[179] Vera Brittain described the legal position of women as hitting an 'all-time low' in the years between 1800 and 1850,[180] while Beatrice and Mary Chapman thought that, for a 30-year period in the middle of the century, women may have 'had less direct influence on public life than at any other period'.[181] By the Reform Act of 1832, women were *explicitly* excluded from the franchise for the first time. Three years later, the Municipal Corporations Act excluded them from the small and dubious share which, up until then, they had had in local politics.[182] By the mid-1840s, most working-class women had withdrawn from radical politics and retreated into their homes.[183] The atmosphere was created in which Coleridge J. could say in *Cochrane* in 1840:

For the happiness and honour of *both* parties [the law] places the wife under the guardianship of the husband, and entitles him, for the sake of both, to protect her from the danger of unrestrained intercourse with the world, by enforcing cohabitation and a common residence.[184]

Conclusion – the Challenge for Nineteenth-Century Feminism

In the nineteenth century the fiction of marital unity operated in subtler and more insidious ways than it had in the seventeenth century. In the seventeenth century the identity of interest between husband and wife was presented as a romantic ideal but was enforced primarily as a religious duty. In the nineteenth century the fiction of unity surrounded itself with a haze of sentimental rhetoric, sanctifying marriage and domesticity and elevating womanhood; women were tempted with compensatory definitions of self-worth. In addition, the married woman's status was presented as being confluent with her physical and psychological make-up.[185]

This made it very difficult for nineteenth-century women to challenge the traditional division of labour between the sexes, particularly as the status of scientific explanation increased. Most women, including many feminists, regarded it as an acceptable and sensible arrangement.[186] John Stuart Mill took it as given that when a woman married and had a family and household to attend to, she would renounce all other occupations 'which [were] not consistent with the requirements of this'.[187] Frances Power Cobbe thought

[t]hat the Home is woman's proper kingdom; that all that pertains to its order, comfort and grace fall under her natural charge, and can by no means be transferred to a man; that a woman's life without such a domestic side must always be looked on as incomplete, or at best exceptional.[188]

In the second half of the nineteenth century, feminist reformers fought to improve the physical and financial conditions of women within the family. They also contended that women were capable of being something *besides* wives and mothers – that the qualities possessed by wives and mothers could valuably be extended into the world beyond the home. However, very few feminists challenged the idea that housekeeping and child-rearing were naturally and exclusively women's work. They did *not* argue that husbands and wives should take equal responsibility for domestic activities and this was to prove a major stumbling-block in their drive to improve women's status. Wives who retained sole responsibility for child care and housekeeping could not hope to compete with men on equal terms in the job market; their financial dependence on their husbands necessarily continued.

Thus, they were deprived of the opportunity to turn the formal legal rights which the feminists had helped to achieve for them, into actual economic power.

Conclusion

J. T. H. Baker claims that 'no one was harmed by fictions'[189] but I would beg to differ. Bentham was closer to mark when he described the fiction as 'a wicked lie'. 'Fiction of use to justice?' he exclaimed: 'Exactly as swindling is to trade.'[190]

The law governing the relationship between husband and wife has not, historically, reflected a fictional unity between husband and wife; it has reflected the patriarchal assumption that women should be subordinate to men – the power principle. The role of the fiction of unity was to *obscure* that reality. The fiction was not a legal principle in the usual sense: it was an ideological structure, designed to legitimate the traditional marital relationship.

And it did more than this. By the nineteenth century it seemed to have acquired an autonomous existence;[191] it had become 'so pervasive in the language and literature of the law that it affected as well as reflected attitudes towards women and marriage'.[192] Oliver Wendell Holmes, writing about fictions, noted that

the mere habit of using these phrases ... makes it likely that other cases will be brought within the penumbra of the same thought on no more substantial ground than the way of thinking which the words have brought about.[193]

The fiction of unity imposed a way of thinking about the marital relationship that would persist far into the twentieth century. It is a testament to the power of ideas and of language that a seventeenth-century device for obfuscation should have become, by the nineteenth century, an independent source of patriarchal theory and practice.

4

The Jackson Decision Revisited

Introduction

We now move on to the second of the two questions posed at the end of Chapter 1. What happened in the second half of the nineteenth century to produce the *Jackson* decision? What did it mean? It has been argued that the husband's right of chastisement lay at the very heart of the legal construction of marriage. Yet, in *Jackson*, the existence of such a right was emphatically rejected. Does this mean that, by 1891, the nature of the marital relationship had radically altered? On the face of it, this is the obvious explanation, for the legal position of wives had improved enormously.

Before 1857 it had been virtually impossible for a woman to terminate her marriage. The ecclesiastical courts offered only divorce *a mensa et thoro* and very few women succeeded in obtaining a parliamentary divorce. The Divorce and Matrimonial Causes Act of 1857 provided for judicial divorce and transferred responsibility for matrimonial matters from the ecclesiastical courts to a newly-created Divorce Court.[1] The position of husband and wife was not equalised: a wife could be divorced for adultery alone; a husband's adultery had to be aggravated by incest, bigamy, rape, sodomy, bestiality, cruelty or desertion. This meant that a woman whose husband was violent but not adulterous was still restricted to divorce *a mensa et thoro*, or judicial separation, as it was now called. However, this had been made more attractive: a woman who obtained a decree of judicial separation was treated as *a feme sole* with respect to any property she subsequently acquired and 'for the purposes of contract, and wrongs and injuries, and suing and being sued in any civil proceedings'. She could not remarry, of course, but she did escape from some of the legal disabilities of wifehood.

In practice, only upper- and middle-class women could take advantage of these changes. Divorce and separation proceedings were very costly and had to be brought in a single divorce court which was situated in London. There was only one provision in the Divorce Act which could conceivably have been of use to working-class wives and that was section 21, which enabled a woman who had been deserted by her husband to apply for a protection order. The effect of such an order was to put the wife in the same position with regard to property and contracts, and suing and being sued, as she would have been in if she had obtained a decree of judicial separation. It was equally available to the poor and the rich because it could be obtained from the magistrates' courts.

The 1857 Act, therefore, did more than enlarge wives' access to divorce; it also improved their property rights; but it did this only in the context of marriages that were effectively at an end. The 1870s, 1880s and 1890s saw legislative reforms which went much further and which transformed the property rights of wives generally. They operated by extending the equitable concept of the married woman's 'separate estate', while dispensing with the need for settlements and trustees. The Married Women's Property Act of 1870 provided that wages and property which a wife earned through her own work would be regarded as her separate property and, in 1882, this principle was extended to all property, regardless of its source or the time of its acquisition.[2]

In effect, all wives acquired a statutory separate estate, along with rights and duties in respect of that estate. A wife could dispose of her separate property during her lifetime or bequeath it in her will. She could enter into contracts and sue in her own name in respect of it. Her husband continued to be jointly liable for her post-nuptial torts, but her separate property bore the liability for her post-nuptial debts and contracts. It was primarily liable for her ante-nuptial debts, contracts and torts: her husband was liable for these to the extent of any property he had acquired under a marriage settlement. She had the same civil and criminal remedies for the protection of her property as a single woman. If her husband interfered with her separate property she could sue him in tort. If he took it and made off she could prosecute him; she was a competent and compellable witness for this purpose.[3]

Another area which had undergone reform was child custody law. Both at common law and at equity, a father was recognised as having an exclusive right to the custody of his legitimate children and this right was so absolute that the courts did not even have jurisdiction to grant the mother a right of access. He had the right to appoint a testamentary guardian to take his place and it was only if he died without doing this that guardianship passed to the mother. If custody was disputed, the common-law courts and, to a greater extent, the Court of Chancery had a discretion to deny the father's claims and appoint an alternative guardian, but they exercised this discretion with extreme circumspection. In practice, some very serious endangerment of the child's health or welfare was required before the father's rights would be abrogated.

In a series of enactments, beginning in the 1830s, Parliament gradually ameliorated the mother's position. Under the 1839 Custody of Infants Act, a mother could petition the Lord Chancellor or the Master of the Rolls for an access order or, if the child was under eight, for a custody order. The Infant Custody Act of 1873 raised the age to sixteen and abolished the rule that denied custody and access to mothers who had been found guilty of adultery. It also stipulated that a private separation deed would be not be invalid simply because it provided for the father to relinquish custody. The 1886 Guardianship of Infants Act went further. It enabled a mother to apply for custody or access to either the Chancery Division of the High Court or to the county court. This applied to any child, regardless of its age. The court was empowered to make such order as it thought fit, having regard to the welfare of the infant, the conduct of the parents and the wishes of the mother as well as of the father.

Gradually, then, the courts' discretion to grant orders in favour of the mother was extended. But none of these Acts gave her automatic rights; in the context of an ongoing marriage, the prima facie position continued to be that parental authority was vested exclusively in the father. Once the marriage was over the parents were dealt with on terms of greater equality. A decree of divorce, nullity or judicial separation gave the divorce court the power to make whatever provision it thought just and proper for the children's custody, maintenance and education.[4] It exercised this power with extreme conservatism, but it is nevertheless significant that the Divorce Act made no reference to the father's superior claim. The mother's position was also improved by the father's death. The 1886 Act provided for a surviving mother to be her children's guardian, even if there were already a guardian appointed by the father or by the court. The two guardians were required to act jointly. It also enabled the mother herself to appoint a guardian although, unless the court ruled that the father was unfitted to act alone, this would only take effect after both parents were dead.[5]

It is clear, therefore, that married women's rights had been greatly enlarged during the second half of the nineteenth century; and, inevitably, this altered the nature of the marital relationship. However, it is argued here that, although they were important part of the background, the *Jackson* decision was not primarily a reflection of these changes. The seeds of *Jackson* lay in other nineteenth-century developments: in the effective abolition of the writ for restitution of conjugal rights; in a protracted parliamentary campaign aimed at increasing the penalties for aggravated assaults on women and children; and in the emergence of wife-beating as an issue of great social concern. It can, of course, be argued that these developments were themselves stimulated by a growing concern for women's rights. However, I shall seek to demonstrate that this was not the case.

The Matrimonial Causes Act, 1884

Before seizing and imprisoning his wife, Mr Jackson had obtained a decree for restitution of conjugal rights; Mrs Jackson had taken no notice. Just twelve years previously, the Divorce Court would have had the power to imprison her for contempt. She would have remained imprisoned indefinitely unless she consented to return to cohabitation, for the court had no power to order release except on obedience.[6]

In 1884 the Matrimonial Causes Act removed this power of attachment. Henceforth, refusal to comply with a decree for restitution of conjugal rights would simply render the offending party guilty of desertion. This entitled the deserted spouse to a judicial separation without having to wait the two years necessary to establish desertion under the 1857 Divorce and Matrimonial Causes Act. If a husband coupled this statutory form of desertion with adultery, his wife was entitled to sue for an absolute divorce.

The 1884 Act provided, in addition, that a husband who refused to return to his wife could be ordered by the court to make her a periodic allowance. Where the wife was the disobedient party, the court could order a settlement to be made of her separate property for the benefit of her husband and their children. If she ran her own business or had separate earnings she could be ordered to make a periodic allowance in the same way as a husband. The court was given the power, finally, to make orders regarding the custody of the couple's children.

Lord Esher M.R. and Fry L.J. attached considerable importance in *Jackson* to the passage of the Matrimonial Causes Act. Jackson's counsel attempted to argue that it had not affected a husband's common-law right to custody of his wife. The power to order imprisonment, it was said, was merely a punishment in respect of a contempt committed by disobeying the court's decree; all that the Act had done was abolish that punitive process. However, the court was not convinced. Fry L.J. felt that if a husband had had a right to the custody of his wife, it could not have survived the 1884 Act:

I cannot think that, after the legislature has taken away the right of the Court to enforce restitution of conjugal rights by attachment, the husband has any right of imprisonment in a case in which he is at once a party, the Judge and the executioner.

Lord Esher M.R. went further:

the passing of the Act of Parliament which took away the power of attachment in such cases is the strongest possible evidence to shew that the legislature had no idea that a power would remain in the husband to imprison the wife for himself; and this tends to show that it is not and never was the law of England that the husband has such a right.[7]

The 1884 Act was popularly known as 'Mrs Weldon's Act'.[8] In 1882 a Mrs Weldon had applied to the Divorce Court for a decree for restitution of conjugal rights. She and her husband had been living apart for a number of years; he paid her a monthly allowance and, on receiving notice of the decree, he offered, in addition, to rent a furnished house for her and supply her with servants. In most cases such an offer would have ended the matter for, in practice, the writ was used by deserted spouses to enforce money demands.[9] However, Mrs Weldon was determined to have her husband live with her again; in 1883 she requested the Divorce Court to issue an attachment for failure to comply with the decree.

The court allowed the attachment, but with great reluctance. Sir James Hannen, the President of the Divorce Court, commended the Scottish law, which resembled the provision later made by the 1884 Matrimonial Causes Act, and said that it was much to be preferred to the English. A husband and wife could not be forced to treat each other with conjugal affection.

The only real advantage, therefore, which a wife can obtain from a decree of restitution is that a suitable dwelling and maintenance may be provided for her, and this could be secured by compelling the husband to allow her proper alimony without requiring him to live with her against his will....[10]

Sir James was not prepared to leave matters as they stood. It was at his instance[11] that the Matrimonial Causes Bill was introduced into the House of Lords in February of 1884. The Bill proceeded rapidly through Parliament with a minimum of discussion. Only one dissenting voice was raised, that of Charles Warton, the Conservative Member for Bridport. Without Warton's obstructionist tactics, the 1882 Married Women's Property Act might have been passed a year earlier. He had condemned it as an engine of 'social revolution' and predicted that it would 'make the woman, instead of a kind and loving wife, a domestic tyrant'.[12] His objections to the Matrimonial Causes Bill were of the same order. He protested against 'the Bill being hurried forward in this abrupt manner, particularly as it contained provisions contrary to what had been the law for centuries', and said that it was scandalous

for the Legislature to interfere in matrimonial causes in this way, and to say that husband and wife should not live together, if one of the parties was disinclined.... [It would] certainly not improve the sanctity of marriage.[13]

Apart from this, the significance of the measure seems to have gone unremarked. Warton's objections were given short shrift by the Bill's supporters. He was told that it had the approval of the President of the Divorce Court and that it had been carefully considered in the House of Lords. In reality, it had passed through the House of Lords in 21 days and had not been debated at all.[14]

While the Matrimonial Causes Act was progressing through Parliament, Mr Weldon was not, as it turns out, languishing in gaol. The issue of the writ of attachment against him had been suspended pending an appeal. He later withdrew the appeal, presumably because the 1884 Act had, by then, been passed, and Mrs Weldon was obliged to apply once again for an order that a writ of attachment should issue. The case was again heard before Sir James Hannen, who decided that the Matrimonial Causes Act was retrospective. Although enforcement by attachment was abolished '[f]rom and after' the passing of the Act, it was not specifically provided that the *decree* must have been pronounced after the passing of the Act.[15] It seems that it would have been more accurately dubbed '*Mr* Weldon's Act'!

By this complicated procedure, the English public was spared '[t]he unedifying spectacle of Mrs Weldon putting her husband in prison for refusing to consort with her'.[16] Earlier in the century a Mrs Barlee had petitioned the ecclesiastical court from Ipswich gaol where she had been imprisoned for over a year rather than return to her abusive husband. She begged to be released on the ground that prison conditions were damaging her health. The court replied that she had offered no proof of her husband's cruelty and that, although they 'very sincerely commiserate[d]', it was not in their power to release her without her husband's consent.[17] So Mrs Barlee remained in gaol and Elizabeth Wolstenholme Elmy tells us that she eventually died there.[18] *This* spectacle was not considered so unedifying as to require immediate reform of the law.

Developments in the Statutory Law of Assaults

Another factor which may have influenced the *Jackson* decision was a parliamentary campaign aimed at increasing the penalties for aggravated assaults on women and children. Only minor success was achieved, but its supporters persisted in their efforts throughout most of the second half of the century.

Until the nineteenth century wife-beaters had been punishable on indictment only. Summary jurisdiction was extended to common assault and battery by the 1828 Offences Against the Person Act, but only very minor penalties could be imposed. The worst punishment that the magistrates could inflict on a wife-beater was a £5 fine with a maximum of two months imprisonment on default.[19]

The Member for Lewes, Mr Fitzroy, raised the matter before Parliament in March of 1853.[20] He argued that these were manifestly inadequate penalties for assaults of an aggravated nature on women and children. Such cases could, if the magistrates saw fit, be remitted to sessions to be tried on indictment,[21] but it was Mr Fitzroy's experience that this alternative power was infrequently exercised. This was because of the strong likelihood that the wife would refuse to give evidence when the case came up for trial; the longer the delay before the hearing, the greater the chances were that she would be coaxed or bullied into silence by her husband. Moreover, the physical evidence of many assaults had disappeared by the time the victim was seen by the jury at sessions. It was impossible, in Fitzroy's view, for wife-beating cases to be dealt with effectively on indictment. The magistrates recognised this and were rightly reluctant to remit cases to the sessions: an inadequate punishment was better than the possibility of none at all.

Fitzroy introduced a Bill designed to enlarge magistrates' powers to inflict summary penalties for brutal assaults on women and children. It provided for a fine of up to £20 or a term of imprisonment, with or without hard labour, not exceeding six months. An amendment granted a further discretionary power to bind the offender over to keep the peace for an additional period of up to six months. In order to facilitate the smallest possible time lapse between the assault and adjudication, cases could be heard outside the normal periods for holding petty sessions.[22]

Some concerns were raised at the Committee stage in the Commons about the dangers of conferring too much power on courts of summary jurisdiction which sat, of course, without juries. In general, though, the proposals met with approval. Fitzroy's Bill received the Royal Assent in June of 1853, and was known as An Act for the better Prevention and Punishment of aggravated Assaults upon Women and Children. One other advantage that it had over the 1828 legislation was that the complaint to the magistrates did not have to be made by 'the party aggrieved'. The complaint could be brought by a third party who had witnessed the assault, perhaps with the result that the husband would be less likely to take violent revenge upon his wife.

While the Bill was progressing through Parliament, an unsuccessful attempt had been made to amend it so as to give magistrates an additional power to order flogging.[23] Fitzroy had suggested that the kind of offenders he had in mind deserved to be flogged, but did not feel justified in proposing such an ignominious penalty to the House. However, the Member for Bath, Mr Phinn, had no such reservations. While

he was not an advocate for corporal punishment in ordinary cases ... in cases of this kind, where men were already reduced below the level of the brute, when all moral sense had gone out of them, he believed it might be applied with good effect.[24]

He proposed that a flogging provision be inserted into the Bill, along with whatever procedural safeguards the House thought necessary.

Although a number of parliamentarians voiced strong support, the flogging amendment was rejected by more than two votes to one.[25] It looked at this time as if the English law was moving towards the elimination of flogging for adults. The whipping of misdemeanants under the common law was falling into disuse, and use of the penalty for adults was becoming restricted, for practical purposes, to those repeatedly convicted under the vagrancy legislation.[26] Phinn's proposal was therefore condemned as being 'quite inconsistent with the feeling of the age, and the spirit of modern legislation'.[27]

There were also a number of practical objections. It was thought, first, that if a flogging sentence were mandatory, magistrates would be reluctant to convict offenders. Secondly, a wife would be even less inclined than before to make a complaint or give evidence against her husband when 'so degrading and brutal a punishment' might result. If she did aid the prosecution the chances of a reconciliation between the couple would be greatly diminished, and she might be permanently deprived of economic support. Finally, it was suggested that flogging would arouse public sympathy and make the wife-beater into 'a hero in the eyes of his associates'.[28]

In spite of the decisive rejection of Phinn's amendment, a handful of parliamentarians continued to campaign vigorously for the flogging of those guilty of serious assaults on women and children. At least three flogging bills were introduced during the next seven years.[29] The first of these was the Aggravated Assaults Bill of 1856. It was introduced by the Member for Swansea, Mr Dillwyn, who argued that the penalties under the 1853 legislation had been ineffective in curbing violent assaults on women and children. He recommended that all such assaults be punished by a short prison sentence in conjunction with a mandatory flogging. This, he said, would sharply diminish the number of assaults, whilst offenders' wives would be spared the financial hardship that often resulted from lengthy prison sentences. He suggested that the flogging be administered at least a week before the prisoner's release so as to reduce the chances of his returning to his family in a vengeful state of mind. He felt that public opinion concerning flogging 'had undergone a great change during the last few years', and there may have been some truth in this, for the motion that the Bill be read a second time was rejected by a majority of only 38. He reintroduced the Bill the following year but it was rejected once again, more decisively this time.[30]

Later in 1857 Viscount Raynham proposed that a committee be appointed to inquire into the operation of the 1853 Act. This, he hoped, would reveal the inadequacy of the current measures and persuade the House that 'corporal punishment was the only proper punishment for this crime'. He failed to persuade the House. Some denied that there was any reason to believe that the 1853 Act had been ineffective; others felt that it was too soon to judge. The motion to set up an inquiry was rejected.[31]

In 1860 Raynham introduced an Aggravated Assaults Amendment Bill. Had it been successful, it would have given magistrates a discretion to impose flogging for a first offence, while rendering it compulsory for a second. He also recommended longer prison sentences. The Bill was twice debated at some length, but was prevented by a large majority from going into Committee.[32]

The 1856, 1857 and 1860 Bills all met with substantially the same objections as had been raised to Phinn's original flogging proposal. Some felt that flogging would be ineffective or counter-productive in the kind of cases under discussion: women would be discouraged from complaining;[33] magistrates would be reluctant to convict;[34] men who were treated like brutes would become more brutal than ever[35] and return home determined to wreak vengeance on their families.[36] Some objected to flogging on principle.[37] There were others who did not oppose flogging *per se*, but were strongly resistant to the idea of a whipping sentence being imposed summarily: it was 'the right of every Englishman', they said, 'not to be subjected to corporal punishment except after ... trial by jury'.[38]

It was only by making a number of concessions to these objectors that Raynham got his Bill as far as the Committee stage. He agreed to amend the Bill to permit an appeal to quarter sessions, with the possibility of bail being granted in the interim. He would also have been prepared, he said, to support a provision which gave magistrates the power to inflict whipping at quarter sessions only. However, in doing this, he laid his proposals open to the kind of practical objections that were discussed earlier: if serious cases were remitted to sessions the delay before the hearing would reduce the likelihood of women testifying; if husbands were sentenced to flogging at petty sessions but then released on bail pending appeal their wives would be in even greater danger, for there would be a strong incentive to prevent them from giving evidence at the sessions.[39]

This succession of frustrated attempts appears to have discouraged the campaigners. When the law of assault was revised by the 1861 Offences Against the Person Act the provisions in the 1853 Act were re-enacted without change,[40] and a decade of parliamentary inactivity commenced.

The 1870s brought renewed agitation and, by this time, attitudes towards flogging seem to have been hardening.[41] An 1872 flogging bill[42] was abandoned after just a few weeks,[43] but the question was being taken much more seriously by the middle of the decade. In May of 1874 Colonel Egerton Leigh made a colourful speech in the House of Commons on the subject of wife abuse. England, he said, was considered 'the Paradise of women', but if steps were not taken to curb 'outrageous and cowardly attacks ... by men', it would soon be transformed into 'the Hell of women'. Thought also had to be given to the trouble that was being stored up for the future, for 'what the children in some families saw was enough to infernalize a whole generation'.[44]

He suggested that flogging be authorised and that the number of lashes be tailored to the number of times the offence had been repeated. Prime Minister Disraeli assured him that this was 'a subject on which there [could not] be any difference of opinion' but hoped that his 'hon. and gallant Friend' would not press for an immediate decision as the matter was to be thoroughly examined by the Secretary of State for the Home Department.[45] Leigh amiably agreed to withdraw his motion, remarking that he only sought 'fair play for the fairer sex' – one of those condescending quips which Frances Power Cobbe found so 'inexpressibly sickening'.[46]

Six months after Colonel Leigh had thus 'broken a lance in defence of the tortured women', the Government commissioned an inquiry into the law on brutal assaults. Richard Cross, the Home Secretary, sent a questionnaire to the judges, the chairmen of quarter sessions, the recorders and the stipendiary magistrates of the metropolitan police courts. In it they were asked whether flogging, which had been authorised for garrotting in 1863,[47] should be extended to further forms of violence, in particular, assaults on women and children. A further circular was sent to the commissioners of police and chief constables.

Of the seventeen judges of the High Court, eleven were clearly in favour of flogging for brutal assaults, while another four expressed qualified support. Cleasby B. opposed flogging for assaults on wives because he felt that it would embitter marital relations. Only Keating J. objected on grounds of principle. Support for the penalty was no less pronounced among chairmen of quarter sessions and recorders although, like many of the judges, they were opposed to giving the power to order whipping to magistrates sitting in petty sessions. This means that they would not necessarily have supported the various flogging Bills. The majority of police court magistrates favoured flogging for serious assaults, but not for 'usual and ordinary cases of wife-beating'. Senior London police officers, on the other hand, were unanimously in support of an extension of flogging.[48]

The Home Secretary subsequently introduced a Bill which would have given judges discretion at assizes to order corporal punishment of up to 25 lashes, once or twice, for, among other things, assault and battery on women and children.[49] Leon Radzinowicz has observed that the response to attempted extensions of flogging during this period was 'a truly unpredictable toss-up'[50] and the fate of Cross's Bill demonstrates the truth of this. Unexpectedly strong opposition was encountered.

In addition to the usual practical objections, there was a vigorous denunciation of the principle of corporal punishment. Opponents claimed that flogging had been abolished in every civilised nation save England: 'Russia even has thrown down the Knout, and Her Majesty's Government stoops to pick it up!' They insisted that it would increase rather than diminish the acts complained of, for violence could not be stamped out 'by torture and blood'. Mr P. A. Taylor claimed that, in reality, Cross's *Brutal Assaults Report* reflected a 'great diversity of opinion among the judges' and he falsely asserted that Lord Coleridge, Brett J. and Denman J. had 'declared emphatically against flogging'. Mr Shaw-Lefevre admitted that the judges were overwhelmingly in favour of flogging, but said that this was not surprising for '[t]here was something in the position of a Judge which led him to favour retaliatory punishments'. The Second Reading of the Bill was adjourned and it was later withdrawn.[51]

Nancy Tomes has written that 'in 1882, the Wife Beaters Act gave police magistrates the power to have offenders flogged and exposed on a public pillory'.[52] However, it is doubtful whether this was so. A Bill which fitted this description was introduced into Parliament in February of 1882, but it was withdrawn again in May.[53] This appears to have been the last nineteenth-century attempt to increase the penalties for assaults on women and children.

Wife-Beating as a Social Issue

These flurries of parliamentary activity did not occur in a vacuum: from about mid-century wife-beating had become a matter of great public concern in England.[54] Legal and popular journals were full of articles about it. Newspapers of the day gave extensive coverage to the details of wife assault cases, and the regularity with which such reports appeared was the subject of frequent comment. 'The paragraph headed "Horrible Wife Murder" is a familiar sight', one writer reported, 'whilst grievous assaults on wives have become ordinary items of daily news.'[55] Frances Power Cobbe confirmed this: the English public, she said, 'read of the beatings, burnings, kicking, and "cloggings" of ... women well-nigh every morning in their newspapers'.[56]

Politicians who supported increased penalties for assaults on women made heavy use of such accounts,[57] as did concerned lay commentators.[58] Through these various channels, the public were made familiar with a terminology and a geography of abuse: they learnt about the 'kicking districts' of Liverpool; about trampling and 'purring' (which meant '"digging" the women with wooden clogs tipped and heeled with iron') in the North; about smashing and vitriol-throwing in London.[59]

In 1857 a Society for the Protection of Women and Children from Aggravated Assaults was set up. It functioned mainly as an advisory and prosecuting agency, but it also advertised for information about wife-beating, published occasional dossiers of its cases and pressed for legal reform. Its usefulness was limited by its obscurity and by precarious funding, but it played a part, nevertheless, in publicising the problem, particularly during the 1870s when public concern was at its height.[60] In 1876 the subject was debated at the annual conference of the National Association for the Promotion of Social Sciences, a social reform organisation founded by Lord Brougham.[61]

Some abused women, like Caroline Norton, became personally famous. A more typical case, perhaps, was that of Susannah Palmer.[62] Susannah had been systematically abused by her husband. He had knocked out her teeth, sold her possessions and turned her out into the street at night to make room for another woman. She had appealed to the law for protection, but had been told that nothing could be done as her husband had not deserted her. Finally she took a knife and slightly wounded him, was charged with assault and sent to

Newgate Prison 'where she expressed perfect contentment because her husband could not get at her'.[63] Here she was found in 1869 by Frances Power Cobbe who solicited aid on her behalf and helped to publicise her plight. The case was seized upon by the feminist press and the suffrage movement and Susannah became a kind of national heroine.

Charivaris

It was also during this period that wife-beaters became the prime target of popular rituals known as 'charivaris'. These rituals operated as a kind of community policing system. They had a long history and could take many forms.[64] The offending member of the community might, for example, be forced to 'ride the stang' or to 'ride skimmington'. This involved being paraded through the town astride a pole, or seated backwards on a donkey, accompanied by a jeering crowd. He would be pelted with mud or pitched into the local duck-pond and, sometimes, severely beaten. If the offender himself were not available he would be represented by an effigy, or by a substitute rider.

Alternatively, he might be treated to a session of 'rough music'. His home would be surrounded at night by a crowd beating on pots and pans, and he would be reminded of his sins by a raucous rendition of appropriate verses. The following is an example:

> This is to give notice that Tom Trotter
> Has beaten his good wo-man;
>
> .   .   .   .
>
> He beat her black, he beat her blue;
> When old Nick gets him,
> He'll give him his due;
> Ran, tan, tan; ran, tan, tan;
> We'll send him there in this old frying pan....

Before the nineteenth century wife-beating had not normally been a focus for these rituals. In fact, all the available evidence suggests it was violent or domineering *wives* who were the occasion of the vast majority of charivaris in the early modern period. Wives who beat their husbands, nagging wives, adulterous wives, scolds and viragos: all of these were common victims. Also at risk were submissive husbands who allowed themselves to be 'hen-pecked' or cuckolded. They had failed to assert the proper authority and were liable to find themselves dragged through the streets dressed in women's clothes as a representation of the reversal of traditional roles that had occurred.

Clearly, the early charivari was designed to reinforce patriarchal values and relations, and to set firm boundaries on permissible sexual and marital behaviour. In practical terms, deviants were frightened or shamed into conformity. But there was more to it than this. As Martin Ingram has pointed out, there were subtle and complex aspects to the way in which the charivari performed its function.[65] The conflict between the patriarchal ideal and the expectations it produced and the everyday realities of married life generated tension within families and communities: the boisterous humour and derision which accompanied the charivari helped to relieve that tension. By means of symbols – the victim riding backwards on the donkey, or the man dressed as a woman – the reversal of the 'natural' order which had occurred was recreated, but in a way that was amusing rather than threatening. Communal mockery of the deviant behaviour reassured the participants that their collective value system was a valid one.

So, why did the focus shift in the nineteenth century to wife-beating? Did it reflect a change in society's value system? Or was it simply the case that wives were in greater need of protection than ever before?

Incidence of Wife-Beating

Wife-beating was undoubtedly a widespread and serious problem at this time. Working from the figures provided by chief constables in Cross's *Brutal Assaults Report*, Cobbe estimated that about 1,500 women were brutally assaulted in England and Wales each year. This amounted to more than four assaults on women each day, and it was Cobbe's belief that the majority of these victims were wives. She emphasised that the figures related only to aggravated assaults, to cases, that is, which will often have involved trampling, burning, blinding and broken bones.[66]

No consistent statistics were kept on convictions for common assaults on women but Tomes estimates that they were between nine and 25 times more prevalent.[67] Cobbe also emphasised that the 1875 statistics were based only on those cases which had come to the attention of the authorities:

for every one of these *published* horrors, [there are] at least three or four which *never are reported at all,* and where the poor victim dies quietly of her injuries like a wounded animal, without ever seeking the mockery of redress offered her by the law.[68]

Other commentators agreed that the 'dark figure' was a high one. Anna Martin, who studied the matrimonial experiences of poorer working-class women at the end of the nineteenth century, thought that as few as one in 50 abused wives took legal action.[69]

Clearly, then, there was a high incidence of wife-beating. The important question, however, is whether it was higher than usual. A dramatic increase in wife-beating during this period would afford a straightforward explanation for the upsurge of public interest and concern.

Much of the debate in Parliament focused on this question. Those who supported severer penalties for wife-beaters were naturally eager to demonstrate that Fitzroy's 1853 Act was not working. Citing returns showing the number of convictions under the Act in the London magistrates' courts, they argued that wife-beating was not diminishing and, later, that it was increasing.[70] However, their evidence was unconvincing. First, it was impossible to compare their figures with pre-1853 statistics for, up until that year, offences against women and children were not distinguishable from other offences against the person in the national returns.[71] And secondly, the returns did not show a rise in the number of convictions; they seem, in fact, to have stayed more or less steady.

An unvarying conviction rate does not necessarily imply an unvarying crime rate. There are good reasons for believing that a greater proportion of the total number of wife-beaters were being successfully prosecuted than ever before. First, it had become much easier to bring a criminal prosecution and, as a result, the number of prosecutions generally was increasing massively. There were two main reasons for this. One was the extension of summary jurisdiction; the other was the establishment, in 1829, of the police force.[72] The abused wife benefited from these developments. Since 1828 she had been able to pursue a prosecution for common assault without the expense and delay of a jury trial. The 1853 Act extended this benefit to aggravated assaults. Cases which would previously have been dismissed at sessions, because of the wife's refusal to testify, could now be dealt with adequately by the magistrates.[73] The police were now available to make arrests and to prosecute offences. The 1853 Act permitted persons other than the 'party aggrieved' to bring the complaint and the 1861 Offences Against the Person Act relaxed the position as regards common assault to permit the complaint to be brought 'by or on behalf of the person aggrieved'.[74] These were undoubtedly advantages,[75] but the benefits conferred by the police force should not be overestimated. The police were always very reluctant to meddle in family matters. If they attempted to control wife-beating at all, they were inclined to use the same informal methods – surveillance, reproaches and sometimes threats – that friends and neighbours had been using for years.[76] If they did exercise their formal powers there was no guarantee that the public and the courts would support them: in 1871 a police constable was fined for common assault after he stopped a man from beating his wife.[77]

This was also a period of rapid population growth. Between 1850 and 1914 the population of England and Wales as a whole doubled. In the urban areas it trebled. This means that the growth in population outstripped the growth in the overall number of criminal prosecutions.[78]

The fact that conviction rates under the 1853 Act remained more or less constant in the face of these developments suggests that the total number of wife-beating incidents was, in fact, diminishing. Opponents of the flogging Bills insisted that this was so and historians Nancy Tomes and Margaret May, agree with them.[79] This would have been in line with general trends. Recorded crime rates were declining steadily throughout the second half of the nineteenth century. Between 1867 and 1906, taking the increase of population into account, recorded offences against the person fell by a fifth.[80] There is no reason to believe that wife-beating trends were out of line with this.

The Social, Political and Economic Climate

Although wife-beating may have been diminishing this was not what people believed at the time. There was a strong public perception that the practice was becoming more and more common. Not only was the number of assaults thought to be high and 'ever-increasing',[81] it was believed that England was being disgraced in the eyes of her neighbours. 'There is not ... any class in the world so subjected to brutal personal violence as English wives', one writer claimed, while Cobbe warned that the wife-murder was becoming 'the opprobrium of the land'.[82] So how is this to be explained? How do we reconcile the reality that wife-beating was almost certainly diminishing with the widely-held belief that it was spiralling out of control?

To make sense of this paradox we have to consider it in the context of broader social, political and economic developments in the second half of the nineteenth century. At first glance this provides little enlightenment and, indeed, adds to the mystery, for this was the famous 'age of equipoise'. Britain appeared to have escaped the revolutionary upheavals which had affected other nations. By 1848 Chartism had been routed and 'no comparably popular or politically subversive working-class movement [had arisen] to take its place'. Class relations seemed to have undergone a remarkable transformation. This was 'an epoch "when the great man helped the poor man and the poor man loved the great", decades socially happier and more harmonious by far than the more anxious and turbulent decades which preceded and followed them.' Industrial expansion and rising living standards produced a belief in national progress and a strong mood of self-confidence. Recorded crime rates had begun a decline which continued steadily until the turn of the century.[83] By 1876 the eminent Victorian crime historian, L. O. Pike, felt able to assert with confidence that 'there never was, in any nation of which we have a history, a time in which life and property were so secure as they are at present in England'.[84]

It was natural for the 1850s and 1860s to appear peaceful and stable after the social disorder of the 1830s and 1840s. However, the transformation was neither as complete nor as instantaneous as contemporary commentators suggested. The disorders of the Hungry Forties were not replaced overnight by the mid-Victorian era of peace and prosperity. Concentrating specifically on the battle against crime, Radzinowicz and Hood have developed a more refined chronology.[85] They divide the century into three eras. In the first 40 years the outlook was one of 'unrelieved pessimism'. Towards the end of the 1840s this gave way to a period of 'qualified optimism', but it was not until the 1870s that the era of 'unfaltering optimism' set in. Only then did the Victorians believe that the war against crime was really being won.

It was with the era of qualified optimism that the period of greatest concern about wife-beating coincided. Crime levels were improving at this time but the Establishment was still haunted by the 'spectre of a dangerous and alienated class'.[86] The fear that law and order were on the point of breaking down had not entirely receded and the level of violent crime in particular still provoked anxiety. The situation was exacerbated in the 1850s by the abolition of transportation and by the introduction of a 'ticket-of-leave' system for prisoners serving penal servitude sentences. It was widely feared that hordes of ex-convicts would soon be roaming the country and even isolated outbreaks of violent crime had the power to increase this fear to a fever-pitch.[87]

The 'garrotting' panic of 1862 is an example of this. In London in that year, a number of people were throttled and robbed, including a Member of Parliament returning home from the House of Commons in the early hours of the morning. While it is true that there was an unusually large number of violent robberies in 1862, it seems that relatively few of them actually involved garrotting. These may all, in fact, have been the work of a small gang that was quickly put out of operation. However, events became blown out of all proportion; the public wailed that law-abiding citizens could no longer 'go about their lawful avocations in peace and safety'. In spite of forceful opposition from Sir George Grey, a flogging bill was swept through the House of Commons by a majority of three to one. It became possible for an adult convicted of robbery with violence or garrotting to receive 150 lashes, in addition to penal servitude for life. The new legislation was widely acclaimed by the judiciary as having been 'admirable medicine for the disease of garrotting' and, indeed, the number of offences fell sharply after its passage. However, some of the claims that were made about the instant and beneficial effect produced by the imposition of flogging sentences seem to have been exaggerated; the crime may, in fact, have been put down by long terms of penal servitude.[88]

In spite of the short duration of the garrotting episode, the belief endured that all forms of public violence were on the increase and that more stringent counter-measures were required if order were to be maintained. In 1867 William Reade warned that

the lawlessness which has temporarily grown up among the dangerous classes will have terrible results. Already rowdyism and ferocity seem to have infected the mob in many places to an unusual degree, and the sooner the lesson is taught that the Law is above all in England, the better for everyone's welfare.[89]

The close association between the fear of violence and disorder and contemporary attitudes to the working classes is clearly represented here. There was a connection in the upper- and middle-class Victorian mind between crime and popular rebellion and this was a time when widespread popular rebellion still seemed like a possibility. Just as concern about wife-beating was part of a more general disquiet about violence, this, in its turn, was part of an upper- and middle-class urge to regulate working-class behaviour.

There were economic as well as political factors at play. Sensitivity to working-class attitudes and habits was being heightened by the demands and problems of industrial capitalism and rapid urbanisation. There was a need for training in 'industrial discipline' if the system of factory production were to operate effectively. The response to these needs was the middle-class campaign for the reform of manners and morals.[90]

As we have seen, this campaign had far-reaching consequences. What began as an Evangelical mission to inculcate respect for discipline,

virtue and seriousness had become, by the 1830s and 1840s, a programme for the transformation of the working class in the image of
the bourgeoisie. It was hugely successful. The Criminal Registrar
reported in 1901 that there had been

a great change in manners: the substitution of words without blows for blows
with or without words; an approximation in the manners of different classes;
a decline in the spirit of lawlessness.[91]

In V. A. C. Gatrell's view,

the process of social pacification, integration, or stabilization (however it be
described) ... was arguably the most remarkable social characteristic of later
Victorian England.[92]

Middle-class morality was brought to bear in numerous areas of
working-class life. Restrictions were imposed, for example, on traditional
leisure activities. Bear and cock-fighting had almost disappeared by
mid-century, whilst fairs had become controlled. Music halls and
dancing saloons were effectively licensing themselves by the 1890s.
These kinds of pastimes were objected to because they were thought
to provide opportunities for immorality and disorder and, more importantly, for drinking. Drinking was the 'besetting sin of the working class',
the chief source, it was believed, of indolence and crime. Drunkards
became prime targets for religious and secular missionaries, along with
prostitutes, vagrants and juvenile delinquents.[93]

When religious and moral propaganda failed, there was the criminal
law to fall back on. The law, it was said, had 'the forming of the
character of the lowest classes in its own hands'. It was 'the one
channel through which the sentiments of the well-conducted part of the
community [could be] made operative perforce on the vilest and
worst'.[94] It was used extensively. Indeed,

[a]ttempts to regulate social conduct in the second half of the century accounted
for the only real growth area in recorded criminal behaviour, and for many of
the sudden fluctuations in the crime rate.[95]

By the end of the century, drunkenness was the single most common
charge in the courts.[96]

However, the criminal law could not be used indiscriminately for
this might stigmatise otherwise useful members of society. In the first
half of the century 'the criminal class', 'the poor' and 'the working
class' had been virtually interchangeable terms. In the second half of
the century, social commentators developed the notion that there was
an irredeemably 'criminal' or 'dangerous class' which was distinct from
the respectable, law-abiding poor and which was responsible for the

vast majority of crime.[97] In 1863 *The Times* reported: 'We have an entire class, though perhaps not a very numerous one, whose freedom is fraught with peril to the rest of the community.'[98]

Dividing up the working classes in this way served two purposes: it proved a clearly defined set of 'folk devils' on to which the public could project their anxieties about violence and disorder;[99] at the same time, it furthered the process by which the deserving, respectable poor were 'integrate[d] ... into the culture of those whom the economic and political system served best'.[100]

Central to this transformation of the working classes was the universalisation of bourgeois family norms. These dictated that men entered the public world as bread-winners and office-holders, while the woman's sphere was the home. It was important for a number of reasons that the working classes live in conventional family units and be encouraged to fulfil their family obligations. First, it provided children with a 'proper' home-life; and the home, it was well-known, was 'the first and most important school of character'.[101] Secondly, it cultivated the work ethic: the stable family, consisting of male bread-winner and dependent wife and children, was 'the only known way of ensuring with any approach to success, that one generation will exert itself in the interest and for the sake of another'.[102]

It had once been very common for working-class couples to cohabit or to marry informally but, from about 1850, this began to change. Working-class couples came under growing pressure to regularise their unions. The practice of 'living tally' was increasingly stigmatised and the harsh provisions of the 1834 Poor Law code discouraged unwed motherhood. The number of church and civil weddings rose steeply. It also became more common for wives to stay at home rather than go out to work. Many families could not manage without the woman's wage but, for those which could, it was an important symbol of respectability.[103]

Brutes, Angels, Martyrs and Viragos

This then was the background to the emergence of wife-beating as a recognised social problem. These were the ideas and the concerns which informed the contemporary debate: they influenced parliamentarians' and social commentators' perception of the problem; indeed, to a large extent, they created the perception of wife-beating *as* a problem. Ultimately, they dictated the proposed solutions.

First, it was very widely assumed that wife-beating was monopolised by the working classes. While the problem was one which required 'consideration of almost everything that relates to the social and moral improvement of what are called the "lower orders"',[104] it was not perceived as having anything to do with the nature of the marital relationship generally. This approach was challenged only once in Parliament. In 1860 a Mr Walter suggested that, if the Members were to extend their research beyond the records of the police courts to those of the Divorce Court, they might uncover alarming similarities of behaviour.[105] However, most preferred to believe that cutting words and cold silences were the greatest cruelties to which respectable ladies were ever submitted. 'Upper class men rarely lifted their hands against their wives', J. W. Kaye explained: 'This is not their mode of expressing resentment.'[106]

The horror and revulsion constantly expressed in Parliament and elsewhere, conveys the impression that the working-class propensity for conjugal violence was a recent discovery. This was false. Social commentators had been remarking on the phenomenon throughout the nineteenth century, although generally in an uncritical fashion. Violence was widely regarded as an accepted part of lower-class family life. Like their drunkenness, their street-brawling and their brutal sports and pastimes, wife-beating simply reflected the generalised savagery of the poor. Some recognised that poverty and squalid, overcrowded accommodation might contribute to this behaviour, but environmental explanations were often intertwined with the cultural assumption that violence was so common among the poor that no one, not even abused wives, questioned its use.[107] There were probably many who believed, along with a coster-boy of Henry Mayhew's acquaintance, that working-class women 'axually liked a feller for walloping them. As long as the bruises hurted, she was always thinking on the cove as gived 'em her'.[108]

However, later in the century, the upper and middle classes were less inclined to be indulgent of working-class wife-beating. It was now perceived in a threatening light precisely *because* it was regarded as but one facet of a generalised savagery. Establishment Victorians were no longer confident that they could control that savagery. Wife-beating was seen as an index of the level of violence in society generally. 'Nothing more demonstrates a weakness in a State,' it was said, 'than the insecurity of its women's safety.'[109] Not only that, it was felt that violence in the home had the potential to spill out into the streets. Men accustomed to striking their wives on whim would not necessarily exercise greater restraint with strangers, whilst children who grew up in violent homes were likely to become the street-corner hooligans of the future.[110] Assaults on women were punished 'by the infliction of trumpery fines', complained Reade, and, as a result,

[t]he savage spirit animating the ruffianism of London ... has full swing.... The wifebeaters, the villains who offer violence to women, the smashers of bones with pokers and hobnailed boots, the cannibals who bite off ears and noses, the ruffians who use quart-pots as lethal weapons, and the vitriol throwers are the worst criminals in England.[111]

There were also economic reasons for discouraging wife-beating. It was assumed that the type of man who beat his wife was unlikely to be a good provider. If he *was* employed, he probably spent his wages on drink, leaving his wife and children to become burdens on the parish: 'Drink and idleness, drink and dirt, drink and misery, drink and cowardly cruelty, are in close alliance'.[112] A blow struck at one aspect of this assemblage of vices was regarded as a blow struck at them all.[113]

Finally, it was feared that wife-beating was making marriage a less attractive option than cohabitation. Social investigators found evidence of a conscious resistance to matrimony among some working-class women who believed that the legal contract would alter the balance of power between them and their partners; 'it always seems to lead to blows and rows', they said. M. E. Loane, a nursing visitor, reported the case of a hard-working and respectable mother who steadfastly refused her long-term partner's proposals of marriage: 'she didn't choose to be knocked about, nor to see her children treated bad, neither'! The advantages of the single state were clear. If the male partner became violent, the woman could leave him and support herself and her children by her own efforts. There was no danger of him seizing her possessions, earnings and children, as he would have had a right to do if they had been married. However, Victorian policy-makers took a different view. Obviously, it was better for a family to be supported by the mother than by the parish and, indeed, a kindly desire to facilitate this was one of the factors which motivated reform of the married women's property law, but, otherwise, arrangements which maximised pressure on male partners to provide, and therefore to work, were much to be preferred.[114]

For all these reasons, wife-beating was no longer to be tolerated. It had become important that working-class family life conform to the bourgeois norm, and wife-beating was a deviation from that norm. Some parliamentarians and commentators thought that the husband would always be the deviant party; others were inclined to think that, more often than not, it was the wife who was to blame. However, whether they worked from a 'suffering wife and feckless husband' model or a 'suffering husband and termagant wife' model made little difference in practice.

The 'suffering wife and feckless husband' approach was more common and was favoured by most of the parliamentarians, supporters and opponents of the flogging proposals alike. Wife-beating incidents were characterised in the parliamentary debates as 'dastardly and cowardly assaults ... perpetrated upon defenceless women by brutes who called themselves men'. The wife-beater was a man 'of brutal and savage nature' who lacked the capacity to control his emotions, an ability that was central to the Victorian conception of manliness. They vented their 'ferocious passions' on the very people they were 'bound to protect', and who were least capable of defending themselves. It would have been less dastardly, apparently, to have attacked another man's wife, for she 'had her own husband to guard her from injury'. Wife-beaters were usually bad providers and invariably drunkards to boot.[115]

It seems that this 'savage race of cruelty-mongers' had been almost universally blessed with loving, docile and industrious wives. J. W. Kaye describes, with an element of prurient enjoyment, how these martyred creatures would 'cling, with wonderful tenacity, even to the hand that smites them, and kiss the feet that treads them in the dust'.[116] The most lowly of these women was 'as worthy of protection as our gracious Sovereign' (since 1842 attempting to shoot at the Queen could be punished by flogging), and yet the criminal law set a greater value on donkeys, poodle dogs, ladies' lap dogs, King Charles' spaniels, vegetables, dried wood, shrubs and walnut trees![117]

Much was made in Parliament and elsewhere of the abused woman's proverbial reluctance to testify against her husband in court. Especially pathetic tales, like that of the woman who declared to a magistrate that she had bitten her own nose, were recounted with grim relish. J. W. Kaye observed with approval: 'No tender-hearted woman will carry her complaints to a police court. She will rather suffer in silence, let her sufferings be what they may'.[118]

This sentiment was echoed in Parliament:

everyone who was acquainted with the feelings of women ... even [women] of the lower classes, among whom these offences generally took place, would agree ... that there was that instinctive tenderness and delicacy in the female mind which would induce a woman to shrink from prosecuting her husband.[119]

Many of the parliamentarians recognised that intimidation or fear of economic hardship could deter women from testifying, but none of them considered the possibility that women might consciously decide to lay a complaint, but go no further, in the hope that this would be sufficient to frighten their husbands into leaving them alone. Nor was there any discussion in Parliament of the role of magistrates, many of whom believed that it was 'in the nature of women to forgive and forget', and who consequently encouraged women to drop charges.[120] Nor, finally, was any mention made of a practice described in an 1856 newspaper report of a wife-assault case:

On the wife leaving the court, the poor woman was assailed by several scoundrels with the foulest abuse – a course now frequently adopted to deter wives from prosecuting.[121]

When wife-beaters were perceived in the manner described above, it followed logically that flogging was the appropriate solution to the problem. The stigma of imprisonment alone could never deter these kind of men for 'they were too depraved in character to feel any shame for that'. However, being great bullies, it could be depended upon that they were also great cowards, and that physical punishment would hold real fear for them. While some kinds of offender might be further brutalised by flogging, 'there was no possible means of reducing to a lower step of brutalisation ruffians who could be guilty of [beating their wives]'.[122] There were many outside Parliament who echoed these sentiments, including members of the progressive National Association for the Promotion of Social Science.[123]

It is clear that it was not the mere fact of having assaulted a woman or a child which turned a man into a brute who deserved to be flogged: there were a number of other qualifying factors. Chief among these was membership of the lower orders. Witness a hypothetical situation posed by an anxious parliamentarian: a Member of Parliament meets 'some saucy boy', gives him a box on the ear and is found guilty of aggravated assault. Was it possible that he might be flogged too? The anti-flogging Member, P. A. Taylor, thought it most unlikely: 'the first cut of the lash touching the tender back of a gentleman' and flogging, he suspected, would 'be swept away forever'.[124]

Other important factors included dishonesty, drunkenness and, most especially, fecklessness. Where fecklessness was lacking there was less certainty about the appropriateness of flogging. The grounds for this hesitation were well-expressed in a magistrate's letter reproduced in Cross's *Brutal Assaults Report*:

The class ... with which the legislation now contemplated would have to deal would be a non-criminal class, that is to say, a working class, providing honestly means of the support of themselves and their families ... Have we not good reason to doubt that the extensive use of the lash as proposed may have the effect of hardening and self-abasing many of the men to whom it was employed, and destroying their usefulness as members of the community?[125]

Viscount Raynham had no scruples of this kind, for he was convinced that wife-beaters were invariably bad supporters. However, J. W. Kaye suspected that 'very bad men are often very good workmen' and he reluctantly questioned the wisdom of flogging in his 1856 article, 'Outrages on Women'.[126]

Other commentators and a few parliamentarians took a different approach to the problem, and argued that 'the beaten wife [was] seldom a good one'. By deviating from the bourgeois ideal of femininity, which demanded passivity, gentleness and industriousness, she had driven her long-suffering husband to violence.[127]

One of the strongest proponents of this view was the court recorder and magistrate Edward Cox. In 1877 in his influential handbook on sentencing, *Principles of Punishment*, he derided the popular image of 'the loving wife and submissive slave brutally beaten by her brutal husband, without provocation or resistance'. The reality, in his experience, was altogether different. The beaten wife was usually

an angel of the fallen class, who has made her husband's home an earthly hell, who spends his earnings in drink, pawns his furniture, starves her children, provides for him no meal, lashes him with her tongue when sober and with her fists when drunk, and if he tries to restrain her fits of passion, resists with a fierceness and strength for which he is no match. He is labouring all day to feed and clothe her and his children and when he returns home at night this is his greeting. The law gives him no redress, no help. He cannot send her away – he cannot obtain a divorce. He is tortured and taunted to the verge of madness. He drinks to drown care. In his cups he vows vengeance, and excited by liquor he assumes unwonted courage, he commands obedience, he threatens punishment, she resists, there is a struggle, he to maintain his authority, she defying it; he for once has the best of it.[128]

In Cox's view, there were instances of wife-beating which were almost justified and very few for which flogging would be an appropriate penalty. He thought that recognisances and articles of the peace should be used where possible, for more severe punishments would diminish the husband's authority in the home. At the 1876 Congress of the National Association for the Promotion of Social Science, the chaplain of Liverpool prison confirmed the existence of Cox's formidable ter-magant, and inquired whether a man could really be blamed for raising his hand to such a woman.[129]

Other commentators were more gentle. There were many working-class wives who could not be blamed for their shortcomings, they said. They had been 'brought up for the most part by ignorant mothers and by bad examples'. No effort had been made to instil habits of neatness and cleanliness when they were girls. They had not been taught household management and no one had explained the importance of making themselves agreeable and attractive to their husbands.[130]

However, much could be done to remedy this. In this respect, Kaye commended to his readers that 'earnest, kindly little work' of Mrs Brewster's, entitled *Sunbeams in the Cottage*, in which she described the change which 'a bright little fireside, a comfortable armchair, a singing tea-kettle, a tidied room, and merry children' could effect in a weary and discontented husband. All that was necessary, commentators suggested, was a cadre of altruistic ladies who could 'elevate and instruct their poor sisters in reference to their domestic duties as wives', and wife-beating would diminish remarkably. There was, of course, the danger that the poor would imagine that they were being patronised but, fortunately, this misapprehension could be avoided by 'insinuat[ing] ... advice in cheery, pleasant talk, as we insinuate physic-powders into the favourite food of young children'.[131]

On the face of it, those who spoke and wrote about wife-beating were divided between two contradictory constructions of the typical wife-beating incident. According to Nancy Tomes, these two constructions were based on very different ideas about the marital relationship. Most of the parliamentarians envisaged wives suffering meekly at the hands of their 'natural protectors'; their role was a passive and dependent one. By contrast, Cox's powerful, provoking wife was a positive image : it allowed that women might be strong and independent and capable of defending their own interests.[132] However, this analysis is questionable. Those who worked from the 'suffering wife and feckless husband' model assumed that all women conformed naturally to the bourgeois ideal of femininity; those of the 'termagant wife and suffering husband' school were disinclined to believe that this was so. But both approaches were based on the same image of how things *ought* to be. They were both based on exactly the same understanding of the problem : the problem was one of deviation from middle-class notions about femininity, masculinity and the relationship between the sexes. Cox was happy to accept that when a wife-beating case *did* involve 'unprovoked brutality and cruelty to a helpless and submissive woman [then it demanded] the highest degree of punishment, even penal servitude'.[133]

Conversely, Kaye was adamant that termagant wives were 'not the sufferers whom we most care to protect'.[134] The warnings were clear : aggressive, independent women should not expect to be protected from violent husbands. Just as a man had to do more than beat his wife to merit flogging, a woman had to do more than get beaten to merit protection : she had to be a particular kind of woman, a woman who did not challenge middle-class notions about femininity and marital relations.

The Nineteenth-Century Feminist Analysis of Wife-Beating

It is no longer as widely believed as it used to be that '[w]omen-battery was uncovered by feminists in the early 1970s'.[135] However, there is still a tendency to assume that pre-twentieth-century analyses of the problem were, at best, superficial and, at worst, misguided. According to M.D.A. Freeman, '[w]hat [Victorian reformers] failed to understand is that violence is endemic in any society which treats women as unequal'.[136] This is clearly a valid criticism of the mainstream debate, but it is an injustice to the considerable body of nineteenth-century feminist think-ing on the subject. It is true that many feminists chose to concentrate their energies on issues which they perceived as being more fundamental to women's oppression, issues like education, employment, property rights and the vote, but there were others for whom wife-beating was central to an understanding of patriarchalism.[137] Chief among these were Frances Power Cobbe, Matilda Blake and Mabel Sharman Crawford. All these women wrote articles dealing specifically with wife-abuse. In addition, there were numerous feminist writers who commented on wife-beating in the context of general surveys of the laws relating to women.[138] This kind of article appeared frequently in contemporary periodicals, particularly in the progressive *Westminster Review*. They had an important ally, finally, in John Stuart Mill, who emphasised in Parliament and in his influential *Subjection of Women* that wife-beating was inextricably linked to women's social, legal and political disabilities.[139]

It cannot be denied that the feminist writers shared many of the assumptions and beliefs of the more conventional commentators. Many of them accepted, for example, that cruelty between upper-class spouses was confined to mental abuse. Cobbe thought that, as a general rule,

the better sort of Englishmen are ... exceptionally humane and considerate to women, [while] the men of the lower class of the same nation are proverbial for their unparalleled brutality.[140]

Her typical wife-beaters had all the familiar attributes: they were 'chiefly the drunken, idle, ruffianly fellows who lounge about the public houses instead of working for their families'. This characterisation was echoed by Crawford and by Catherine Louisa Shore.[141] Wife-beaters were classed with 'roughs', 'drunkards', 'illiterates' and 'liberated con-victs' and it was argued that only a comprehensive programme of reforms could effect any change: 'Foul words, gross acts, drink, dirt, and vice, oaths, curses, and blows, it is all, alas! *in keeping* – nor can we hope to cure one evil without the rest.[142]

Like the parliamentarians, feminist writers emphasised the cowardice and shamefulness of violence towards women 'whose lot in life [was] entrusted entirely to their [husbands'] kindness', women who, for the most part, were emphatically decent and respectable. They too collected accounts of especially shocking cases from the newspapers and published court reports. They used them to demonstrate both the wanton savagery of many attacks and the scandalous inadequacy of the law's response.[143]

The failure of the law to respond decisively to wife-abuse was a recurring theme in their writing. Not only were the penalties provided for in the law of assault manifestly inadequate, they represented only the *maximum* sentences that could be imposed. The decision to leave the actual amount of punishment to the discretion of the magistrate had resulted, they argued, in 'monstrously lenient sentences'. In Mill's experience, prison sentences were only imposed when the offender could not afford to pay a fine, thereby creating a 'power of compounding by payment of blood money'. Even these fines were commonly set at a level well below the possible maximum. As the feminists demonstrated, violence to a wife could be punished less severely than violence to a cat or even a municipal park-bench!'[144] When violence to *men* was in issue, the contrast was even more striking. One writer compared the legislature's response to wife-beating with that provoked by the 1862 garrotting episode; she concluded that while

[i]t had been the custom from time immemorial that wives should be exposed to the full violence of their lords and masters ... that a free-born citizen should incur the same danger was not to be endured for a moment.[145]

Very few wife assaults attracted the more severe sentences that could be imposed on indictment. Of the 8,075 assaults of all kinds (including those which resulted in death) committed against women in 1891, only 43 were punished by more than two years imprisonment. The killing of a wife frequently resulted in a manslaughter rather than a murder charge.[146].

As regards the proposed remedy of flogging, there was a certain amount of feminist acquiescence here also. Surprisingly perhaps, John Stuart Mill and Harriet Taylor Mill were strongly in favour. In an article in which they discussed the merits of Fitzroy's 1853 Bill, they expressed their hope that Phinn's flogging amendment would be accepted. While, in general, they considered corporal punishment to be odious, they believed that only a mandatory flogging sentence could make any impression upon the kind of offender in question:

Those who presume on their consciousness of animal strength to brutally illtreat those who are physically weaker, should be made to know what it is to be in the hands of a physical strength as much greater than their own, as theirs than that of the subjects of their tyranny.[147]

Others responded equivocally. Neither Blake nor the female author[148] of 'The Law in Relation to Women' expressed any opinion as to the appropriateness of flogging generally. However, they were both convinced that the failure to punish wife-beating as severely as some property offences reflected and encouraged disregard for women's safety:

If it be right that robbers are to be punished by flogging ... it would surely be only suitable that those gentlemen who beat their wives, knock them down and dance upon them, dig them with knifes or carve them with reaping-hooks should have a taste of the same punishment.[149]

They thought that wife-beaters deserved to be flogged 'as richly as any garrotter'. Similarly, Cobbe regarded the Government's failure to increase the penalties for assaults on women after the detailed and expensive official inquiry of 1875 which revealed that the majority of the judges favoured flogging, as a clear indication of the low value set on women's lives.[150]

So much for what the feminist and the mainstream commentators had in common. What is more important is how they differed. Some of the differences were admittedly a question of emphasis; others went much further. The feminist writings reflect perceptions and concerns which rarely or never appeared in the parliamentary debates.

First, they subjected the assumption that men of education and refinement scorned the use of violence to greater scrutiny. Cobbe, as we have seen, subscribed to the orthodox view that wife-beating was a working-class preserve. She believed that it was rare for wealthy men to injure their wives. However, she admitted the possibility that it was only the fear of scandal which held them in check:

the gentleman or tradesman somehow manages to bear in mind the disgrace he will incur if his outbreak be betrayed by his wife's black eye or broken arm, and he regulates his cuffs or kicks accordingly.[151]

Blake and Crawford drew attention to the damage that upper-class men did in their capacity as judges and magistrates and as makers and administrators of the law: even if they were not personally given to beating their wives, their failure to respond decisively to working-class wife-abuse suggested a general acquiescence in the practice.[152]

The feminists accepted that beaten wives were sometimes slovenly and careless, that they nagged and drank and pawned the furniture. Cobbe, for one, was not prepared to deny the existence of the 'worrying, peevish killjoy, ... with a voice like a file and a face like a ferret, who bores on, night and day, till life is a burden'. However, she suspected that few had the courage to meddle with these 'terrible harpies' in cold blood. If they got beaten at all, it was usually in the course of a drunken brawl in which they had been active participants if not instigators.

The point was that the 'hateful virago' was rare and bore little resemblance to the majority of wives described in the courts as 'nagging' or 'provoking'. Cobbe thought that men were inclined to take a broad view of what constituted 'aggravating' behaviour:

I have no doubt that every husband who comes home with empty pockets, and from whom his wife needs to beg repeatedly for money to feed herself and her children, considers that she 'nags' him. I have no doubt that when a wife reproaches such a husband with squandering his wages in the public-house, or on some wretched rival, while she and her children are starving, he accuses her to all his friends of intolerable 'nagging'.[53]

This is supported by Nancy Tomes' study of wife-beating cases in London between 1841 and 1875. One husband hit his wife on the head with a walking stick because she had tried to prevent him from emptying the till of their coffee-house to buy liquor. Another was beaten when she informed her husband that he would get no supper, because 'he had left her no money to purchase anything'. One wife who took her husband's wages was beaten to death. 'We had a few words about money matters', he told the police. 'I never meant to kill her, she should have kept her hand out of my pocket.'[54]

Even if wives *were* nagging or slovenly or drunken, the feminists persisted, did this make it 'fit and proper for the Queen's peace to be broken[and the woman's bones along with it[?]' Cobbe thought it significant that faults which, in men, were never punished by more than a five shilling fine, should effectively become capital offences when found in a wife. She had always believed it to be the mark of a civilised country that lynching was disapproved of, but the husband of a nagging wife was apparently entitled to take the law into his own hands. She urged her readers to remember how many women resorted to drink only after years of toil and childbearing had destroyed their health, and violence and contempt, their self-respect.[55]

As we have seen, the feminists were unanimously of the opinion that existing legal responses to wife-beating were inadequate. However, when it came to proposing solutions they were less self-assured than the reforming parliamentarians. It was pointed out in Parliament that it was difficult to punish a wife-beater effectively without making his wife and children suffer also and feminist writers took this concern very seriously. As Crawford explained, both fines and prison sentences affected the beaten wife just as much as her attacker:

[the one] taxed the means required for the support of [her] family, [the other] entailed on her the penalty of hard labour to keep herself and her children from starvation.[156]

Severer penalties could only increase wives' reluctance to make complaints. Already women were deterred from taking action by the fear that their husbands would revenge themselves when they were released from gaol. In Crawford's view, this was a justified fear. She cited examples of husbands who murdered their wives after having been imprisoned for assaults upon them. In fact, a large proportion of wife murderers had several previous convictions for wife-assault. She concluded that 'the infliction of the lash would be manifestly unwise'.

Crawford would like to have seen wife-beaters treated less leniently, but only if it could be done without further jeopardising the safety of the wife. This was impossible, she thought, while the couple remained bound to continue living together after the punishment.[157] Cobbe and the author of 'The Laws Relating to Women' also advised against flogging and emphasised the need to release women from violent marriages. Mill, as we have seen, supported flogging, but he too argued that 'it was contrary to reason and experience to suppose that there [could] be any real check to brutality, consistent with leaving the victim still in the power of the executioner'.[158]

Clearly what was required was an escape route for victims of abuse. The 1857 reform of the divorce law had failed to provide this. An abused wife could not get a divorce unless, first, her husband was also an adulterer and, secondly, she could afford the considerable expense. She could get a judicial separation on grounds of cruelty but, again, this was expensive. She could only get a protection order from the magistrates if her husband had deserted her. If it was she who had left then she was ineligible, even if she had been driven out by ill-treatment.

The possibility of divorce or judicial separation being made more easily accessible to abused wives had been mooted occasionally in Parliament, and also by Kaye and by various members of the National Association for the Promotion of Social Science.[159] However, the suggestion aroused little interest. Mr Dillwyn pointed out that divorce 'was a very large question, affecting the social and domestic relations of the whole people', and said that 'he did not wish to mix [it] up ... with the question which he had now brought before the House'.[160]

It was Cobbe who was responsible for the advances made in this area. She considered the matter seriously and methodically and, with the help of Alfred Hill, a Birmingham magistrate, drafted a Bill 'for the Protection of Wives whose Husbands have been convicted of assaults upon them'.[161] A provision based on this Bill was incorporated into a Bill of Lord Penzance's, concerning the costs of intervention by the Queen's Proctor in matrimonial causes, and was introduced into Parliament in February of 1878. It was accepted with a minor amendment and became part of the Matrimonial Causes Act of 1878. The Act gave magistrates and judges the power to grant a judicial separation to a wife whose husband had been convicted of an aggravated assault upon her. She could also be awarded custody of any children under ten years of age and weekly maintenance.[162] Cobbe hoped that this promise of protection from renewed violence would greatly increase the number of wives prepared to press criminal charges against their husbands.

Unfortunately, the Act gave the judge or magistrate a wider discretion than Cobbe had envisaged. He could grant an order if he was 'satisfied that the future safety of the wife [was] in peril'. This, besides 'seem[ing] to indirectly sanction personal violence that did not actually endanger life', meant that a wife had no guarantee when she went to court that she would be released from her marital obligations. Also, the Act made no special provision for the enforcement of maintenance orders. Cobbe, anticipating that these would be a highly unreliable source of income, had suggested that the payments be made by the Poor Law Guardians, who would then be responsible for recovering the money from the husband. However, this idea met with disapproval at the Committee stage in the House of Lords and Lord Penzance had readily agreed to an amendment.[163]

However, we should not underestimate Cobbe's achievement. The effectiveness of the 1878 Act and of the Summary Jurisdiction (Married Women) Act which extended it in 1895, are discussed further in the concluding chapter. Suffice it to say here that Cobbe's Bill paved the way for a limited summary jurisdiction in matrimonial matters which, for many years, helped to make up for poor people's limited access to the Divorce Court. She herself regarded it as one of the best things she ever did.[164]

Not for a moment, though, did Cobbe imagine that her scheme for judicial separations was the solution to the wife-beating problem. She freely admitted that the practice would not disappear as a result; it would take a great deal more than an Act of Parliament to achieve that. The most that could be hoped for was that the sufferings of its victims would be partially alleviated.[165]

Which brings us to the most important difference between the mainstream and the feminist commentators – their analysis of why wife-beating occurred. In discussing the catalysts of wife-assault, Cobbe listed all the familiar factors: alcohol; prostitution; the natural savagery of the lower classes; the 'interminable, inevitable propinquity' enforced by over-crowded accommodation; the noise and filth and ugliness of urban slums. However, she was emphatic that these were but 'incidental and minor causes'. Like other feminist writers including Crawford, Shore and the Mills, Cobbe believed that the 'fatal root' or 'underground spring' of wife-beating lay in the legal, social and political inequality of women and, in particular, of wives.[166] Reformers could not hope to eradicate wife-beating, she said, while

the position of a woman before the law as wife, mother and citizen, remains so much below that of a man as husband, father and citizen, that it is a matter of course that she must be regarded by him as an inferior.

Every young boy knew that his mother was not his equal: even if he did not see her 'daily scoffed at, beaten and abused', he would learn that the laws of his country denied her the rights of citizenship and did not even think her fit to be his guardian.[167] Harriet Taylor Mill was just as explicit about the cause and effect relationship:

The truly horrible effects of the law among the lowest of the working population, is exhibited in these cases of hideous maltreatment of their wives by working men, with which every newspaper, every police report teems. Wretches unfit to have the smallest authority over any living thing, have a helpless woman for their household slave. These excesses could not exist if women both earned, and had the right to possess, a part of the income of the family.[168]

The feminists did not believe, as Freeman has suggested, that the removal of formal, legal inequalities, or even the extension to women of the franchise, would, in itself, eliminate wife-beating. It was clear to them that a thoroughgoing revision of society's attitudes and values was necessary before that would happen. Most importantly, perhaps, men would have to realise that the existing relations between the sexes, and between spouses in particular, degraded and limited them almost as much as it did women.[169] Mill argued that the patriarchal family nurtured the worst male qualities: men learnt to 'worship their own will as such a grand thing that it [was] actually the law for another rational being'.[170] In deriving their sense of worth and their sexual identity from their dominance over women, women, moreover, who had been purposely bred for inferiority and weakness, they lost the opportunity to develop fully as human beings. Men who feared equality in their most intimate relationships with others deprived themselves of self-knowledge and thereby stunted their own moral development. Such men, Mill concluded, could have little to contribute to the creation of a more just and rational society.

While political reform could not, in itself, effect this required transformation in consciousness, it was an important first step. The feminists argued that only when women obtained the franchise and could influence the making of laws would their legal position improve significantly. It was foolish to depend on male chivalry to protect women's interests in this respect, for male and female interests were so obviously opposed on many issues. They knew that legal reforms could not, any more than the vote, eliminate violence against wives, but they believed strongly in the power of the law to educate. Rather than 'rendering [a woman] *more* helpless, *more* dependent than inferior strength would naturally make her', the law should be used 'to surround her social status with every equal right and dignity'. It was hoped that if husbands saw their wives 'placed by the state on an equal footing' with them, they would find it less easy to regard them as property, while if wives believed that they had a right not to be beaten, they would be encouraged to resist abuse and press their cases in court.[171]

The Feminists and the Parliamentarians

The feminist analysis of wife-beating had little or no impact on the mainstream debate. Parliamentarians spoke of their duty to protect helpless women from violence, not of wives' right not to be beaten. There was much talk of the sufferings of women, but none of suffrage for women.[172] It was never suggested that wife-beating might have anything to do with the nature of the marital relationship generally. Indeed, when one of the leading newspapers suggested that Mr Dillwyn was interfering between husbands and wives in seeking to increase the penalties for aggravated assaults on women he was hotly indignant. This was an 'entirely mistaken' view of his objective:

In reality, it was not a question between a man and his wife, but between man and woman – between brute force and helpless weakness.... He hoped, therefore, that there would be no misapprehension that he intended to interfere between a man and his wife.[173]

Feminists at this time were actively involved in the campaigns to reform the law on divorce, child custody and married women's property rights, but they played no part in the campaign to increase the penalties for wife-beating. Women who attempted to make their views known to the reforming parliamentarians were disregarded or treated with contempt. In 1856, while Dillwyn's Aggravated Assaults Bill was progressing through Parliament, a resolution was passed at a women's meeting in Leicester in which flogging was denounced as a 'barbarous and obsolete mode of punishment' which could only serve to further brutalise those on whom it was imposed. When Mr Dillwyn's attention was drawn to this fact at the Bill's Second Reading, he replied that

he could not attach much importance to that meeting. He had never expected that women would hold meetings *in favour* of the Bill, or take any public part in its advocacy. By doing so, women must of course have exposed themselves to a great deal of personal ridicule, and their compassionate, long-suffering, uncomplaining spirit would indispose them to plead their own cause, and to demand such a remedy as this. The women felt no doubt that they might safely leave their cause in the hands of a Parliament of men.

He went on to express his belief that the majority of women supported his proposals, but that, in any event, wife-beating was more of a man's question than a woman's question. These 'unmanly assaults', he explained, ultimately had a more injurious effect on those who committed them than on those who endured them.[74]

Colonel Egerton Leigh was no more impressed with a women's rights paper which he was sent whilst the 1875 flogging Bill was being debated. It was suggested in this publication that educating men might be more efficacious in the long term than flogging them, a point of view which, in Leigh's opinion, demonstrated that '[w]omen themselves could not be trusted to deal with this question'.[75]

Women who had their own views on how they wished to be helped, challenged the image of the pitiful female suffering in silence which formed such an important part of the reforming parliamentarians' rhetoric. Their views were dismissed or marginalised.

The Jackson Decision Revisited

It is time now to return to *R. v. Jackson* and consider how it fits into the picture. When the decision was announced Elizabeth Wolstenholme Elmy was ecstatic. ' "Coverture" is dead and buried', she announced. 'It is the grandest victory the women's cause has ever yet gained, greater even than the passing of the Married Women's Property Acts.' Henceforth, 'the relative claims of the parties to the conjugal relation [would] have to be considered and established in accordance with the rule of personal freedom.'[76] If this is, in fact, what the *Jackson* judges set out to do, then their view of the marital relationship was very different from the one which had informed the law for centuries. It was a view, moreover, which bore little relation to that of the parliamentarians who had attempted to reform the law of assault. The parliamentarians had no interest in the civil liberties of married women, nor any intention of interfering with the traditional marriage relationship. Their concern was with the deviation from bourgeois family norms which wife-beating represented.

If the *Jackson* judges approached the problem from a vastly different perspective, it is not evident in the kind of language they used. Lord Halsbury's tone throughout was one of genteel indignation:

Is it nothing that a lady coming out of church on a Sunday afternoon is to be seized by a number of men and forcibly put into a carriage and carried off? Must not the element of insult involved in such a transaction be considered?

Not only this, it appeared that on gaining the house Mr Jackson had pulled off his wife's bonnet and thrown it into the fire. Lord Halsbury LC confessed

to regarding with something like indignation the statement of the facts of this case, and the absence of a due sense of the delicacy and respect due to a wife whom the husband has sworn to cherish and protect.

Lord Esher M.R. too stressed the 'extreme insult' involved in the manner of Mrs Jackson's seizure. She had been carried off and 'insultingly imprisoned' in her husband's house. A lawyer's clerk and a nurse had been employed 'to help to keep watch over her and control her. That in itself is insulting.' 'Could *anything*, in fact, have been 'more insulting?'[77]

This blustering is understandable given the preoccupations of the age: efforts were being made to break the working classes of their brutal habits and encourage them to adopt the chivalrous code of their betters. Working-class men were being urged to behave like gentleman and to treat their wives like ladies. It was a bad time for a respectable middle-class man to seize his wife in public and then to come into court arguing that he had been acting within his rights as laid down by the common law of England. Mr Jackson was an embarrassment. The judges were understandably anxious to demonstrate that, if a husband had ever possessed such rights at law, they had long since ceased to exist and to express their amazement at the vulgar misapprehension which had arisen. They were not concerned with the legal status of wives. They had no more intention than the parliamentarians had of transforming the nature of the marital relationship.

However, others took a different view of what they had done. The decision was seen in many quarters as having radical and far-reaching implications. Any suggestion that Jackson was an anachronistic figure whose behaviour reflected a long outmoded understanding of the marital relationship was belied by the remarkable public response.[178]

A week after the hearing Mrs Jackson set off for home with her sister and brother-in-law. Two miles from Clitheroe their carriage was mobbed. A crowd surrounded their house that night and the police had to be called. *The Times* reported that:

[g]roans, hisses and yells were given for Mrs Jackson, and cheers, with the singing of 'He's a jolly good fellow' for her husband. The midnight scene was an extremely stormy and threatening one, the police being hard-pressed to prevent violence. The crowd continued outside nearly the whole of the night.

The disturbances continued for a number of days. On the Saturday night the crowd made an effigy of Mrs Jackson and paraded it through the streets. They stopped at the homes of her two sisters and hooting and yelling quickly turned into stone-throwing.[179] In short, the response bore a striking resemblance to a charivari – the popular ritual which had long been used to discipline transgressors of society's sexual and marital norms.

It was not only 'the mob' who supported Mr Jackson. A number of prominent Blackburn men, including the bishop and the town clerk, lent their names to an appeal for funds to enable him to take his case to the House of Lords. However, in the event, there was no further legal action. In a series of editorials in *The Times*, the *Jackson* judges were taken to task. It was felt that Jackson had been 'hardly used':

[F]orce ... is always disagreeable, especially when applied to a lady; but, if ladies and their relatives refuse to regard the law, and the husband is armed by the law with special rights, it is hard to blame him for proceeding to extremities.... we very much doubt whether the public will echo those easy denunciations of Mr Jackson's 'brutality' of which Lord Esher was so prodigal.

The judges were told that they should have concentrated on the limited question of fact and law which came before them instead of 'trifling' with the marriage law.[180]

Lord Halsbury and Lord Esher were subjected to hostile questioning in the House of Lords. Did the decision really have the effect that it appeared to have? Did the Government propose legislation on the subject? Were they aware that some magistrates had responded by threatening not to grant any more separation orders 'or otherwise interfere for the protection of married women'? The beleaguered judges responded defensively. All that *Jackson* had decided was that a man could not imprison his wife. They could think of no other decision which had been so misunderstood![181]

Public consternation seems to have been widespread. Contemporary writers described the 'clamour' and the 'hubbub' created by a 'bewildered populace', while an amused American lawyer remarked on the 'great tribulation in the breasts of English husbands' on discovering that they could no longer imprison their 'chaste but reluctant wives'.[182] In an article in *The Nineteenth Century*, the fiercely anti-feminist writer Lynn Linton announced that

[m]arriage, as hitherto understood in England, was suddenly abolished one fine morning last month! ... the sceptre of sovereignty is in the hands of the weaker, and the stronger has to beg for bare justice. Our law lords have destroyed the old balance as completely as if a tornado had passed over a stately shrine and flung the holy image to the winds.

She went on to describe the 'deep shock of surprise and indignation [that was] thrilling through the country'. Henceforth, it seemed, if a woman tired of her household duties or objected to her husband's taste in ties or in music, or to his habit of smoking a pipe, she could simply pack up her bags and leave him to drift 'over the domestic sea a veritable rudderless and water-logged derelict'. The grievance did not have to be any more substantial than the

shadowy distaste of the famous Clitheroe paradigm, which seems to have been founded on nothing more solid than the froth of caprice and 'I have changed my mind.'

Not only could the abandoned husband never remarry unless his wife committed adultery but, in spite of being deprived of her services and her property, perhaps even denied an heir to inherit his estate and carry on his name, he was obliged to continue maintaining her. In the absence of a broadening of the grounds for divorce this situation was intolerable. Mrs Linton knew, if others did not, where 'the prancing desires of the free lovers and the grimmer designs of the woman's rights women' were tending – to 'social anarchy', to 'chaos and universal topsyturvydom', to 'the true beginning of the end'. 'It is all a muddle,' she concluded in distress.[183]

'[T]hat bastion of male conservatism', *Punch*,[184] had a field-day:

FOR BETTER OR WORSE!

(*Two Views of the Same Subject.*)

POSSIBLE ROMANCE

SCENE – *A Dungeon beneath the Castle Moat. Wife chained to a post, with bread and water beside her. Enter Husband, with cat-o'-nine-tails.*

Husband. And now, after ten days' seclusion, will you make over your entire property to me, signing the deed with your life's blood?
Wife (*in a feeble voice*). Never! You may kill me, but I will defy you to the last!

Husband. Then die!

[*He is about to leave the dungeon, when he is met by a Messenger from the Court of Appeal.*]

Messenger. In the name of the Law, release your prisoner!

Husband. Foiled!

[*Joy of Wife, and tableau, as the Curtain falls.*]

PROBABLE REALITY

SCENE – *The Church-door of a fashionable Church. Wife bidding adieu to Husband.*

Husband. Surely, now that my name and fortune are yours, you will reconsider your decision, and at least accompany me back to our wedding breakfast?

Wife (*in a firm voice*). Never! You may kill me, but I will defy you to the last!

Husband. This is rank nonsense! You must take my arm.

[*He is about to leave the Church-porch, when he is met by a Messenger from the Court of Appeal.*]

Messenger. In the name of the Law, release your prisoner!

Husband. Sold!

[*Joy of Wife, and tableau, as the Curtain falls.*][185]

Lawyers were no less surprised than lay-people to learn that a husband's right of custody and control had long since lapsed. To them, the reviled *Cochrane* decision had read 'very plainly and sensibly'[186] and they made no attempt to hide their disgust. Nevill Geary wrote in his 1892 manual on the law of marriage:

[I]f ... the wife elects to use the matrimonial domicile as a hotel, coming and going at her own pleasure, it does not seem that ... a husband has any remedy; and this is the result of *R. v. Jackson.*[187]

In *The Law Relating to Married Women*, also published in 1892, Joseph Matthews echoed Mrs Linton's concerns. By a wife's caprice a husband could be condemned to lifelong celibacy, although still liable to maintain her. Surely this was not right?

When it is considered that a wife upon her marriage undertakes in the most solemn manner to obey, serve, love, honour and keep her husband ... and how essential it is to the preservation of society that the marriage tie should be held sacred, it might be supposed that the husband would at least have the right to compel the wife to live with him, and render to him marital rights, ... *Queen v. Jackson* ... seems to show that this view is very far from being correct.[188]

Legal resistance continued long after March of 1891. In 1906 Edward Fellows suggested that it was time to face up once again to 'the unchangeable facts of nature.... it should be recognised that the wife's primary duty is to live with her husband'. He recommended the revival of enforcement of restitution of conjugal rights by imprisonment and that a deserting wife's income should become the property of her husband. Only thus could the courts regain 'some control over women who refused to do their duty'.[189]

Other legal academics set about salvaging the remnants of the husband's authority. The judges in *Jackson* had hinted that there might be some circumstances in which a wife could lawfully be restrained. This was seized upon. Eversley suggested in the 1906 edition of *The Law of Domestic Relations* that it was still permissible for a husband to 'detain his wife within the walls of the matrimonial domicile ... when apprehensive of her doing some injury to his honour or property'.[190] Crawley's 1892 *Law of Husband and Wife* went further. Crawley refused to accept that a husband's rights had actually been abolished. He argued that they had simply become unenforceable as a result of the 1884 Matrimonial Causes Act and advised his readers that 'even if [the husband] exceed[ed] his rights no action at law for assault or false imprisonment would lie against him'.[191]

In the light of all this, it is not surprising to find feminist writers complaining in the 1890s that the belief in a right to beat and confine still existed and that the judiciary did not discourage it. The *Jackson* decision may, as Stopes put it, have 'reduced the demand for wife-kicking boots', but it was clear that a fair amount of trade was still being carried on in that commodity.'[192]

The reaction to the *Jackson* case, and the treatment meted out to Mrs Jackson personally, must have served as a stern warning to other married women who felt inclined to challenge the traditional view of marital relations. Mrs Jackson had the advantage of strongly supportive relatives. The families of many abused wives will have chosen to ignore the signs of marital strife and the courts seemed keen to encourage this attitude. It will be remembered that the Queen's Bench judges in *Jackson* saved their most acidic comments for the sisters. Similarly, commentators were quick to suggest that the disagreements which brought the Cochranes to court in 1840 were easily explained by the fact that there 'seems to have been a good deal of mother-in-law in the case, and "mother-in-law" is English for bitter beer'.[193]

Conclusion

One of the central aims of nineteenth-century feminist reformers was full legal equality for spouses. They regarded this as a precondition of the truly companionate marriage. Only if wives had the same political and legal rights as their husbands could marriage be transformed from a relation of domination and subordination into an intimate friendship.[194] But there was another reason for focusing specifically on the status of wives. The feminists recognised the interlocking nature of women's subordination in the household and in the state:

Women were kept from the vote and from most remunerative employment because it was assumed that their proper place was in the home, bearing and rearing children. Every woman, married or not, was regarded as a mother, or, more crudely, as a reproductive machine. A woman's sexual and reproductive capacities, not her other abilities, assigned her both her proper sphere in society and her rights under the law.[195]

It was essential for all women that wives acquire the same rights as their husbands to operate in the public sphere.

The feminists tended to assume that political and legal reforms would, in themselves, produce gradual changes in social attitudes. We know now that they were overly optimistic about this. It was not enough for women to possess the same formal, legal rights as men: they also needed the same opportunity to exercise them. In particular, women needed *actual* economic power if their social status was to improve. However, very few feminists challenged the traditional division of labour between the sexes. They accepted that housekeeping and child-rearing were naturally and exclusively women's work and, in doing so, they consigned the vast majority of married women to continued financial dependence on their husbands. Such women could not compete with men in the outside world on equal terms, particularly if they had children.

Of course, it is easy to be critical with the benefit of hindsight. The achievements of the nineteenth-century feminists should not be underestimated: in most respects their analysis of women's oppression was highly sophisticated and the reforms they procured were undoubt-edly 'crucial prerequisites of the reconstruction of gender relations in both the family and the state'.[196]

Unfortunately, that reconstruction was not to take place in their lifetime. In none of the areas of law which they tackled did they come anywhere near achieving the aim of spousal equality. Divorce law was reformed but a wife still had to satisfy more stringent grounds. Child custody law was reformed but a mother still did not have an automatic right to custody during the currency of her marriage. Married women's property rights were reformed but a wife's position was still different from a man's or from a single woman's. She could enter into contracts, but only in respect of her separate property. It was her property that was liable for her post-nuptial debts rather than her personally. She could not be imprisoned if she failed to pay.

Feminists had played an active role in each of these reform cam-paigns; indeed, much of the reforming legislation had its origins in feminist agitation. Ultimately, however, they were dependent on male parliamentarians (whom they had played no part in electing) to represent their point of view. It was easy for their objectives to be distorted or ignored. They asked for equality and were given equity. They asked for rights and were give protection. They asked for a transformation of women's legal status and were given limited reforms directed at particular categories of women; the parliamentarians were quite prepared to stretch a helping hand to women who were very poor or especially vulnerable or particularly deserving, but were extremely resistant to fundamental alterations in women's legal status.

As regards a husband's right to his wife's body, the feminists had even less impact on nineteenth-century developments than they did elsewhere. The changes that occurred were brought about by male judges and parliamentarians for reasons of their own. It is true that the flogging Bills were all rejected whereas Frances Power Cobbe's 1878 Bill was enacted into law. This was because Cobbe was more sensitive to the mood of Parliament as a whole than the floggers were. She deliberately focused her proposals on providing relief to the victim rather than on punishing the offender. Parliamentarians liked protecting poor defenceless women and Cobbe offered them the opportunity to do just that. None of the nineteenth-century changes were designed to alter the nature of the marital relationship. As we have seen, Elizabeth Wolstenholme Elmy jumped to the conclusion that *Jackson* had killed coverture dead and that, henceforth, 'the relative claims of the parties to the conjugal relation [would] have to be considered and established in accordance with the rule of personal freedom'. She quickly discovered her error. She attempted to build on the *Jackson* triumph by seeking the abolition of the marital rape exemption: it clearly followed from the principle enunciated in *Jackson* that a wife had the right to refuse her husband sexual intercourse. She could not even get her Bill introduced.[197]

5
Conclusion

Introduction

My aim in this study has been to illuminate the relationship between wife-beating, coverture and the fiction of marital unity and to use that relationship to explain nineteenth-century developments in the law relating to wife-beating. In this concluding section I recap my arguments in the context of an examination of the abused wife's position at the end of the nineteenth century. To what extent had the events of the preceding 50 years improved her ability to protect herself from marital violence?

The Abused Wife at the End of the Nineteenth Century

By the end of the nineteenth century the legal position of married women had improved considerably. However, for many of the victims of marital abuse, the practical gains were small.

The 1891 decision in *R*. v. *Jackson* was undeniably a legal landmark. Sweeping away centuries of judicial authority, the Court of Appeal finally made it illegal for a husband to beat or imprison his wife. Admittedly, explicit claims to a legal right to beat had largely died away by the nineteenth century; however, as the Lord Chancellor pointed out in *Jackson*, a husband's right to control his wife's movements would mean little unless he were entitled to use whatever physical coercion was necessary to enforce that right.

Jackson represented a significant change in the law. The judges conveyed the impression that the outcome of the case was a foregone conclusion, that they were simply confirming long-established changes in judicial practice; however, this was misleading. In cases like *Cochrane* and *Price* the husband's general right to the custody of his wife's person had been unequivocally affirmed. And these decisions were entirely in line with previous authority; the vigour of the patriarchal rhetoric in which they were couched may have been new but the law was not.

Although there were cases which seemed to suggest that the husband's right had ceased to exist or that it could only be exercised to prevent or punish the wife's misbehaviour, they were all explicable in other ways. Many of these cases concerned husbands who had signed away their general right to custody under the terms of a separation agreement. Others involved husbands who were judged to have acted excessively by, for example, confining their wives in madhouses. A third category of case concerned husbands who sought to use the *habeas corpus* action to have their runaway wives returned to them. Their claims were rejected, not because they lacked a general right to custody, but because this was an inappropriate use of *habeas corpus.*

Thus *Jackson* represented a real advance. It enabled a wife to live apart from her husband in the face of his objections and ensured that, if he seized and imprisoned her, her friends and relatives would be able to secure her release. On the other hand, it did nothing to ensure her ability to survive independently. Fleeing was an unattractive option if the disabilities attendant on wifehood would continue to apply. From this point of view, the reforms in the areas of married women's property rights and divorce law were, potentially, of greater practical significance. The Married Women's Property Acts of the 1870s, 1880s and 1890s made it theoretically possible for the abused wife to support herself and her children by her own efforts; there was no longer the danger of her husband seizing her earnings and possessions. At the same time, the 1857 Divorce Act and, more especially, the Matrimonial Causes Act of 1878 and the Summary Jurisdiction (Married Women) Act of 1895, offered an escape from the other aspects of coverture.

However, the theory and the reality did not match. As we have seen, the 1878 scheme for judicial separations was designed to protect wives who took advantage of the improved offences against the person legislation. However, it failed to live up to even Frances Power Cobbe's modest expectations. This was largely because of the 'permissive form'[1] in which the scheme was enacted; a wife was not entitled to a separation order unless her husband had actually been convicted of an aggravated assault upon her, and then only if the magistrate believed her future safety to be imperilled. Joseph Matthews was of the opinion that magistrates 'construe[d] the statute ... very liberally in favour of their jurisdiction',[2] but feminist assessments of the time suggested otherwise.

In 'Maltreatment of Wives', Mabel Crawford reported the details of 22 wife-beating cases which were decided within a six-week period in 1893.[3] Although many involved appallingly savage violence, and in spite of the fact that several of the wives 'urgently and piteously appealed' to the magistrate for a separation, not a single separation order was granted. Most of the offenders, including some with previous convictions for wife-assault, were simply required to pay a small fine. Even when the justices recognised the seriousness of the offence, as in the case of a Birmingham man who was imprisoned for a year for deliberately setting fire to his wife, the sentence was not accompanied by a separation order. In Crawford's view, the new legislation resembled a 'Dead Sea apple, fair without, and ashes, dust and bitterness within'.[4] It created the illusion that a woman who pressed charges against her husband would be protected; in reality, she might be exposed to greater danger than ever. Moreover, under the 1878 Act, an assaulted woman could only be granted custody of children under ten years of age. Many women must have been deterred from taking action by the prospect of leaving older children to the mercies of a violent father.

The terms of the 1878 Act were broadened in 1895. Under the Summary Jurisdiction (Married Women) Act, a wife could be granted a separation if her husband deserted her, forced her by wilful neglect or persistent cruelty to leave him, or was sentenced on indictment to pay a fine of more than £5 or to a term of imprisonment exceeding two months for assaulting her. Henceforth, she could be granted custody of children below the age of sixteen and be awarded weekly maintenance of up to £2. These extensions, particularly the fact that it was no longer necessary to procure a conviction for assault, represented a substantial advance. The passage of the Act precipitated a flood of applications, revealing, probably for the first time, the real dimensions of the wife-beating problem. Unfortunately, however, the magistrates retained a discretion as to the granting of orders and, in 1905, Elizabeth Wolstenholme Elmy reported that they were

administering the new Act on the old lines, refusing the relief asked for, and telling applicant wives (in direct contravention of the express words of the Act) that the violence complained of must be of such a character as to bring the husband under the Aggravated Assaults Act.[5]

Even if separation orders had been granted freely they could only have been of limited use: they did not enable women to remarry. A husband who could prove that his wife had committed adultery, either before or after separation, was entitled to have the order discharged.[6] In drafting her 1878 Bill, Frances Power Cobbe had deliberately chosen to provide for judicial separation rather than divorce; she feared that marital assaults would increase, and that wives would be tempted to provoke them, if they became a means of acquiring an absolute divorce.[7] As we have seen, an abused wife could only get a divorce if her husband were also an adulterer and if she could afford the considerable expense involved in petitioning the Divorce Court in London.

Cobbe did not regard the difference between separation and divorce as problematic; she believed that the abused wife would usually be grateful for the chance to live out the rest of her life 'like a well-conducted widow'.[8] This reflected a perception of women as asexual beings. More seriously, it ignored economic realities. Unless substantial maintenance was both ordered and paid, the wife would have to support herself and her children through her own efforts. In reality, it was virtually impossible for a woman to earn enough in the poorly-paid occupations that were open to her to keep both herself and a family.[9] Housekeeping and child-rearing were still regarded as a woman's natural occupation and employers continued to operate on the assumption that women would be economically dependent on men. In particular, it was assumed that women with children would have husbands playing the part of main bread-winner. To restore a woman with children to the status of a *feme sole* in a society that was shot through with these attitudes was simply to replace the fiction of marital unity with an equally fictitious image of independence.

The Survival of the Power Principle

Blackstone, as we have seen, thought that the husband's legal right to beat and imprison his wife had arisen as a consequence of coverture. As a husband was liable to be held legally responsible for his wife's conduct, it was essential that he have the power to control it. If this were true it could be seen as providing a plausible explanation of the *Jackson* decision. In the second half of the nineteenth century the disabilities attendant on wifehood had begun to be removed. Slowly but surely coverture was being dismantled and, correspondingly, the husband's need for a legal right of control was diminishing. On this view, *Jackson* simply represented the courts' recognition of these facts.

However, I have argued that Blackstone's approach inverted the true relationship between coverture and wife-beating. An acceptance of the husband's right to beat and imprison was the very *essence* of coverture; it was the *cause* rather than the consequence. It was not coverture but the 'power principle' which lay at the heart of the wife-beating problem. This is the name which I have given to the societal assumption that women were lesser beings, that they should be subject to men and that men had the right to control them. Although the law did not create this belief, it accommodated and supported it. The husband's legal right to beat and imprison and the wife's legal disabilities were all emanations from the power principle.

The abolition of the husband's legal right in *Jackson* and the inroads which reforming legislation had begun to make into the doctrine of coverture did not necessarily signal the demise of the power principle. I would argue that none of these changes went deep enough to engage the root of the problem; the power principle survived and simply manifested itself in different and more subtle ways. It was arguably as potent in the nineteenth century as it had been in Norman times.

The Fiction of Marital Unity

The power principle largely owed its survival to the fiction of marital unity. The fiction of marital unity was regarded by nineteenth-century family lawyers as the fundamental principle underlying the legal construction of the marital relationship. In reality, it was no such thing. It was not a legal principle in the usual sense; it was an ideological structure which was designed to legitimate the legal manifestations of the power principle.

This had not always been its role. When the fiction of unity first began to feature in legal literature, after the Norman Conquest, it simply indicated the canonical doctrines of the unity of flesh and of the indissolubility of marriage. Its legitimating services were not required during this period for the law's acceptance of masculine predominance had not yet come to be regarded as a source of embarrassment. The medieval common lawyers unashamedly attributed the married women's unequal legal status to the power principle.

However, this gradually ceased to be acceptable. In the seventeenth century the power principle came under attack. Out of the religious, political and economic changes which were taking place during this period, the principle of individualism had begun to emerge. And this principle was at odds with the subordination of wives. If all men were free and equal in the eyes of God, the state and the market, how could the subjection of women continue to be maintained? It was in this context that the fiction revealed its chameleon-like nature and transformed itself into a legal maxim which explained and justified the wife's unequal status. The wife was told that she and her husband counted as one in the eyes of the law and that their interests were so similar that she could be politically represented by her husband without injustice. This notion of marital unity was given a coating of religion and romance to make it easier to swallow.

This seventeenth-century settlement held the line for a hundred years or more. However, by the nineteenth century, the power principle was under pressure once again. This time the challenge came from Chartists and Owenites and, later, from feminist law reformers. The fiction of unity responded by undergoing another transformation. It guaranteed its continuing influence by meshing with new religious, social and scientific theories about femininity and woman's place in society. The notion of separate sexual spheres emerged and respectability and domesticity became the ruling Victorian values. Now, although husband and wife were still portrayed as two halves of a whole, each had their own clearly defined role. These roles were very different but, supposedly, equally important. Evangelicalism and the cult of domesticity offered wives compensatory definitions of self-worth; although they were denied any power in the world of work and politics, they were granted unbounded influence in the sphere of home and family. And this influence could extend beyond the private sphere; the home represented a moral power-house where men could recharge their spiritual batteries between forays into the turbulent world outside. Thus wives were given a part to play in the battle to save the world from sin and disorder. Victorian scientists lent their support, assuring women that, physically and emotionally, they were uniquely and exclusively adapted to house-keeping and child-rearing. Only by obeying the dictates of nature and confining themselves to the private sphere could they hope to produce the superior offspring upon which the nation's future depended.

These social and religious ideologies had their origins among the middle classes. However, through the campaign for the reform of manners and morals, which derived its initial impetus from Evan-gelicalism, they acquired an ever-widening sphere of influence. By mid-century the middle-class drive for moral regeneration had spread out to include all social classes. In particular, the bourgeois ideal of the family became a part of the dominant culture; it came to be considered the only proper way to live.

Conclusion

Although the law did not create the power principle, it represented

a mode of reproduction of the existing patriarchal order, minimising social change but avoiding the problems of overt conflict.... [It did] not create patriarchal relations but ... in a complex and often contradictory fashion reproduce[d] the material and ideological conditions under which these relations [could] survive.[10]

Legal changes had to occur in the nineteenth century if overt conflict was to be avoided. As the century progressed, changing attitudes rendered many of the legal manifestations of the power principle unacceptable: the husband's legal right to beat and imprison his wife had to go; the edifice of legal male dominance represented by coverture began to crumble.

At the same time, however, the patriarchy was mounting a counter-offensive; trends were emerging which operated to impede the progression towards female equality. These trends manifested themselves in entrenched notions about femininity, masculinity, the relationship between the sexes and the proper roles of men and women within society. The role which they dictated for women offered little potential for self-determination. It was based on a dream,

the dream of domestic felicity. . . . The women of the early nineteenth-century provincial middle class caught hold of that dream, but when it became a full reality they found their sphere isolated, trivialised and often unable to give the support it had promised. It was in the experience of their daughters and grand-daughters later in the century that the inequalities, the lack of power and resources for control over their own lives, came to be exposed and expressed."

However, the dream proved enduring. The belief that housekeeping and child-rearing were naturally and exclusively female occupations persisted; it prevented those daughters and grand-daughters from taking full advantage of the formal legal rights which they fought so hard to achieve.

The *Jackson* decision and the parliamentary campaign for the reform of the law of assault were both primarily directed towards the maintenance of this convenient dream. They served as vehicles for the propagation of the bourgeois model of the family, the bourgeois code of chivalry and the doctrine of the separate sexual spheres. Far from being a *reflection* of women's improving legal status, they formed part of the *reaction* to it. The law could no longer impose the power principle explicitly; however, it could support religious and social ideologies which would help to ensure that the vast majority of women would continue to be financially, emotionally and, therefore, physically in men's power.

The main vehicle of continued legal support for the power principle was the fiction of marital unity. Like mistletoe, the fiction of marital unity was hemiparasitic; it was partly independent and partly parasitic. Although it had an independent existence within the law it derived much of its strength from contemporaneous social, political, religious and economic developments.

NOTES

Chapter 1: The Jackson Decision and the History of the Law on Wife-Beating

1. The Divorce and Matrimonial Causes Act 1857, s. 17.
2. 10 March 1891, 8.
3. 64 *Law Times*, (*N.S.*) (25 July 1891) 679, 680. See also 55 *Justice of the Peace* (28 March 1891), 199.
4. David Rubenstein, *Before the Suffragettes: Women's Emancipation in the 1890s* (1986), 54–8 at 55. On Lord Halsbury's character, see R. F. V. Heuston, *Lives of the Lord Chancellors 1885–1940* (1964), 67–75.
5. 7 T.L.R. (1890–1) 382, 384, 385.
6. [1891], 1 Q.B. 671. See also 55 *Justice of the Peace* (18 April 1891), 246.
7. *The Times*, 3 April 1891, 9.
8. Ibid., 20 March 1891, 9.
9. See Mary Lyndon Shanley, *Feminism, Marriage, and the Law in Victorian England, 1850–95* (1989), 177–183 at 177.
10. *The Times*, 3 April 1891, 9.
11. 'The Personal Liberty of Married Women', 90 *Law Times* (1890–1), 386.
12. Eliza Lynn Linton, 'The Judicial Shock to Marriage', 171 *The Nineteenth Century* (1891), 691, 692.
13. R. W. Chambers, *Thomas More* (1949, originally 1935), 95–6.
14. See Law Commission Working Paper No. 103, *Criminal Law: Binding Over: The Issues* (1987), 4–30 at 4.
15. See 21 Jac. I, c. 8.
16. 8th edn. (1755), 185 (my emphasis); see also 542.
17. (1599, originally 1581), 137. In later editions the reference to husbands and wives disappears: see *Eirenarcha* (1610), 127.
18. Godb. 215; 72 E.R. 966.
19. See Katherine O'Donovan, 'The Male Appendage – Legal Definitions of Women' in Sandra Burman (ed.), *Fit Work for Women* (1979), 134, 137.
20. I.L., (ed.) T.E. (1632), 128. In the early part of the seventeenth-century, a London regulation forbade wife-beating after nine in the evening because of the noise: see C. V. Wedgewood, *The King's Peace, 1637–1641* (1960, originally 1955), 42.
21. *Countrey Justice* (repr. 1975), 133. See also: Lambarde (1610), 78; *Cloburn's Case* (1629) Hetl. 149; 124 E.R. 414.
22. 1 Keb. 637; 83 E.R. 1157.

23. 'Wife-Torture in England', 32 *Contemporary Review* (1878), 55, 64.

24. (1979), 63.

25. Lawrence Stone, *The Family, Sex and Marriage in England, 1500–1800* (1977), 326.

26. M. Dorothy George (ed.), *Catalogue of Personal and Political Satires in the British Museum* (1978), 5: nos. 6122, 6123 and 6124. See also Stone (1977), plate 19.

27. See PRO KB 21/43.

28. *The Lives of Twelve Eminent Judges of the Last and Present Century* (1846), 1: 19.

29. *The Judges of England; with Sketches of Their Lives* (1864; repr. 1966), 8: 251–2 at 252.

30. A. W. B. Simpson, *Biographical Dictionary of the Common Law* (1984), 87–9 at 88.

31. 7th edn. (1817, originally 1767), 18.

32. See *Pleas of the Crown* (1716–21; repr. 1973), 1: 130. See also *Fletcher* v. *Fletcher* (1788) 2 Cox. 99, 102; 30 E.R. 46, 47.

33. George (1978), 6: no. 7123.

34. Courtney Stanhope Kenny, *The History of the Law of England as to the Effects of Marriage on Property and on the Wife's Legal Capacity* (1879), 154. See also E. P. Thompson, *Customs in Common* (1991), 506 and n. 2.

35. (1846), 1: 19.

36. See, for example: Kenny (1879), 154; Lord Denning, *The Changing Law* (1953), 79. In 'Wife-Beating and Imprisonment', 91 *Law Times* (1891), 321, Irving Browne discussed some nineteenth-century American cases which popularised the reasonable instrument rule.

37. (1613) Godb. 215; 72 E.R. 966.

38. 3 Keb. 433; 84 E.R. 807; 2 Lev. 128; 83 E.R. 482; 3 Salk. 139; 91 E.R. 739.

39. See: Levin L. Schücking, *The Puritan Family: A Social Study from the Literary Sources* (1969), xi–xv, 18–57; Christopher Hill, *The World Turned Upside Down* (1972), 247–60 at 249.

40. See Simpson (1984), 220–2.

41. Quoted in Doris May Stenton, *The English Woman in History* (1957), 106.

42. Quoted in Stone (1977), 197.

43. Quoted in Stenton (1957), 109.

44. (1622; repr. 1976), 389–93 at 390–2.

45. See Leonore Marie Glanz, *The Legal Position of English Women Under the Early Stuart Kings and the Interregnum, 1603–1660* (1973), 45.

46. (1609; repr. 1978), 31–2, 28, 43.

47. (repr. 1973), 1: 130.

48. 9th edn. (1764), 3: 390.

49. 5th edn., 2: 238 n.(e).

50. Quoted in 'The Husband's Dominion Over His Wife', 65 *Law Journal* (1928), 182.

51. 6th edn. (1807), 1: 457.

52. See Edward Manson, 'Marital Authority', 7 *Law Quarterly Review* (1891), 244, 245.

53. See 'The Husband's Dominion Over His Wife', (1928), 182.

54. *Commentaries on the Laws of England*, 15th edn. (1809), 1 : 445.

55. Quoted in B. Hill (ed.), *Eighteenth-Century Women: An Anthology* (1984), 144.

56. Quoted in Eugene A. Hecker, *A Short History of Women's Rights From the Days of Augustus to the Present Time*, 2nd edn. (1971, originally 1914), 126.

57. Anna Laetitia Barbauld (ed.), *The Correspondence of Samuel Richardson* (1804), 6 : 186–7.

58. *Sir Cleave Moore* v. *Ellis Freeman et al* (1725), Bunb. 205 ; 145 E.R. 648. The husband's right of moderate chastisement was upheld in the Canadian courts as late as 1826 : see the discussion of *Hawley* v. *Ham* in Constance Backhouse, *Petticoats and Prejudice: Women and Law in Nineteenth-Century Canada* (1991), 167–76.

59. See, for example : 1755, PRO KB 21/37 (John and Elizabeth Park (Hil. 28 Geo. 2), Christopher and Mary Wallis, Adam and Ellen Lodge (East. 28 Geo. 2)); 1775, PRO KB 21/41 (Thomas and Sarah Giordani (Hil. 15 Geo. 3), Thomas and Mary Higginson (Trin. 15 Geo. 3), Richard and Elizabeth Howells (Mich. 16 Geo. 3)). See also the numerous cases listed in PRO KB 33/20/4.

60. (1810), 13 East. 171 n.(a) ; 2 Stra. 1202.

61. See Roper Samuel Donnison Roper, *A Treatise of the Law of Property Arising from the Relation between Husband and Wife*, 2nd edn. (1826), 2 : 318–19.

62. See Law Commission (1987), 9–10, 66–8.

63. See Peregrine Bingham, *The Law of Infancy and Coverture*, 2nd US ed. (1849), 304–5.

64. See, for example, 1775, PRO KB 21/41 (Sarah and Thomas Giordani (Hil. 15 Geo. 3) and Elizabeth and Richard Howells (Mich. 16 Geo. 3)); 1781, PRO KB 21/42 (Christian and Edward White (Mich. 22 Geo. 3)).

65. See, for example, *R.* v. *Brotherton* (1734), Cas. T. Hard. 74 ; 95 E.R. 46 ; *Lord Vane's Case* (1744), 13 East 171 n.(a) ; *Heyn's Case* (1813), 2 V. & B. 183 ; 35 E.R. 288 ; *Dobbyn's Case* (1814), 3 V. & B. 183 ; 35 E.R. 448.

66. (1717) PRO KB 33/20/4.

67. Or *R.* v. *Bowes* ; 1 T.R. 696 ; 99 E.R. 1327. For further information about this couple, see Susan Staves, *Married Women's Separate Property in England 1660–1833* (1990), 53–5.

68. 'Personal Relations of Husband and Wife', 55 *Justice of the Peace* (4 April 1891), 211, 229.

69. PRO KB 1/12, part 1, Hil. 30 Geo. 2, affdt. of Theophilus Meridith (1 Feb. 1757).

70. Ibid., affdt. of William Meridith (7 Jan. 1757).

71. Ibid., affdt. of William Meredith (26 Jan. 1757).

72. 1 Burr. 631 ; 97 E.R. 483.

73. See Douglas Hay, 'Property, Authority and Criminal Law', in Douglas Hay et al. (eds.), *Albion's Fatal Tree: Crime and Society in Eighteenth-Century England* (1975), 17, 33–4.

74. See Roper (1826), 2 : 319.

75. *Countess of Strathmore's Case* (1787), 1 T.R. 700 ; 99 E.R. 1329.

76. (1757), Amb. 333 ; 27 E.R. 233.

77. See : *R.* v. *Lord George Howard* (1707), 11 Mod. 109 ; 88 E.R. 931 ; *Lord Anglesea's Case* (1701), 12 Mod. 44 ; 88 E.R. 1443.

78. Quoted in Hill (1984), 144.
79. See: *R.* v. *Lord Lee* (1674), 2 Lev. 128; 3 Salk. 139; *Lady Head* v. *Sir Francis Head* (1745), 3 Atk. 295; 26 E.R. 972; (1747), 3 Atk. 547; 26 E.R. 1115; 1 Ves. Sen. 17; 27 E.R. 863; *Ex Parte King* (1757), Amb. 333; 27 E.R. 223.
80. (1735), 32.
81. See *Sim's Case* (1734), 2 Stra. 1207; 93 E.R. 1131; Lambarde (1599 (1581)), 88; Dalton (1975 (1618)), 134; Hawkins (1973 (1716)), 2: 431.
82. 189.
83. See The Laws Respecting Women, As They regard their Natural Rights, or their Connections and Conduct (1777), 55–6.
84. (1632), 128–9.
85. *The Law of Husband and Wife Within the Jurisdiction of the Queen's Bench and Chancery Divisions* (1884), 5. See also: William Pinder Eversley, *The Law of Domestic Relations* (1885), 238; Nevill Geary, *The Law of Marriage and Family Relations: A Manual of Practical Law* (1892), 173–4.
86. (1840), 8 Dowl. 630; PRO KB 1/73, Trin. 3 Vict., *Ex Parte Cochrane*, affdt. of John Espin and Samuel Woodward (28 May 1840).
87. Edward Manson, 'Marital Authority', 7 *Law Quarterly Review* (1891), 244, 250. See also: 'The Husband's Dominion Over His Wife' (1928), 182, 183; Montague Lush, *The Law of Husband and Wife*, 4th edn. (1933), 28–9.
88. Manson, 'Marital Authority' (1891), 250.
89. Prec. Ch. 492; 24 E.R. 220.
90. 1 Burr. 541; 97 E.R. 440; 2 Keny. 279; 96 E.R. 1182.
91. 8 Mod. 22; 88 E.R. 17.
92. See Daniel Defoe, *Moll Flanders* (1981, originally 1722), 62–6 and 356 n. 3.
93. 1 Stra. 478; 93 E.R. 645.
94. See: Lawrence Stone, *Road to Divorce: England 1530–1987* (1990), 149–82, 194–5; Staves (1990), 162–95; C. A. Morrison, 'Contract', in R. H. Graveson and F. R. Crane (eds.), *A Century of Family Law, 1857–1957* (1957), 116, 136–7.
95. See: Staves (1990), 131, 145; Morrison (1957), 116, 126–31; P. M. Bromley, *Family Law*, 3rd edn. (1966), 205–13, 274–8.
96. See: George L. Haskins, 'The Estate by the Marital Right', 97 *University of Pennsylvania Law Review* (1949), 345, 350–1; John D. Johnston, 'Sex and Property: Tradition, The Law School Curriculum, and Developments Toward Equality', 47 *New York University Law Review* (1972), 1034, 1052–6.
97. John Fraser MacQueen, *The Rights and Liabilities of Husband and Wife* (1849), 335–7 at 336.
98. 1 Stra. 478; 93 E.R. 645; 8 Mod. 22; 88 E.R. 17.
99. *R.* v. *Lord Vane* (1747), 1 Black. W. 18; 96 E.R. 9. See also *Lord Vane* v. *Lady Vane* (1740), Barn. C. 135; 27 E.R. 585.
100. Lord Chancellor Eldon, quoted in Stone (1990), 155.
101. *R.* v. *Mary Mead*, 1 Burr. 541; 97 E.R. 440; 2 Keny. 279; 96 E.R. 1182.
102. *R.* v. *Edgar* (1789), Ridg. t. H. 152; 27 E.R. 787.
103. *R.* v. *Turlington*, 2 Burr. 1115; 97 E.R. 741. See also the account given in *The Laws Respecting Women* (1777), 74–5.

104. *Head* v. *Head* (1745), 3 Atk. 295; 26 E.R. 972. See also (1747), 3 Atk. 547; 26 E.R. 1115; 1 Ves. Sen. 17; 27 E.R. 863.
105. [1891] 1 Q.B. 671, 675, 682, 680.
106. *R.* v. *Dr Newton*, 1 Barn. KB 42; 94 E.R. 29; 1 Barn. KB 64; 94 E.R. 44.
107. Quoted in Hill (1984), 145–7 at 146; see also 137–8.
108. Stone (1990), 167–9 at 167.
109. (1809 (1765)), 1 : 445.
110. (1840), 8 Dowl. 630, 635.
111. See R.J. Sharpe, *The Law of Habeas Corpus*, 2nd edn. (1989), 16–20.
112. 15 *Parliamentary History*, H.C., 871–897 at 890.
113. Ibid., H.L., 896–7 at 897.
114. See Sharpe (1989), 68 n. 28.
115. 32 *Parliamentary Debates* H.C., 542–6 at 543.
116. See Sharpe (1989), 174.
117. 18 Q.B. 781; 118 E.R. 295.
118. Or *R.* v. *Anne Brooke and Thomas Fladgate* (1766) 4 Burr. 1991; 98 E.R. 38; PRO KB 1/16/5, Mich. 7 Geo. 3, affdt. of Abraham Gregory (6 Nov. 1766) and affdt. of Ann Gregory (28 Nov. 1766).
119. 1 Stra. 445; 93 E.R. 625.
120. (1871), PRO KB 21/42, Hil. 21 Geo. 3, *R.* v. *Hester Harford*; PRO KB 1/22/1, Hil. 21 Geo. 3, affdt. of Robert Morris (9 Feb. 1871) and affdt. of Hester Harford (12 Feb. 1781); PRO KB 33/20/4, Articles of the Peace against Robert Morris (12 Feb. 1781).
121. (1805), 2 Smith 617; 8 Revised Reports 724.
122. 5 Term Rep. 91; 101 E.R. 51. Geoffrey Best suggests that *R.* v. *Leggatt* brought about a change in the law. However, he does not cite authority and it is not clear that he is comparing like case with like: see *Mid-Victorian Britain 1851–75* (1971), 279–80.
123. See Sharpe (1989), 174.
124. See Geary (1892), 371–8 at 376–7.
125. See: (1850) *Thomas* v. *Roberts*, 14 Jur. 639; (1860) *Nottidge* v. *Prince*, 29 L.J. Chan. 357.
126. See Lee Holcombe, *Wives and Property: Reform of the Married Women's Property Law in Nineteenth-Century England* (1983), 33, 44, 53–4.
127. 2 F. & F. 264; 174 E.R. 1052.
128. See *Shepherd* v. *Mackoul* (1813), 3 Camp. 327; 170 E.R. 1399; *Williams* v. *Fowler* (1825), M'Cle. & Yo. 269; 148 E.R. 413.
129. Offences Against the Person Act 1828, s. 27.
130. See Jennifer S. Davis, 'Prosecutions and Their Context: The Use of the Criminal Law in Later Nineteenth-Century London', in Douglas Hay and Francis Snyder (eds.), *Policing and Prosecution in Britain, 1750–1850* (1989), 397, 399–401, 416–19.
131. *Grindell* v. *Godmond* (1836), 5 Ad. & E. 755; 111 E.R. 1351.
132. Under s. 27 of the Offences Against the Person Act 1828, magistrates could impose a fine of up to £5, with a maximum of two months imprisonment on default.
133. The Divorce and Matrimonial Causes Act 1857.
134. See Stone (1990), 301–67 at 360–2.

135. See: ibid., 192–4, 198–206; A. James Hammerton, 'Victorian Marriage and the Law of Matrimonial Cruelty' (Conference Paper, 1987); Martin Ingram, *Church Courts, Sex and Marriage in England, 1570–1640* (1987), 146, 181–8. On the development of the law relating to alimony awards, see: G. W. Prothero (ed.), *Select Statutes and other Constitutional Documents illustrative of the Reigns of Elizabeth and James I*, 4th edn. (1913), 424–35; R. H. Helmholz, *Roman Canon Law in Reformation England* (1990), 77–9.

136. 2 Lee. 115; 161 E.R. 283.

137. *Waring* v. *Waring* (1813), 2 Hag. Con. 153, 155; 161 E.R. 699, 700.

138. See Ruth Paley, 'The Crown Side of the Court of Kings Bench: Litigants and Litigation in Hanoverian London' (unpublished paper, 1991), 4–8.

139. PRO KB 1/20/1, Mich. 16 Geo. 3, affdt. of John Chandler and others (15 Nov. 1775).

140. MacQueen (1849), 338–9 at 339. See also: James Kent, *Commentaries on American Law*, 11th edn. (1866), 2: 180; Lush (1884), 4–5; Eversley (1885), 238; Geary (1892), 166–7, 174–8; Joseph Bridges Matthews, *A Manual of the Law Relating to Married Women* (1892), 235.

141. 'The Emergence of a Modern American Family Law: Child Custody, Adoption, and the Courts, 1796–1851', 73 *Northwestern University Law Review* (1979), 1038, 1063 n. 97.

142. See (1990), 178–95 at 183–4.

Chapter 2: Wife-Beating, Coverture and the Power Principle

1. 15th edn. (1809, originally 1765–9), 1: 444.

2. 4th edn., 29.

3. *Woman as Force in History: A Study in Traditions and Realities* (repr. 1976), 214. See also Joel Prentiss Bishop, *Commentaries on the Law of Marriage and Divorce*, 5th edn. (1873), 628–9.

4. (1809 (1765–9)), 1: 441–2.

5. *The Law of Husband and Wife Within the Jurisdiction of the Queen's Bench and Chancery Divisions* (1884), 3.

6. *A Treatise of the Law of Property Arising from the Relation Between Husband and Wife*, 2nd edn. (1826), 1.

7. Jeremy Bentham, quoted by John Henry Wigmore, *Evidence in Trials at Common Law*, 8 (McNaughton rev. 1961): 219.

8. On Blackstone's influence on American lawyers, see: Norma Basch, *In the Eyes of the Law: Women, Marriage and Property in Nineteenth-Century New York* (1982), 43–69; Beard (1946; repr. 1976), 88–90, 117–32.

9. See, for example: Roper (1826), 1: 1; Lush (1884), 3; James Clancy, *An Essay on the Equitable Rights, Duties and Disabilities of Married Women, with respect to their Separate Property* (1814), 1; Thomas Barrett-Lennard, *The Position in Law of Women* (1883), xxvii, 1; Basil Edwin Lawrence, *The History of Laws Affecting the Property of Married Women in England* (1884), 1; Nevill Geary, *The Law of Marriage and Family Relations: A Manual of Practical Law* (1892), 163.

10. See Basch (1982), 66–7.

11. The sources drawn on in the discussion of coverture include: Lee Holcombe, *Wives and Property: Reform of the Married Women's Property Law in*

Nineteenth-Century England (1983), 18–36; Susan Staves, *Married Women's Separate Property in England, 1660–1833* (1990); C. A. Morrison, 'Tort', in R. H. Graveson and F. R. Crane, *A Century of Family Law, 1857–1957* (1957), 88; C. A. Morrison, 'Contract', in Graveson and Crane (1957), 116; G. D. Nokes, 'Evidence', in Graveson and Crane (1957), 143; D. Mendes da Costa, 'Criminal Law', in Graveson and Crane (1957), 165; Sir William Holdsworth, *A History of English Law*, (1908; rpr. 1966), 3: 525–33; Montague Lush, 'Changes in the Law Affecting the Rights, Status and Liabilities of Married Women', in *A Century of Law Reform: Twelve Lectures on the Changes in the Law of England During the Nineteenth Century* (1901), 342, 358–63; Maud Isobel Crofts, *Women Under English Law*, 2nd edn. (1928), 32–47; Glanville Williams, 'The Legal Unity of Husband and Wife', 10 *Modern Law Review* (1947), 16.

12. I.L., (ed.) T.E. (1632), 129.
13. See: George L. Haskins, 'The Estate by the Marital Right', 97 *University of Pennsylvania Law Review* (1948–9), 345, 350–1; John D. Johnston, 'Sex and Property: Tradition, the Law School Curriculum, and Developments Towards Equality', 47 *New York University Law Review* (1972), 1034, 1052–6.
14. See Holcombe (1983), 46.
15. *The First Part of the Institutes of the Lawes of England; or, a Commentary Upon Littleton* (1812, originally 1628), 112a.
16. See, for example: John Comyns, *A Digest of the Laws of England*, 5th edn. (1822, originally 1762–7), 2: 219 ff; *Baron and Feme: A Treatise of the Common Law concerning Husbands and Wives* (1700; repr. 1979), 5.
17. (1809 (1765–9)), 1: 442. See also I.L. (1632), 122.
18. See *Lectures on the Relation between Law and Public Opinion in England during the Nineteenth Century* (1905; repr. 1962), 371.
19. *A New Abridgment of the Law*, 6th edn. (1807, originally 1736–6), 1: 476, 495.
20. 70.
21. *Woman Under the English Law from the Landing of the Saxons to the Present Time* (1896), 135–8.
22. *Ecclesiastical Law*, 7th edn. (1809, originally 1763), 4: 49–57.
23. *The Law of Baron and Femme* (1816; repr. 1981), 137–60.
24. See: Holdsworth (1908; repr. 1966), 3: 542–4; Sir Frederick Pollock and Frederic Maitland, *The History of English Law before the Time of Edward I* (1895), 2: 426–8.
25. (34 & 35 Hen. 8, c.5), s.14. This Act 'concerning the explanation of wills' was passed two years after the 1540 Statute of Wills.
26. (1807 (1736–66)), 1: 483.
27. Literally, 'under the power of the husband'.
28. (1812 (1628)), 112b. See also: *The Laws Respecting Women, As They regard their Natural Rights, or their Connections and Conduct* (1777), 178–80; William Noy, *The Principal Grounds and Maxims with an Analysis of the Laws of England*, 3rd US from the 9th London edn. (1845, originally 1641; repr. 1980), 39.
29. (1809 (1765–9)), 1: 443–4.
30. I.L. (1632), 123.
31. See: Blackstone (1809 (1765–9)), 1: 442; Comyns (1822 (1762–7)), 2: 219–20.

32. See Coke (1812 (1628)), 112a.
33. See, for example, Dicey (1905; repr. 1962), 373.
34. 'The Changing Status of a Married Woman', 13 *Law Quarterly Review* (1897), 187, 193.
35. See: Pollock and Maitland (1895), 2: 432–3; Holdsworth (1908; repr. 1966), 2: 528–30; James Kent, *Commentaries on American Law*, 11th edn. (1866), 2: 137–8.
36. See (1883), 119–20.
37. (1816; repr. 1981), 98.
38. (1809 (1765–9)), 1: 444. See also: Coke (1812 (1628)), 112a; Reeve (1816; repr. 1981), 89–90, 98.
39. See (1866), 2: 137. See also Charles Crawley, *The Law of Husband and Wife* (1892), 25.
40. *Baron and Feme* (1700; repr. 1979), 125. See also Joel Prentiss Bishop, *Commentaries on the Law of Married Women* (1871), 1: 19–20.
41. 1 Mod. 124, 126; 86 E.R. 781, 783.
42. *A Treatise on the Law of Husband and Wife as Respects Property (Partly Founded upon Roper's Treatise)* (1850), 2: 5.
43. See, for example: Bishop (1871), 1: 19–20; Reeve (1816; repr. 1981), 89–90, 98.
44. See: *Baron and Feme* (1700; repr. 1979), 125–41; Noy (1845 (1641); repr. 1980), 37–8; Kent (1866), 2: 138–9; Comyns (1822 (1762–7)), 2: 230–1, 233–5. For another example of this principle, see: *Laws Respecting Women* (1777), 172; Comyns (1822 (1762–7)), 2: 239–40; Noy (1845 (1641); repr. 1980), 39; Kent (1866), 2: 138.
45. For the reasoning behind this, see Morrison (1957), 116, 117–18.
46. See: Blackstone (1809 (1765–9)), 1: 442–3; Clancy (1814), 3.
47. *The History of the Law of England as to the Effects of Marriage on Property and on the Wife's Legal Capacity* (1879), 129.
48. Holdsworth (1908; repr. 1966), 3: 531.
49. 36–40 at 40; for a contemporary, and hostile, review of *The Hardships of the English Laws*, see 6 *Gentleman's Magazine* (1736), 648. See also Bacon (1807 (1736–66)), 1: 485.
50. See (1816; repr. 1981), 68–70.
51. (1735), 40–1.
52. It was not totally agreed upon in the nineteenth century that this was the case: there was authority going both ways, but the much more commonly accepted view was that a wife was capable of committing a tort. It is difficult, otherwise, to understand why she had to be joined in suits with her husband or, indeed, how there could be a suit at all: see: Barrett-Lennard (1883), xxvii, 16–17; E. Ling-Mallison, *Law Relating to Women* (1930), 2; John Fraser MacQueen, *The Rights and Liabilities of Husband and Wife* (1849), 124–5; Holdsworth (1908; repr. 1966), 3: 531–2; Lush (1884), 252; Reeve (1816; repr. 1981), 72; Kenny (1879), 96.
53. See MacQueen (1849), 124–5.
54. See: Julius Goebel (ed.), *Cases and Materials on the Development of Legal Institutions* (1946), 493–4; Leo Kanowitz, *Women and the Law: The Unfinished Revolution* (1969), 37–8.

55. However, it seems that in the eighteenth century there was an arbitration or formal compounding process in operation on the criminal side of the King's Bench, which abused wives could use to force their husbands to agree to regular maintenance payments: see: Ruth Paley, 'Londoners and the King's Bench (Crown Side) in the Eighteenth and Early Nineteenth Centuries' (Conference paper, 1991), 7–11; Ruth Paley, 'The Crown Side of the Court of King's Bench: Litigants and Litigation in Hanoverian London' (Unpublished paper, 1991), 28; *R.* v. *Peck* (1755), PRO KB 1/12/1, Hil. 29 Geo. 2; *R.* v. *Ewbank* (1773), PRO KB 1/19/1, East. 13 Geo. 3 (2), 38.

56. Blackburn J. in *Phillips* v. *Barnet* [1876] 1 Q.B. 436, 438 (per Blackburn J.).

57. [1991] 3 W.L.R. 767.

58. See, for example: Barrett-Lennard (1883), 5; William Pinder Eversley, *The Law of the Domestic Relations*, 3rd edn. (1906), 173; Lush (1933), 29.

59. See: James Fitzjames Stephen, *A Digest of the Criminal Law*, 3rd edn. (1883), 186; Christine Boyle, 'Violence Against Wives – The Criminal Law in Retreat?', 31 *Northern Ireland Legal Quarterly* (1980), 35, 37–8; Jocelynne Scutt, 'Consent in Rape: The Problem of the Marriage Contract', 3 *Monash University Law Review* (1977), 255, 257–64; David Lanham, 'Hale, Misogyny and Rape', 7 *Criminal Law Journal* (1983), 148, 153–5.

60. See ibid., 148, 155.

61. (1847, originally 1678), 1 : 629.

62. 'The Subjection of Women' (1868), Alice S. Rossi (ed.), in *Essays on Sex Equality* (1970), 125, 160.

63. (1866), 16 QBD 772.

64. See: Rupert Cross, *Evidence* (1958), 173–5; Rupert Cross and Colin Tapper, *Cross on Evidence*, 7th edn (1990, originally 1958), 204–6.

65. See Herman Cohen, *Spouse-Witnesses in Criminal Cases* (1913), 22.

66. (1812 (1628)), 66. See also: Dalton, *The Countrey Justice* (1618; repr. 1975), 377; Hale (1847 (1678)), 2 : 279.

67. *Pleas of the Crown* (1716–21; repr. 1973), 2 : 431.

68. (1809 (1765–9)), 1 : 443.

69. *An Introduction to the Law Relative to Trials at Nisi Prius*, 7th edn. (1817, originally 1767), 286a.

70. See: 2 (Chadbourn rev. 1979): 856–62; 8 (1961): 211–22.

71. Ibid., 216.

72. See, for example: Coke (1812 (1628)), 66; Hawkins (1716–21; repr. 1973), 2 : 431; Buller (1817 (1767)), 286a; *Barker* v. *Dixie* (1736), Cas. t. Hardwicke 264; 95 E.R. 171.

73. See Cross (1958), 175.

74. See Holdsworth (1908; repr. 1966), 9 : 197 n.3.

75. Hale (1847 (1678)), 2 : 279.

76. *Hoskyn* v. *Commissioners of Police for the Metropolis* (H.L.) [1979] A.C. 474, 495 (per Lord Salmon). In this case (now reversed by s. 80 of the Police and Criminal Evidence Act 1984) the Lords held that a wife who had been assaulted by her husband and was, therefore, competent at common law to testify against him, could not be compelled to do so.

77. Wigmore, 8 (1961): 212.

78. See: Cross (1958), 174; Cross and Tapper (1990), 204–5.
79. See: Wigmore, 8 (1961): 246–7; Cohen (1913), 30–1.
80. 2 Lew. 279, 287–8; 168 E.R. 1154, 1156.
81. See: Wigmore, 8 (1961): 242; *Reeve* v. *Wood* (1864), 10 Cox. C. C. 58.
82. *Bentley* v. *Cooke* (178a), 3 Doug. 422, 424; 99 E.R. 729.
83. See Cohen (1913), 22–3.
84. 3 St Tr. 401, 402.
85. See, for example: *R.* v. *Azire* (1716), 1 Stra. 633; 93 E.R. 746; *R.* v. *Pearce* (1840), 9 Car. & P. 667; 173 E.R. 1003. See also Buller (1817 (1767)), 286a-87a.
86. *Anonymous* (1701), 12 Mod. 454; 88 E.R. 1447. See also Hawkins (1716–21; repr. 1973), 2 : 431. For further discussion of the scope of this exception, see: Cohen (1913), 25–7, 29–30; O. M. Stone, 'When a Wife May Testify', 14 *Modern Law Review* (1951), 341.
87. (1847 (1678)), 1 : 48, 301.
88. (1817 (1767)), 286a. See also *Baron and Feme* (1700; repr. 1979), 329.
89. See: Wigmore, 8 (1961): 253; Cross and Tapper (1990), 205.
90. (1913), 23–5.
91. See Offences Against the Person Act 1828, s.2.
92. See: (25 Edw. III. st 5, c. 2); Shelley Gavigan, 'Petit Treason in Eighteenth Century England: Women's Inequality Before the Law', 3 *Canadian Journal of Women and the Law* (1989–90), 335; Frank McLynn, *Crime and Punishment in Eighteenth-Century England* (1991), 118–24.
93. (1809 (1765–9)), 4 : 75. See also: J. Chitty, *A Practical Treatise on the Criminal Law* (1816), 3 : 742: Hale (1847 (1678)), 1 : 381.
94. Edward Hyde East, *A Treatise of the Pleas of the Crown* (1803), 1 : 336.
95. See An Act for discontinuing the Judgment which has been required by Law to be given against Women convicted of certain Crimes, and substituting another Judgment in lieu 1790, s. 1.
96. See: Ruth Campbell, 'Sentence of Death by Burning for Women', 5–6 *Journal of Legal History* (1984–5), 43; Hale (1847 (1678)), 1 : 382; Edward Coke, *The Third part of the Institutes of the Law of England* (1644), 311; Blackstone (1809 (1765–9)), 4 : 93, 204.
97. See: Gavigan (1989–90), 335, 359–63; McLynn (1991), 121–2.
98. 19 *Gentleman's Magazine* (1749), 486–8.
99. See Douglas Hay, in 'Property, Authority and the Criminal Law', in Douglas Hay et al. (eds.), *Albion's Fatal Tree: Crime and Society in Eighteenth-Century England* (1975), 17, analyses the role that the criminal law plays in maintaining and legitimising the traditional power structure.
100. See: *R.* v. *Maddy*, sub nom. *R.* v. *Manning* (1671), T. Raymond, 212; 1 Vent. 158; 86 E.R. 108; Hale (1847 (1678)), 1 : 486; *R.* v. *Pearson* (1835), 2 Lew. 216; 168 E.R. 1133.
101. *R.* v. *Greening* [1913] 3 KB 846.
102. See *R.* v. *Rothwell* (1871), 12 Cox. C. C. 145; *R.* v. *Jones* (1908), 72 J.P. 215.
103. *R.* v. *Kelly* (1848), 2 Car. & K. 814; 175 E.R. 342 (per Rolfe B.).
104. See, for example: Hawkins (1716–21; repr. 1973), 1 : 93, 192; Anthony Fitzherbert, *The New Natura Brevium* (1704, originally 1516), 256; Hale (1847 (1678)) 1 : 513.

105. See *De Legibus et Constuetudinibus Angliae* (1878, originally 1250; repr. 1964), 3: fol. 151b (p. 519).
106. See, for example: Dalton (1618; repr. 1975), 252; Coke (1644), 108; Hale (1847 (1678)), 1: 47, 621; Hawkins (1716–21; repr. 1973), 1: 1; 2: 320; East (1803), 2: 559.
107. (1842), 1 Car. & K. 185; 174 E.R. 768.
108. (1849), 3 Cox. C. C. 425.
109. (1849), 2 Car. & K. 887, 904 n. a; 175 E.R. 372, 379 n. a.
110. (1716–21; repr. 1973), 2: 320. See also: Dalton (1618; repr. 1975), 252; Coke (1644), 108.
111. See ibid.; Coke seems to have been the first learned writer to state that the criminal law placed the husband in a different position from the wife in this respect. See also: Hale (1847 (1678)), 1: 47; Hawkins (1716–21; repr. 1973), 1: 1; 2: 320; East (1803), 2: 559.
112. See (1878 (1250); repr. 1964), 3: fol. 151b (p. 519).
113. (1847 (1678)), 1: 47.
114. See William Oldnall Russell, *A Treatise on Crimes and Misdemeanors*, 7th edn. (1909), 1: 93–4.
115. See (1716–21; repr. 1973), 1: 1.
116. See (1847 (1678)), 1: 434.
117. See (1930), 55.
118. See: Hawkins (1716–21; repr. 1973), 1: 1; Hale (1847 (1678)), 1: 45, 47, 434; Blackstone (1809 (1765–9)), 4: 29; Eversley (1885), 244; James Fitzjames Stephen, *A Digest of the Criminal Law*, 6th edn. (1904), 23; Courtney Stanhope Kenny, *Outlines of Criminal Law*, 4th edn. (1909), 71–2.
119. 8 Car. & P. 19; 173 E.R. 381.
120. 8 Car. & P. 541; 173 E.R. 610.
121. (1909), 71; (1904), 23; but see Ling-Mallison (1930), 55–6.
122. Ibid., 56; *Criminal Law: The General Part* (1953), 603.
123. See: William Pinder Eversley, *The Law of Domestic Relations* (1885), 243–4; Ling-Mallison (1930), 54; Kenny (1909), 71; Russell (1909), 99–100.
124. See Holdsworth (1908; repr. 1966), 3: 444.
125. See: Hawkins (1716–21; repr. 1973), 1: 1; East (1803), 2: 559; Hale (1847 (1678)), 1: 45, 46, 434, 516, 621; Carol Z. Weiner, 'Is a Spinster an Unmarried Woman?', 20 *American Journal of Legal History* (1976), 27.
126. See, for example: *R. v. Hughes* (1813), 2 Lewin 228; 168 E.R. 1137; *R. v. Smith* (1858), Dears. & Bell. 553; 169 E.R. 1117; but see *R. v. Brooks* (1853), Dears. 184; 169 E.R. 688 which seemed to lay down that a wife could *never* be convicted of receiving stolen goods from her husband.
127. See Glanville Williams, *Criminal Law, The General Part*, 2nd edn. (1961), 762–3 at 763.
128. *R. v. Smith* (1916), 12 C.App.R. (1917), 42, 43; *R. v. Archer* (1826), 1 Mood 143; 168 E.R. 1218; *R. v. Cohen* (1868), 11 Cox. C. C. 99.
129. See *Crime and the Courts in England, 1660–1800* (1986), 238, 414.
130. The Criminal Justice Act 1925, s. 47 provides:

on a charge against a wife, for any offence other than treason or murder, it shall be a good defence to prove that the offence was committed in the presence of and under the coercion of the husband.

On the modern defence, see: J. F. Garner, 'The Defence of Coercion', [1954] *Criminal Law Review*, 448; J. Edwards, 'Compulsion, Coercion and Criminal Responsibility', 14 *Modern Law Review* (1951), 297, 309–13; P. J. Pace, 'Marital Coercion – Anachronism or Modernism?', [1979] *Criminal Law Review*, 82; David Marshall, 'Coercion is the Oppression of Wives: An Introduction to a Criminal Law Defence' (Occasional paper, 1987), esp. 16–22; Williams (1961), 764–8; Philip Levy, 'More Equal Than Others?', 142 *New Law Journal* (13 March 1992), 355.

131. 188 H.C. Deb. col. 875 (20 Nov. 1925).

132. Referred to in *R.* v. *Cruse* (1838), 8 Car. & P. 541, 543–4; 173 E.R. 610, 615.

133. See, for example: James Fitzjames Stephen, *History of the Criminal Law of England* (1883), 106; Stephen (1904), 398–9; Kenny (1909), 72; Sir Alfred Denning, *The Changing Law* (1953), 82–3; Kanowitz (1969), 89–90.

134. On benefit of clergy, see: Holdsworth (1908; repr. 1966), 3: 294–302; J. H. Baker, *An Introduction to English Legal History*, 3rd edn. (1990), 586–9; Cynthia Herrup, *The Common Peace: Participation and the Criminal Law in Seventeenth-Century England* (1987), 48–50, 143.

135. (1909), 72.

136. See Marshall (1987), 6–16.

137. Quoted in ibid., 7. See also Christine Fell, Cecily Clark and Elizabeth Williams, *Women in Anglo-Saxon England and the Impact of 1066* (1984), 59

138. Quoted in Marshall (1987), 11–12.

139. See (1878 (1250); repr. 1964), 2: fol. 151b (p. 519).

140. (1618; repr. 1975), 237.

141. See: Hale (1847 (1678)), 1: 45–6; Williams 1961), 763.

142. See: John Beattie, 'The Criminality of Women in Eighteenth-Century England', 8 *Journal of Social History* (1974–5), 80, 113 n.56; Beattie (1986), 238, 414; Marshall (1987), 5; but see: Carolyn Conley, *The Unwritten Law: Criminal Justice in Victorian Kent* (1991), 69; G. S. Rowe, 'Femes Covert and Criminal Prosecution in Eighteenth-Century Pennsylvania', 32 *American Journal of Legal History* (1988), 138.

143. See: Francis Bacon, *Maxims of the Law* (1596) in *The Works of Francis Bacon* (1826), 34; William Lambarde, *Eirenarcha* (1599, originally 1581), 275–6; Dalton (1618; repr. 1975), 236–7; I.L. (1632), 206; Hale (1847 (1678)), 1: 45–6; Hawkins (1716–21; repr. 1973), 1: 1; East (1803), 1: 351; 2: 559–60; Stephen (1904), 396–8; Stephen (1883), 2: 105; Holdsworth (1908; repr. 1966), 3: 443, 444 and n.1.

144. See: (1809 (1765–9)), 1: 444; (1807 (1736–66)), 1: 486. See also *Laws Respecting Women* (1777), 70–1, 346.

145. *R.* v. *Green* (1913) 9 Cr.App.R. 228, 231 (per Issacs C.J.).

146. See, for example: Lush (1884), 12; Eversley (1885), 243–5.

147. Blackburn J., quoted in Conley (1991), 69.

148. See: Ruth Kittel, 'Women Under the Law in Medieval England, 1066–1485', in Barbara Kanner (ed.), *The Women of England From Anglo-Saxon Times to the Present: Interpretative Bibliographical Essays* (1980), 124, 130–1; Barbara Hanawalt Westman, 'The Peasant Family and Crime in Four-teenth-Century England', 13 (2) *Journal of British Studies* (1974), 1, 12–14;

Lawrence Stone, *The Family, Sex and Marriage in England, 1500–1800* (1977), 201; Carol Z. Weiner, 'Sex Roles and Crime in Late Elizabethan Hertfordshire', 8 *Journal of Social History* (1975), 38; J. A. Sharpe, *Crime in Early Modern England, 1550–1750* (1984), 108–11; Beattie (1974–5), 80; McLynn (1991), 116–32; George Rude, *Criminal and Victim: Crime and Society in Early Nineteenth-Century England* (1985), 61–4; Conley (1991), 68–72.

149. See: Weiner (1975), 38, 39 and n. 12; Beattie (1974–5), 80, 95–6.
150. See: Weiner (1976), 27, 31; Hale (1847 (1678)), 1: 45, 46, 434, 516, 621.
151. Hawkins (1716–21; repr. 1973), 1: 1.
152. Sharpe (1984), 109.
153. See Marshall (1987), 1, 12–13.
154. See Hay (1975), 17, 18.
155. McLynn (1991), 129.
156. 'The Case of the Married Spinster: An Alternative Explanation', 21 *American Journal of Legal History* (1977), 260, 264.
157. (1826 (1596)), 34. See also: Noy (1845 (1641); repr. 1980), 29; *Hardships of the English Laws* (1735), 21–7; Cleveland (1896), 113–14.
158. Dalton (1618; repr. 1975), 177.
159. (1809 (1765–9)), 4: 29.
160. (1735), 24.
161. See: Johnston (1972), 1034, 1046–50; Basch (1982), 42–69; Norma Basch, 'Invisible Women: The Legal Fiction of Marital Unity in Nineteenth-Century America', 5 *Feminist Studies* (1979), 346, 352–3.
162. See, for example: Holdsworth (1908; repr. 1966), 3: 531; Sir Arthur Underhill, *The Law Reform (Married Women and Tort-feasors) Act, 1935* (1936), 3.
163. See, for example, Goebel (1946), 493–4.
164. See, for example, Jeremy Bentham, 'Principles of the Civil Code', in John Bowring (ed.), *The Works of Jeremy Bentham* (1838–43; repr. 1962), 1: 299, 355–6.
165. *A profitable book upon domestic law – Essays for English Women and Law Students* (1875), 66.
166. See, for example, Eversley (1885), 236–7.
167. See, for example: Bacon (1807 (1736–66)), 1: 483; Bright (1850), 2: 37–8.
168. Alfred Fellows, 'Changes in the Law of Husband and Wife', 22 *Law Quarterly Review* (1906), 64.
169. See, for example, Bright (1850), 2: 37–8.
170. *Phillips v. Barnet* [1876] 1 Q.B. 436, 441 (per Field J.).

Chapter 3: Wife-Beating and the Fiction of Marital Unity: History of an Idea

1. See for example: William Pinder Eversley, *The Law of Domestic Relations* (1885), 237–8; P. M. Bromley, *Family Law*, 3rd edn. (1966), 270.
2. *Commentaries on the Law of Married Women* (1871), 1: 21.
3. 4th edn. (1933), 58.
4. Montague Lush, *The Law of Husband and Wife Within the Jurisdiction of the Queen's Bench and Chancery Divisions* (1884), 5.
5. The fiction has never been abolished outright by legislation. However, in

Midland Bank Trust Co. Ltd v. *Green (No. 3)* [1981] 3 All E.R. 744, the Court of Appeal held that, having regard to the changes in the legal position of wives over the past hundred years, the fiction should no longer be regarded as a part of the common law.

6. See: Sir Frederick Pollock and Frederic Maitland, *The History of English Law before the Time of Edward I* (1895), 1 : 468; 2 : 403–4, 411, 415, 417.

7. 'What Causes Fundamental Legal Ideas? Marital Property in England and France in the Thirteenth Century', 78 *Michigan Law Review* (1979), 59, 64–6 at 64.

8. For support for Maitland's interpretation, see: Sir William Holdsworth, *A History of English Law* (1908; repr. 1966), 3 : 524, 526; George L. Haskins, 'The Estate by the Marital Right', 97 *University of Pennsylvania Law Review* (1948–9), 345, 345–7; Glanville Williams, 'The Legal Unity of Husband and Wife', *Modern Law Review* (1947), 16, 18.

9. See: *De Legibus et Consuetudinibus Angliae* (1878, originally 1250; repr. 1964), fol. 429 b (p. 393).

10. See Haskins (1948–9), 345, 347.

11. John D. Johnston, 'Sex and Property: Tradition, the Law School Curriculum, and Developments Towards Equality', 47 *New York University Law Review* (1972), 1034, 1047.

12. See (1947), 16, 19–20, 26.

13. Ibid., 16, 24.

14. Ibid., 16, 31.

15. See: *Woman as Force in History: A Study in Traditions and Realities* (1946; repr. 1976), 87–214.

16. See also: Mary Bateson, *Borough Customs*, in *The Publications of the Selden Society*, vols. 20 and 21 (1906), 2 : c–cxv; A. Beatrice Wallis Chapman and Mary Wallis Chapman, *The Status of Women Under the English Law* (1909), 7–9, 20–2; Leonore Marie Glanz, *The Legal Position of English Women Under the Early Stuart Kings and the Interregnum, 1603–1660* (Ph.D. dissertation, 1973), 1–2, 42.

17. See also Katherine O'Donovan, 'The Male Appendage – Legal Definitions of Women', in Sandra Burman (ed.), *Fit Work for Women* (1979), 134, 137–8.

18. Beard (1946; repr. 1976), 208.

19. See also Sir William Holdsworth, *Some Makers of English Law: The Tagore Lectures, 1937–8* (1966), 111–32.

20. (1946; repr. 1976), 96.

21. Ibid., 102.

22. Ibid., 92.

23. Ibid., 96.

24. Ibid., 103, 88, 131, 95.

25. Ibid., 111–12.

26. *British Freewomen, Their Historical Privilege* (1894), 99–112.

27. 33–4 *Women Lawyers Journal* (1947–8), 7, 9.

28. See: Norma Basch, *In the Eyes of the Law: Women, Marriage, and Property in Nineteenth-Century New York* (1982), 30–6, 64–6; Peggy A. Rabkin, *Fathers to Daughters: The Legal Foundations of Female Emancipation* (1980), 5–7, 75–7.

29. Basch (1982), 35.
30. Pollock and Maitland (1895), 2 : 401.
31. Basch (1982), 21.
32. Lord Thurlow, quoted in Lee Holcombe, *Wives and Property: Reform of the Married Women's Property Law in Nineteenth-Century England* (1983), 42.
33. (1946; repr. 1976), 110.
34. See e.g. ibid., 127.
35. Ibid., 88.
36. See 'The Injustice of the English Law as it Bears on the Relationship of Husband and Wife', 9 *Contemporary Review* (1868), 114.
37. See (1908; repr. 1966), 3 : 528–9.
38. *The Hardships of the English Laws in Relation to Wives, With an Explanation of the Original Curse of Subjection Passed upon the Woman* (1735), 51, 52.
39. (1982), 27. See also: ibid., 15–19, 42–3, 49–50, 61–2, 67–9, 229–31; Norma Basch, 'Invisible Women: The Legal Fiction of Marital Unity in Nineteenth-Century America', 5 *Feminist Studies* (1979), 346.
40. See: Basch (1982), 17; Basch (1979), 346, 347.
41. See Williams (1947), 16, 16–17.
42. See Edward Coke, *The First Part of the Institutes of the Lawes of England; or, a Commentary Upon Littleton* (1812, originally 1628), ss. 168, 291, 665.
43. See *The New Natura Brevium* (1704, originally 1516), s. 116k (p. 256).
44. Ranulf Glanvil, *A Treatise on the Laws and Customs of the Kingdom of England* (1812, originally, 1187), 356.
45. Hencricus de Bracton, *De Legibus et Consuetudinibus Angliae* (1878, originally 1250), 5 : fol. 371 b (p. 423).
46. Ibid., 3 : fol. 208 (p. 371).
47. See Sheila C. Dietrich, 'An Introduction to Women in Anglo-Saxon Society (c. 600–1066)', in Barbara Kanner (ed.), *The Women of England from Anglo-Saxon Times to the Present: Interpretative Bibliographical Essays* (1980), 32, 39.
48. Christine Fell, Cecily Clark and Elizabeth Williams, *Women in Anglo-Saxon England and the Impact of 1066* (1984), 14.
49. Ibid., 56.
50. See: Fell, Clark and Williams (1984), esp. 7–21, 56–107; Dietrich (1980), 32; Marc A. Meyer, 'Land Charters and the Legal Position of Anglo-Saxon Women', in Kanner (1980), 57; Florence Griswold Buckstaff, 'Married Women's Property in Anglo-Saxon and Anglo-Norman Law and the Origin of the Common-Law Dower', 4 *Annals of the American Academy of Political and Social Science* (1893–4), 233; Courtney Stanhope Kenny, *The History of the Law of England as to the Effects of Marriage on Property and on the Wife's Legal Capacity* (1879), 10, 12, 21–37; Arthur Rackham Cleveland, *Woman Under the English Law from the Landing of the Saxons to the Present Time* (1896), 35–44, 62–3; Basil Edwin Lawrence, *The History of Laws Affecting the Property of Married Women in England* (1884), 1–2; S. A. Leathley, *The History of Marriage and Divorce* (1916), 57–8; Pollock and Maitland (1895), 2 : 362–3, 400–1.
51. See: Fell, Clark and Williams (1984), 148–71; Donahue (1979), 78; Basch (1982), 17–19; Buckstaff (1893–4), 250–61; Pollock and Maitland (1895), 2 :

399–400, 405, 425–31; Beard (1946; repr. 1976), 186–204; Lawrence (1884), 168–9.

52. Glanvil (1812 (1187)), 116–18.
53. Ibid, 163.
54. See Lawrence (1884), 2; Kenny (1879), 11–12.
55. See: Fell, Clark and Williams (1984), 13–14, 149; Doris May Stenton, *The English Woman in History* (1957), 29–30; Julius Goebel (ed.), *Cases and Materials on the Development of Legal Institutions* (1946), 456–9, 488; Cleveland (1896) 81.
56. See: Frances and Joseph Gies, *Marriage and the Family in the Middle Ages* (1989, originally 1987), 47; Pollock and Maitland (1895), 2: 364; Goebel (1946), 444; Leathley (1916), 55–6; but see Fell, Clark and Williams (1984), 20.
57. See: ibid., 13, 14, 152: Baker, *An Introduction to English Legal History*, 3rd edn. (1990), 146–9; Pollock and Maitland, (1895), 2: 364–6; Leathley (1916), 99.
58. See: Fell, Clark and Williams (1984), 13, 14, 152–4; Mary Daly, *The Church and the Second Sex, With a Feminist Postchristian Introduction and New Archaic Afterwords by the Author* (1985), 20–34, 74–98; R. Emerson Dobash and Russell Dobash, *Violence Against Wives: A Case Against the Patriarchy* (1979), 40–3; Capri Montgomery O'Neal, *Marriage and the Status of Women in Medieval Law Codes* (LL.M thesis, 1983), 15–18.
59. See for example: 1 Corinthians 7: 4 (For the wife does not rule over her own body, but the husband does; likewise the husband does not rule over his own body, but the wife does.); 1 Corinthians 11: 11–12 (Nevertheless in the Lord woman is not independent of man nor man of woman; for as woman was made from man, so man is now born of woman. And all things are from God.); Ephesians 5: 28–29 (Even so husbands should love their wives as their own bodies. He who loves his wife loves himself. For no man ever hates his own flesh, but nourishes and cherishes it, as Christ does the church.).
60. Quoted in Dobash and Dobash (1979), 40.
61. 1 Corinthians, 7: 9. See Goebel (1946), 445–7.
62. See: Stenton (1957), 30; *Midland Bank Trust Co. Ltd* v. *Green (No. 3)* [1979] 1 Ch. 496, 511–14.
63. Bracton 1878 (1250), 5: fol. 414 (p. 265). See also: ibid., 1: fol. 6 b (p. 47); L.J. Downer (ed.), *Leges Henrici Primi* (1972, originally 1201–1330), c. 453 (p. 155).
64. Yearbook (1363–4), H., 38. Ed. III, 3 a, in *Select cases in the Court of King's Bench Under Edward III*, in *The Publications of the Selden Society*, vol. 82 (1965), 4: 133.
65. Glanvil (1812 (1187)), 281.
66. See: *Midland Bank Trust Co. Ltd. V. Green (No. 3)* [1981] 3 All E.R. (C.A.) 744, 751; Sybil Wolfram, *In-laws and Outlaws: Kinship and Marriage in England* (1987), 16–19; Sybil Wolfram, '"Husband and Wife are one Person: the Husband" (Nineteenth-century English Aphorism),' in A-J. Arnaud and E. Kingdom (eds.), *Women's Rights and the Rights of Man* (1990), 158, 161–4; Reginald Haw, *The State of Matrimony: An Investigation of the Relationship between ecclesiastical and civil marriage in England after the Reformation* (1952), 10, 23–7; Goebels (1946), 493 n. 23; Leathley (1916), 47–8, 85.

67. Ephesians 5: 31.
68. T. A. Lacey, quoted in Haw (1952), 10.
69. See: Gies and Gies (1989 (1987)), 100–1, 104–6, 108; Pollock and Maitland (1985), 2: 362–3, 400–1.
70. See: Fell, Clark and Williams (1984), 57; Gies and Gies (1989 (1987)), 57, 108–9; Margaret Bowker, 'Marriage and the Role of Women in English History', 31–41 *Quis Custodiet* (1971–3), 76, 79–80; Leathley (1916), 99; Cleveland (1896), 49–50; Keith Thomas, 'The Double Standard', 20 *Journal of the History of Ideas* (1959), 195, 200.
71. [1979] 1 Ch. 496, 513.
72. I.L., (ed.) T.E. (1632), 124–5 (translation added).
73. (1967), 33–6, 51–70, 83–5.
74. Ibid., 35.
75. See Dobash and Dobash (1979), 48.
76. See: Christopher Hill, *The World Turned Upside Down: Radical Ideas During the English Revolution* (1972), 121–47; J. A. Sharpe, *Early Modern England: A Social History, 1550–1760* (1987), 227–53; Keith Thomas, 'Women and the Civil War Sects', 13 *Past and Present* (1958), 42; Lawrence Stone, *The Family, Sex and Marriage in England, 1500–1800* (1977), 337–8.
77. Hill (1972), 124.
78. Quoted in Sharpe (1987), 239.
79. Quoted in Thomas (1958), 42, 48.
80. Carole Pateman, *The Problem of Political Obligation: A Critical Analysis of Liberal Theory* (1979), 6, 11–14 at 12.
81. *The Sexual Contract* (1988), 39–40.
82. See: Hill (1972), 247–60; Thomas (1958), 42, 45, 51–2, 57; Sharpe (1987), 241; Sheila Rowbotham, *Hidden from History*, 3rd edn. (1977; repr. 1990), 8–12.
83. Quoted in Hill (1972), 251.
84. Rowbotham (1977; repr. 1990), 10
85. See Stenton (1957), 143–4.
86. *Domesticall Duties* (1622; repr. 1976), the Epistle Dedicatory.
87. See: Stenton (1957), 142; D. E. Underdown, 'The Taming of the Scold: the Enforcement of Patriarchal Authority in Early Modern England', in Anthony Fletcher and John Stevenson (eds.), *Order and Disorder in Early Modern England* (1985), 116, 116–19.
88. For example: *Baron and Feme: A Treatise of the Common Law concerning Husbands and Wives* (1700; repr. 1979); *A Treatise of Feme Coverts: Or the Lady's Law* (1732; repr. 1974); *The Hardships of the English Laws in Relation to Wives* (1735).
89. See I.L., (ed.) T.E. (1632), A Preface to the Reader.
90. Ibid., 146.
91. See: Rowbotham (1977; repr. 1990), 10; Stone (1977), 338–40; Stopes (1894), 108–9.
92. Ibid., 109.
93. See: Chapman and Chapman (1909), 22, 32–3; Stopes (1894), 99–100; Edward Coke, *The Fourth Part* of *the Institutes* of *the Laws* of *England* (1797, originally 1644), 5–6

94. Teresa Brennan and Carole Pateman, '"Mere Auxiliaries to the Commonwealth": Women and Liberalism', 27 *Political Studies* (1979), 183, 184.

95. 'Reflections Upon Marriage' (1706), in Bridget Hill (ed.) *The First English Feminist: Reflections Upon Marriage and other writings by Mary Astell* (1986), 69, 76. See also Ruth Perry, *The Celebrated Mary Astell: An Early English Feminist* (1986).

96. Pateman (1988), 40.

97. See: ibid., *passim*; Carole Pateman, '"God Hath Ordained to Man a Helper": Hobbes, Patriarchy and Conjugal Right', in Mary Lyndon Shanley and Carole Pateman (eds.), *Feminist Interpretations and Political Theory* (1991), 53; Carole Pateman, *The Disorder of Women* (1989); Pateman (1979); Brennan and Pateman (1979), 183; See also Mary Lyndon Shanley, 'Marriage Contract and Social Contract in Seventeenth Century English Political Thought', 32 *Western Political Quarterly* (1979), 79.

98. Quoted in Pateman (1988), 52–3.

99. Quoted in Pateman (1991), 53, 67.

100. Ibid.

101. See: Basch (1982), 47; Basch (1979), 346, 350–1, 353–5; Norma Basch, 'Equity v. Equality: Emerging Concepts of Women's Political Status in the Age of Jackson', 3 *Journal of the Early Republic* (1983), 297, 305.

102. *Commentaries on the Laws of England*, 15th edn. (1809, originally 1765–9), 1: 171.

103. See Chapman and Chapman (1909), 24.

104. 'Criminals, Idiots, Women and Minors' 78 *Fraser's Magazine* (1868), 777, 780–2, 787–8.

105. See: Levin L. Schücking, *The Puritan Family: A Social Study from the Literary Sources* (1969), xi–xv, 18–57; Hill (1972), 247–50; Stone (1977), 135–42; Dobash and Dobash (1979), 51–3; Thomas (1959), 195, 203–5.

106. William Perkins, 'Christian Oeconomy', in Ian Breward (ed.), *The Work of William Perkins* (1970), 411, 419

107. John R. Gillis, *For Better, For Worse: British Marriages, 1600 to the Present* (1985), 14.

108. Ibid.; but see Kathleen M. Davies, 'Continuity and Change in Literary Advice on Marriage', in R. B. Outhwaite (ed.), *Marriage and Society: Studies in the Social History of Marriage* (1981), 58.

109. 'Philogamus', *The Present State of Matrimony: Or, The Real Causes of Conjugal Infidelity and Unhappy Marriages* (1739; repr. 1985), 55.

110. See for example: William Whately, *A Bride-Bush, or a direction for married persons* (1617); John Sprint, *The Bride-Woman's Conseller* (1699); Gouge (1622; rep. 1976); R. Cawdry, *A Godlye Forme of Household Government* (1614); Richard Braithwaite, *The English Gentlewoman Drawne out to the full Body* (1631); Joseph Swetnam, *The Arraignment of Lewde, idle, froward and unconstant women* (1615); Lord Halifax, *The Lady's New Year Gift, or Advice to a Daughter* (1688), in H. C. Foxcroft, *Life and Letters of George Savile, Marquis of Halifax* (1898), 2: 388. For discussion of this kind of literature, see: Davies (1981), 58; Stenton (1957), 107–9, 141–51, 202–8; Stone (1977), 197–9.

111. See: Stenton (1957), 104–7; Stone (1977), 198; Dobash and Dobash (1979), 55–6.

112. Quoted in Stenton (1957), 106.
113. Quoted in Stone (1977), 198.
114. 'Philogamus', (1739; repr. 1985), 48.
115. (1922; repr. 1976), 356.
116. Quoted in Martin Ingram, *Church Courts, Sex and Marriage in England, 1570–1640* (1987), 143.
117. Quoted in Stenton (1957), 153–4.
118. See: Stone (1977), 202; Dobash and Dobash (1979), 56; Susan Staves, 'Where is History but in Texts? Reading the History of Marriage', in John M. Wallace (ed.), *The Golden and the Brazen World: Papers in History and Literature* (1985), 125, 128.
119. *The Morality of Marriage, and Other Essays on the Status and Destiny of Woman* (1897), 136–7.
120. Brennan and Pateman (1979), 183, 190.
121. For example: 'Woman's Law: Mrs Norton's Letter to the Queen', 23 *Law Review* (1855–6), 334, 341. See also J. W. Kaye, 'The Non-Existence of Women', 23 *North British Review* (1855), 536, *passim*.
122. Lush, 'Changes in the Law Affecting the Rights, Status and Liabilities of Married Women', in *A Century of Law Reform: Twelve Lectures on the Changes in the Law During the Nineteenth Century* (1901), 342, 343.
123. Thomas Lee, notes to Blackstone's *Commentaries on the Laws of England*, 18th edn. (1829) 1: 443. See also Barbara Bodichon, *A Brief Summary in Plain Language of the Most Important Laws Concerning Women* (1854), 6.
124. (1868), 777, 789.
125. (1897), 107.
126. Caroline Norton, *Caroline Norton's Defense: English Laws for Women in the Nineteenth Century* (1854: repr. 1982), 165.
127. See: Mary Poovey, *Uneven Developments: The Ideological Work of Gender in Mid-Victorian England* (1989), 21, 51–88; Margaret Forster, *Significant Sisters: The Grassroots of Active Feminism, 1839–1939* (1985), 15–52.
128. Caroline Norton, *Letter to the Queen on Lord Cranworth's Marriage and Divorce Bill* (1854), in Carol Bauer and Lawrence Ritt (eds.), *Free and Ennobled: Source Readings in the Development of Victorian Feminism* (1979), 182, 186.
129. For example: (1854: repr. 1982), esp. 156–61; *A Plain Letter to the Lord Chancellor on the Infant Custody Bill* (1839).
130. (1979 (1854)), 182, 184.
131. R. A. Soloway, *Prelates and People: Ecclesiastical Social Thought in England 1783–1852* (1969), 26–9 at 29. See also: Malcolm I. Thomis and Peter Holt, *Threats of Revolution In Britain 1789–1848* (1977), 6–28; Stone (1977), 677.
132. Leonore Davidoff and Catherine Hall, *Family Fortunes: Men and Women of the English Middle Class 1780–1850* (1987), 155.
133. See: Rowbotham (1977; repr. 1990), 20–2; Mary Poovey, *The Proper Lady and the Woman Writer: Ideology as Style in the Works of Mary Wollstonecraft, Mary Shelley and Jane Austen* (1984), 48–81; Margaret Walters, 'The Rights and Wrongs of Women: Mary Wollstonecraft, Harriet Martineau, Simone de Beauvoir', in Juliet Mitchell and Ann Oakley (eds.), *The Rights and Wrongs of Women* (1976; repr. 1983), 304, 304–29.

134. See: Thomis and Holt (1977), 85–116; David Thomson, *England in the Nineteenth Century (1815–1914)* (1950: repr. 1963), 56–8, 83–7; Leonore Davidoff, 'Mastered for Life: Servant and Wife in Victorian and Edwardian England', 7 *Journal of Social History* (1974), 406, 411.

135. Rowbotham (1977; repr. 1990), 34.

136. See: Dorothy Thompson, *The Chartists* (1984), 120–51; Dorothy Thompson, 'Women and Nineteenth-Century Radical Politics', in Juliet Mitchell and Ann Oakley (eds.), *The Rights and Wrongs of Women* (1976: rep. 1983), 112; Jane Rendall (ed.), *Equal or Different: Women's Politics 1800–1914* (1987), 7–8.

137. Quoted in Thompson (1976; repr. 1983), 112, 123.

138. Quoted in Thompson (1984), 125.

139. See: Barbara Taylor's splendid *Eve and the New Jerusalem: Socialism and Feminism in the Nineteenth Century* (1983; repr. 1991); Pateman (1988), 136; Rowbotham (1977; repr. 1990), 44–6; Rendall (1987), 7–8; Thompson (1976: repr. 1983), 112, 128–9.

140. See: Taylor (1983; repr. 1991), 17, 22–4, 34–5, 50, 68n-9n, 215, 240, 251; Pateman (1988), 94, 123–4, 136, 156–60; Stopes (1894), 134–6; Stenton (1957), 320–3, 332–3.

141. Quoted in William Thompson, *The Appeall of one Half of the Human Race, Woman, against the Pretensions of the other Half, Men, to retain them in Political, and thence in Civil and Domestic Slavery* (1983, originally 1825), 9.

142. Ibid., 24.

143. Ibid., 60.

144. Ibid., 55–6.

145. Ibid., 65.

146. Ibid., 18.

147. My discussion of Evangelicalism and the cult of domesticity draws throughout on the following sources: Davidoff and Hall (1987), 18–19, 73–192, 450–4; Catherine Hall, 'The Early Formulation of Victorian Domestic Ideology', in Sandra Burman (ed.), *Fit Work for Women* (1979), 15; Taylor (1983; repr. 1991), 12–16, 25–6, 79, 110–12, 123–9, 136–42, 171, 200–2, 221–2, 262–3; Stone (1977), 666–80; Norman St John Stevas, 'Women in Public Law', in R. H. Graveson and F. R. Crane (eds.), *A Century of Family Law* (1957), 256, 258–9.

148. Davidoff and Hall (1987), 83.

149. Ibid., 82.

150. Quoted in Stone (1977), 667.

151. Davidoff and Hall (1987), 178.

152. Ibid., 173.

153. Quoted in ibid., 115.

154. Ibid., 111.

155. Ibid., 118.

156. Ibid., 112.

157. Christopher Lasch, *Haven in a Heartless World: The Family Beseiged* (1977), 6–7.

158. See Jane Lewis, *Women in England, 1870–1950: Sexual Divisions and Social Change* (1984), 45–7.

159. Davidoff and Hall (1987), 115.
160. See Basch (1982), 227.
161. Patricia Branca, *Silent Sisterhood: Middle-Class Women in the Victorian Home* (1975: repr. 1977), 22.
162. 'The Laws Concerning Women', 79 *Blackwood's Edinburgh Magazine* (1856), 379, 387.
163. See: Lewis (1984), xi, 12, 16; Branca (1975; repr. 1977), 74–113; Carol-Ann Hooper, 'Child sexual abuse and the regulation of women: Variations on a theme', in Carol Smart (ed.), Regulating Womenhood: Historical Essays in Marriage, Motherhood and Sexuality (1992), 53, 59–63.
164. Ibid., 74.
165. Ibid., 111–23.
166. William Wilberforce, quoted in Hall (1979), 15, 26.
167. T. Binney, quoted in Davidoff and Hall (1987), 116.
168. 'Women, Work and Politics in Nineteenth-Century England: The Problem of Authority', in Rendall (1987), 57, 81.
169. Davidoff and Hall (1987), 136.
170. Ibid., 175.
171. See Lewis (1984), 46–7, 91.
172. See Branca (1975: repr. 1977), 152.
173. See Lewis (1984), 113–15.
174. See Davidoff (1974), 406, 421.
175. See: Cynthia Eagle Russett, *Sexual Science: The Victorian Construction of Womanhood* (1989), esp. 1–15; Lewis (1984), 75, 81–8.
176. Russett (1989), 3–4.
177. See, for example, the experience of socialist feminist, Edith Lanchester, who in 1895 was committed to an insane asylum by a leading mental specialist on the ground that she was determined 'to live in illicit intercourse with a man in a station of life much below her own', and thus avoid 'becoming the chattel of any man'. She was later pronounced by the Commissioners of Lunacy to be 'very foolish' but 'perfectly sane', and released: see David Rubinstein, *Before the Suffragettes: Women's Emancipation in the 1890s* (1986), 58–62.
178. (1856), 379, 381. For a biography, see Merryn Williams, *Margaret Oliphant: A Critical Biography* (1986).
179. See Stone (1987), 666.
180. *Lady into Woman: A History of Women from Victoria to Elizabeth II* (1953), 23.
181. (1909), 39.
182. See William L. O'Neill, *The Woman Movement* (1969), 17–18.
183. See: Thompson (1984), 122, 132; Thompson (1976: repr. 1983), 112, 137–8; Rendall (1987), 8.
184. (1840) 8 Dowl. 630, 636.
185. See Basch (1982), 69; Taylor describes how many of these ideas found echoes even within radical thought: see (1983; repr. 1991), 30–31, 221–37.
186. See Lewis (1984), 82.
187. Quoted in Pateman (1988), 162–3.
188. 'The Final Cause of Women', in Bauer and Ritt (1979), 66, 67. See also Kaye (1855), 536, 558.

189. (1990), 231.
190. *Legal Fictions*, in C. K. Ogden, *Bentham's Theory of Fictions*, 2nd edn. (1951, originally 1932), 141.
191. See: Basch (1982), 42–3, 68–9, 229–31; Basch (1979), 346, 347, 359–60.
192. Ibid., 346, 359.
193. 'Agency', 4 *Harvard Law Review* (1891), 345, 351.

Chapter 4: The Jackson Decision Revisited

1. See ss. 2, 6, 7, 16, 21, 25, 26 and 27. See also Mary Lyndon Shanley, *Feminism, Marriage, and the Law in Victorian England, 1850–1895* (1989), 35–48.
2. See also the Married Women's Property Act 1884 and the Married Women's Property Act 1893.
3. See: Lee Holcombe, *Wives and Property: Reform of the Married Women's Property Law in Nineteenth-Century England* (1983), chs. 8–10; Shanley (1989), chs. 2 and 4; C. A. Morrison, 'Tort', in R. H. Graveson and F. R. Crane (eds.), *A Century of Family Law, 1857–1957* (1957), 88, 91–104; C. A. Morrison, 'Contract', in Graveson and Crane (1957), 116, 117–26.
4. Divorce and Matrimonial Causes Act 1857, s. 35; Matrimonial Causes Act 1859, s. 4.
5. See: P. H. Pettit, 'Parental Control and Guardianship', in Graveson and Crane (1957), 56, 56–75; Shanley (1989), 25 and ch. 5; Lawrence Stone, *Road to Divorce: England 1530–1987* (1990), 170–80, 390.
6. See Nevill Geary, *The Law of Marriage and Family Relations: A Manual of Practical Law* (1892), 376–7.
7. [1891] 1 Q.B. 671, 676–7, 686, 684.
8. See: Joseph Bridges Matthews, *A Manual of the Law Relating to Married Women* (1892), 238 n.(e); Alfred Fellows, 'Changes in the Law of Husband and Wife', 22 *Law Quarterly Review* (1906), 64, 66.
9. See *Marshall* v. *M.* (1879), 5 P.D. 19 at 23 (per Sir James Hannen, Pres.).
10. *Weldon* v. *Weldon* (1883), 9 P.D. 52, 56.
11. See 292 H.C. Deb. col. 356 (8 August 1884).
12. Holcombe (1983), 200–1 at 201.
13. 292 H.C. Deb. cols. 405 (9 August 1884) and 356 (8 August 1884). See also 287 H.C. Deb. cols. 247–9 (21 April 1884).
14. See: 284 H.C. Deb. cols. 294 (8 February 1884) and 995 (15 February 1884); 285 H.C. Deb. cols. 1 (26 February 1884), 60 (28 February 1884) and 188 (29 February 1884).
15. *Weldon* v. *Weldon* (1885), 10 P.D. 72.
16. Edward Manson, 'Marital Authority', 7 *Law Quarterly Review* (1891), 244, 251–2.
17. *Barlee* v. *Barlee* (1822), 1 Add. 301; 162 E.R. 105.
18. See 'Ignota', 'Judicial Sex Bias', 149 *Westminster Review* (1898), 147, 279, 286.
19. s. 27.
20. See 124 H.C. Deb. cols. 1414–19 (10 March 1853).
21. Offences Against the Person Act 1828, s.29.

22. See: 124 H.C. Deb. col. 1417 (10 March 1853); 125 H.C. Deb. cols. 684–5 (6 April 1853, Mr Packe) and 669–74.
23. See ibid., cols. 674–84 (6 April 1853).
24. 124 H.C. Deb. cols. 1414–15 and 1419 (10 March 1853).
25. See: ibid., col. 1421 (Mr Phillimore); 125 H.C. Deb. cols. 678 (6 April 1853, Mr Newdegate), 679 (Mr Aglionby and Lord Lovaine) and 684 (Sir John Pakington).
26. See Leon Radzinowicz and Roger Hood, *A History of English Criminal Law and its Administration from 1750* (1986), 5: 689–92.
27. 125 H.C. Deb. col. 677 (6 April 1853, Mr Fitzroy).
28. See ibid., cols. 677, (Mr Fitzroy), 680 (Viscount Palmerston), 678 (Captain Scobell), and 683 (Mr Walpole).
29. See also The Aggravated Assaults Amendment Bill, 153 H.C. Deb. col. 1040 (29 March 1859) and the Offences Against the Person Bill, 154 H.C. Deb. col. 477 (30 June 1859) and 155 H.C. Deb. col. 139 (20 July 1859). Neither Bill got beyond the First Reading stage and they were never debated, but the former especially may have been a flogging bill.
30. See: 141 H.C. Deb. cols. 24–8 (12 March 1856); 142 H.C. Deb. cols. 165–77 at 177 (7 May 1856); 145 H.C. Deb. cols. 211–15 (12 May 1857) and 540–1 at 541 (19 May 1857).
31. See ibid., cols. 994–9 (28 May 1857).
32. See: 157 H.C. Deb. col. 15 (6 March 1860); 158 H.C. Deb. cols. 519–36 at 519–20 (2 May 1860); 159 H.C. Deb. cols. 733–40 at 740 (20 June 1860).
33. See, for example: 142 H.C. Deb. cols. 175 (7 May 1856, Captain Scobell) and 177 (Mr Stuart Wortley); 158 H.C. Deb. cols. 524 (2 May 1860, Mr Clive), 528 (Mr Sotherton Estcourt), 530 (Sir George Lewis) and 530–1 (Colonel North).
34. See, for example: ibid., cols. 524–5 (2 May 1860, Mr Clive); 159 H.C. Deb. col. 739 (20 June 1860, Mr Deedes).
35. See, for example: 142 H.C. Deb. col. 174 (7 March 1856, Mr Barrow); 159 H.C. Deb. col. 734 (20 June 1860, Viscount Enfield).
36. See, for example: 142 H.C. Deb. col. 174 (7 May 1856, Sir George Grey); 158 H.C. Deb. col. 534 (2 May 1860, Mr Clay).
37. See, for example: 141 H.C. Deb. cols. 27–8 (12 March 1856, Mr Massey); 158 H.C. Deb. col. 531 (2 May 1860, Mr Conningham); 159 H.C. Deb. cols. 734 (30 June 1860, Mr Hardy), 736 (Colonel North) and 736, 738 (Sir George Lewis).
38. 142 H.C. Deb. col. 174 (7 May 1856, Mr Barrow). See also: ibid., col. 171 (7 May 1856, Sir George Grey); 158 H.C. Deb. cols. 524–5 (2 May 1860, Mr Clive), 527 (Mr Henley) and 529–30 (Sir George Lewis); 159 H.C. Deb. col. 735 (20 June 1860, Mr Hardy).
39. See ibid. cols. 734 (20 June 1860, Viscount Enfield), 740, 734 (Viscount Enfield), 736 (Mr W. Ewart) and 739 (Mr Deedes).
40. s. 43.
41. See Radzinowicz and Hood (1986), 693.
42. See *Sessional Papers* H.C. (1872), 3: 479–80.
43. See: 210 H.C. Deb. col. 1753 (24 April 1872); 211 H.C. Deb. col. 499 (8 May 1872).

44. 219 H.C. Deb. cols. 396–8 (18 May 1874).
45. Ibid., col. 399.
46. 'Wife-Torture in England', 32 *Contemporary Review* (1878), 55, 78.
47. An Act for the further Security of the Persons of her Majesty's Subjects from Personal Violence 1863.
48. 'Report to the Secretary of State for the Home Department on the State of the Law Relating to Brutal Assaults etc.' (C. 1138), *Sessional Papers* H.C. (1875), 61: 29, 33–48, 50–142, 158–9, 176–96.
49. See 244 H.C. Deb. col. 209 (7 May 1875).
50. Radzinowicz and Hood (1986), 696.
51. See: 224 H.C. Deb. cols. 1853–78 (14 June 1875); 226 H.C. Deb. cols. 54–5 (26 July 1875).
52. '"A Torrent of Abuse": Crimes of Violence Between Working-Class Men and Women in London, 1840–1875', 11 *Journal of Social History* (1878), 328, 340.
53. See: 266 H.C. Deb. col. 142 (8 February 1882); 269 H.C. Deb. col. 381 (10 May 1882). For the text of the Bill see *Sessional Papers* H.C. (1882), 6: 755–6.
54. See: Margaret May, 'Violence in the Family: An Historical Perspective', in J.P. Martin (ed.), *Violence and the Family* (1978), 135, 143; R. Emerson Dobash and Russell Dobash, *Violence Against Wives: A Case Against the Patriarchy* (1979), 3–5.
55. Mabel Sharman Crawford, 'Maltreatment of Wives', 139 *Westminster Review* (1893), 292.
56. (1878), 55, 56.
57. See, for example: 124 H.C. Deb. cols. 1415–16 (10 March 1853, Mr Fitzroy); 127 H.C. Deb. col. 551 (26 May 1853), Earl Granville); 141 H.C. Deb. col. 27 (12 March 1856, Mr Dillwyn); 145 H.C. Deb. 213–14 (12 May 1857, Mr Dillwyn); 158 H.C. Deb. col. 523 (2 May 1860, Viscount Raynham).
58. See, for example: J.W. Kaye, 'Outrages on Women', 25 *North British Review* (1856), 233, 233–4; Matilda Blake, 'Are Women Protected?' 137 *Westminster Review* (1892a), 43, 44; Cobbe (1878), 55, 74–6; Crawford (1893), 292, 294–6.
59. Cobbe (1878), 55, 59; 219 H.C. Deb. col. 397 (18 May 1874, Colonel Egerton Leigh); William Reade, 'Our Judges, Our Persons, and Our Purses', 24 *Law Magazine and Review* (3rd Ser.) (1867–8), 118, 121.
60. See May (1978), 135, 145–6.
61. See 'What Legislation is Necessary for the Repression of Crimes of Violence' and discussion, *Transactions NAPSS 1876* (1877), 345–61. For a brief discussion of the aims and composition of this organisation, see Dorothy M. Stetson, *A Woman's Issue: The Politics of Family Law Reform* (1982), 65–6.
62. See: Holcombe (1983), 144; Cobbe (1878), 55, 69 n. 70; May (1978), 135, 147.
63. Bertrand Russell, 'Rights Husbands Had Once', *Sunday Referee* (15 December 1935), 12.
64. See: E.P. Thompson, *Customs in Common* (1991), ch. 8; E.P. Thompson,

'Rough Music: Le Charivari Anglais', 27 *Annales Economies Societes Civilization* (1972), 285, esp. 296–8, 300–3; John Gillis, *For Better, For Worse: British Marriages, 1600 to the Present* (1985), 76–81, 130–4; D. E. Underwood, 'The Taming of the Scold: the Enforcement of Patriarchal Authority in Early Modern England', in Anthony Fletcher and John Stevenson (eds.), *Order and Disorder in Early Modern England* (1985), 116, 127–36; Russell P. Dobash and R. Emerson Dobash, 'Community Response to Violence Against Wives: Charivari, Abstract Justice and Patriarchy', 28 (5) *Social Problems* (1981), 563; Martin Ingram, 'Ridings, Rough Music and the "Reform of Popular Culture" in Early Modern England', 105 *Past and Present* (1984), 79; Carol Z. Weiner, 'Sex Roles and Crime in Late Elizabethan Hertfordshire', 8 *Journal of Social History* (1975), 38, 44; Robert Chambers (ed.), *Book of Days: A Miscellany of Popular Antiquities*, 2 vols. (1862–4; repr. 1967), 2: 510. See also the description of a skimmington-ride in Thomas Hardy, *The Mayor of Casterbridge* (1987, originally 1886), 332–4, 350–7 and 435 n.334.

65. See (1984), 79, 96–9.
66. See (1878), 55, 71–2.
67. See (1978), 328, 330.
68. (1878), 55, 73–4 (emphasis in original).
69. See Iris Minor, 'Working-class Women and Matrimonial Law Reform, 1890–1914', in David Martin and David Rubinstein (eds.), *Ideology and the Labour Movement* (1979), 103 at 117.
70. See: 141 H.C. Deb. cols. 24–5 (12 March 1856, Mr Dillwyn); 145 H.C. Deb. cols. 214 (12 May 1857, Mr Dillwyn), 997 (28 May 1857, Mr Bentinck) and 994–5 (Viscount Raynham); 151 H.C. Deb. col. 2036 (23 July 1858, Mr Dillwyn); 158 H.C. Deb. cols. 526 (2 May 1860, Mr Warner), 528 (Mr Dillwyn) and 530 (Mr Brady).
71. See May (1978), 135, 136.
72. See Jennifer Davis, 'Prosecutions and Their Context: The Use of the Criminal Law in Later Nineteenth-Century London', in Douglas Hay and Francis Snyder (eds.), *Policing and Prosecution in Britain, 1750–1850* (1989), 397, 399–400.
73. See 142 H.C. Deb. col. 171 (7 May 1856) and 145 H.C. Deb. col. 996 (28 May 1857, Sir George Grey).
74. s. 42.
75. See 142 H.C. Deb. col. 171 (7 May 1856).
76. See Tomes (1978), 328, 335–7.
77. See Carolyn Conley, *The Unwritten Law: Criminal Justice in Victorian Kent* (1991), 76.
78. See V. A. . C. Gatrell, 'The Decline of Theft and Violence in Victorian England', in V. A. C. Gatrell, Bruce Lenman and Geoffrey Parker (eds.), *Crime and the Law: The Social History of Crime in Western Europe since 1500* (1980), 238, 240 and n. 9.
79. See: 142 H.C. Deb. col. 176 (7 May 1856, Mr Stuart Wortley); 145 H.C. Deb. col. 215 (12 May 1857, Sir George Grey); 158 H.C. Deb. cols. 526–7 (2 May 1860, Mr Henley) and 529 (Sir George Lewis); 159 H.C. Deb. cols. 736–7 (20 June 1860, Sir George Lewis); 224 H.C. Deb. cols. 1863

(14 June 1875, Mr P. A. Taylor) and 1875–6 (Mr Henley); 257 H.C. Deb. col. 1025 (20 January 1881, Sir William Harcourt); Tomes, (1978), 328, 329–30, 338, 340–1; May, (1978), 135, 136, 160, 162; but see Ellen Ross, '"Fierce Questions and Taunts": Married Life in Working-Class London, 1840–1914', 8 *Feminist Studies* (1983), 575, 591.

80. See Radzinowicz and Hood (1986), 117–18.
81. Crawford (1893), 292, 302. See also 211 H.C. Deb. col. 285 (6 May 1872, Mr Montague Guest).
82. 'The Political Disabilities of Woman', 97 *Westminster Review* (1872), 50, 68; Cobbe (1787), 55, 56. See also 219 H.C. Deb. col. 398 (18 May 1874, Colonel Egerton Leigh).
83. Davis (1989), 397–9 at 397; Geoffrey Best, *Mid-Victorian Britain 1851–1875* (1971), 228–81 at 229; John Stevenson, *Popular Disturbances in England 1700–1870* (1979), 275–6 at 275.
84. Quoted in Radzinowicz and Hood (1986), 115.
85. see ibid. 113–24, esp. 114–15.
86. Ibid., 114.
87. See: ibid., 114–15, 490–515, 524–52; May (1978), 135, 143, 148.
88. See: Radzinowicz and Hood (1986), 243–4, 525, 692, 703–5; Jennifer Davis, 'The London Garrotting Panic of 1862: A Moral Panic and the Creation of a Criminal Class in Mid-Victorian England', in Gatrell, Lenman and Parker (1980), 190.
89. (1867–8), 118, 121.
90. See David Jones, *Protest, Community and Police in Nineteenth-Century Britain* (1982), 23–5.
91. Quoted in Gatrell (1980), 238, 241.
92. Ibid., 238, 252–3.
93. See: Jones (1982), 24–5; Robert Storch, 'The Policeman as Domestic Missionary: Urban Discipline and Popular Culture in Northern England, 1850–1880', 9 *Journal of Social History* (1976), 481; Henry Mayhew, *London Labour and the London Poor* (1851–62; repr. 1967), 1: 40–2, 484–5.
94. John Stuart Mill, 'Remarks on Mr Fitzroy's Bill for the More Effectual Prevention of Assaults on Women and Children', (1853), in John Robson (ed.), *Essays on Equality, Law and Education* (1984), 21: 103, 107: See also Gatrell (1980), 238, 252–61, 277.
95. Jones (1982), 23. See also Radzinowicz and Hood (1986), 119.
96. See Jones (1982), 23, 25.
97. See: J.J. Tobias, *Crime and Industrial Society in the Nineteenth Century* (1967), 52–6; Gatrell (1980), 238, 272; Davis (1980), 190, 198–203, 210–13.
98. Quoted in ibid., 190, 202.
99. See ibid., 190, 201.
100. Gatrell (1980), 238, 256.
101. Samuel Smiles, quoted in Lawrence Stone, *The Family, Sex and Marriage in England, 1500–1800* (1977), 667.
102. Helen Bosanquet, quoted in Jane Lewis, *Women in England, 1870–1950: Sexual Divisions and Social Change* (1984), 11–12. See also Jones (1982), 26.
103. See: Gillis (1985), 196–209, 231–59; Conley (1991), 77–8; Stephen Parker, *Informal Marriage, Cohabitation and the Law, 1750–1989* (1990), ch. 4.

104. Kaye (1856), 233, 246. See also: 142 H.C. Deb. cols. 175 (7 May 1856, Mr Muntz) and 176 (Mr Stuart Wortley); 158 H.C. Deb. cols. 522 (2 May 1860, Viscount Raynham) and 532 (Mr Walter); Arthur Rackham Cleveland, *Women Under the English Law from the Landing of the Saxons to the Present Time* (1896), 241.
105. See 158 H.C. Deb. col. 532 (2 May 1860).
106. (1856), 233, 235.
107. See May (1978), 135, 139–43, 161–2.
108. (1851–62; repr. 1967), 1: 36.
109. Reade (1867–8), 118, 123.
110. See: May (1978), 135, 143, 162–3; 219 H.C. Deb. cols. 397–8 (18 May 1874, Colonel Egerton Leigh); Crawford (1893), 292, 303.
111. (1867–8), 118, 119–21.
112. Thomas Holmes, *Pictures and problems from London Police Courts* (1900), 77.
113. See, for example, 158 H.C. Deb. cols. 520, 536 (2 May 1860, Viscount Raynham) and 531 (Colonel North).
114. See: May (1978), 135, 145, 160; Carol Bauer and Lawrence Ritt, 'Wife-Abuse, Late Victorian English Feminists, and the Legacy of Frances Power Cobbe', 6 *International Journal of Women's Studies* (1983b), 195, 199; Minor (1979), 103, 114; Lewis (1984), 12, 46–7; Jane Lewis, 'The Working-Class Wife and Mother and State Intervention, 1870–1918', in Jane Lewis (ed.), *Labour and Love: Women's Experience of Home and Family, 1850–1940* (1986; repr. 1989), 99, esp. 104; Jo Sutton, 'Modern and Victorian Battered Women: A Look at an Old Pattern', in University of Bradford, Occasional Paper No. 4, *Battered Women and Abused Children* (1979), 9, 13.
115. 124 H.C. Deb. col. 1414 (10 March 1853, Mr Fitzroy); 142 H.C. Deb. cols. 166–7 (7 May 1856, Mr Dillwyn) and 170 (Sir George Grey); 158 H.C. Deb. cols. 520, 536 (2 May 1860, Viscount Raynham); 159 H.C. Deb. col. 738 (20 June 1860, Mr Bonham Carter); 125 H.C. Deb. col. 680 (6 April 1853, Viscount Palmerston); 145 H.C. Deb. col. 212 (12 May 1857, Mr Dillwyn); 158 H.C. Deb. cols. 527 (2 May 1860, Mr Henley), 529 (Sir George Lewis) and 531 (Colonel North): See also Kaye (1856), 233, 242.
116. Ibid., 233, 236. See also J. W. Kaye, 'The Non-Existence of Women', 23 *North British Review* (1855), 536, 547.
117. 159 H.C. Deb. col. 740 (20 June 1860, Viscount Raynham); 124 H.C. Deb. col. 1418 (10 May 1853, Mr Fitzroy); 125 H.C. Deb. col. 675 (6 April 1853, Mr Phinn); 128, H.C. Deb. col. 551 (26 May 1853, Earl Glanville); Radzinowicz and Hood (1986), 703.
118. (1856), 233, 242.
119. 158 H.C. Deb. col. 532 (2 May 1860, Mr Walter): See also: 124 H.C. Deb. col. 1417 (10 March 1853, Mr Fitzroy); 125 H.C. Deb. 671 (6 April 1853, Mr Henley); 158 H.C. Deb. col. 123 (2 May 1860, Viscount Raynham).
120. See: 224 H.C. Deb. col. 187 (14 June 1875, Colonel Egerton Leigh); Jennifer Davis, 'A Poor Man's System of Justice: The London Police Courts in the Second Half of the Nineteenth Century', 23 *Historical Journal* (1984), 309, 322; Tomes (1978), 328, 333; Edward Cox, *Principles of Punishment as Applied in the Administration of Criminal Law by Judges and Magistrates* (1877), 104.

121. Quoted in Kaye (1856), 233, 234; see also 236.
122. 142 H.C. Deb. cols. 167 (7 May 1856, Mr Dillwyn) and 174 (Mr Bentinck):
     See also 124 H.C. Deb. col. 1419 (10 March 1853, Mr Phinn).
123. See: F.W. Newman (attrib.), 'Corporal Punishment, and Penal Refor-
     mation', 71 *Fraser's Magazine* (1865), 154, 159, 164–6; Reade (1867–8), 118,
     121–3; Rev. J.T. Bart, 'On the Adaptation of Punishment to the Causes
     of Crime', *Transactions NAPSS* 1857 (1858), 315, 319; Mr Sergeant Pulling,
     'Crimes of Violence' and discussion, *Transactions NAPSS* 1876 (1877), 345,
     349, 351–2 (Mr A. O. Charles), 352 (Rev. Morris Joseph), 353–4 (Mr Groom
     Napier), 355–6, (Mr J.T. Foard), 359 (Mr Serjeant Pulling), 359–60 (Mr
     Barwick Baker, Chairman); William Tayler, 'On Criminal Offences and
     the Repression of Crime', *Transactions NAPSS* 1874 (1875), 353, 354–5.
124. 142 H.C. Deb. cols. 174 (7 May 1856, Captain Scobell); 224 H.C. Deb.
     col. 1859 (14 June 1875).
125. (C. 1138) *Sessional Papers* H.C. (1875), vol. 158.
126. 158 H.C. Deb. cols. 520–35 (2 May 1860); Kaye (1856), 233, 241–6.
127. See: 142 H.C. Deb cols. 175–6 (7 May 1856, Mr Muntz); 145 H.C. Deb.
     col. 999 (28 May 1857, Mr Clay); 158 H.C. Deb. cols. 524 (2 May 1860,
     Mr Clive) and 533–4 (Mr Clay); Kaye (1856), 233, 247.
128. (1877), 101–2.
129. Ibid., 99–103; *Transactions NAPSS* 1876 (1977), 358 (Rev. D. Morris). See
     also: Dobash and Dobash (1981), 563, 572; Tomes (1987), 328, 331–3;
     Minor (1979), 103, 116.
130. *Transactions NAPSS* 1876 (1877), 357 (Mr J.W. Sully); Kaye (1856), 233,
     247–55: See also May (1978), 135, 145; Dobash and Dobash (1981), 563,
     572–3.
131. (1856), 233, 248–9, 253; *Transactions NAPSS* 1876 (1877), 375 (Mr J.W.
     Sully).
132. (1978), 328, 338–9, 341–2.
133. (1877), 102.
134. (1856), 233, 242.
135. Maria K. Pastoor, 'Police Training and the Effectiveness of Minnesota
     "Domestic Abuse" Laws', 2 *Law and Inequality* (1984), 53. See also Dobash
     and Dobash (1979), 3–5.
136. *Violence in the Home: A Socio-legal Study* (1979; repr. 1980), 128–9 at 128.
137. See: Carol Bauer and Lawrence Ritt, '"A Husband is a Beating Animal",
     Frances Power Cobbe Confronts the Wife-Abuse Problem in Victorian
     England', 6 *International Journal of Women's Studies* (1983a), 99; Bauer and
     Ritt (1983b), 159. For the United States see: Elizabeth Pleck, 'Feminist
     Responses to "Crimes Against Women", 1868–96', 8 *Signs* (1982–3), 451;
     Elizabeth Pleck, *Domestic Tyranny: The Making of Social Policy Against Family
     Violence from Colonial Times to the Present* (1987), chs. 4, 5 and 6.
138. See, for example: 'The Laws Relating to Women', 20–1 *Law Review* (1854–
     5), 1, 24–5; Alfred Dewes, 'The Injustice of the English Law as it Bears
     on the Relationship of Husband and Wife', 9 *Contemporary Review* (1868),
     114, 122–3; 'The Political Disabilities of Women' (1782), 50, 62, 67–9;
     Louisa Catherine Shore, 'The Emancipation of Women', 102 *Westminster
     Review* (1874), 137, 145–6; 'The Law in Relation to Women', 128 *Westminster*

Review (1887), 698, 700–1, 704–6, 708–9; Matilda Blake, 'The Lady and the Law', 137 *Westminster Review* (1892b), 364–7; 'Ignota' (Elizabeth C. Wolstenholme Elmy), 'The Present Legal Position of Women', 163 *Westminster Review* (1905), 513, 520–3.

139. (1868), in Alice S. Rossi (ed.), *Essays on Sex Equality* (1970), 125, 140–2, 158–67. See also: May (1978), 135, 146–7; Bauer and Ritt (1983a), 99, 101–2.

140. (1878), 55, 56. See also: 'The Law in Relation to Women' (1887), 698, 700; 'The Laws Relating to Women' (1854–5), 1, 24; Mill (1868), 125, 163–4; 'The Political Disabilities of Women' (1872), 50, 68; Shore (1874), 137, 145; Crawford (1893), 292, 296, 298, 302; Bierne Stedman, 'Right of Husband to Chastise Wife', 3 *Virginia Law Register* (N.S.) (1917), 241, 247.

141. Cobbe (1878), 55, 66; Crawford (1893), 292, 297; Shore (1874), 137, 144–5.

142. Cobbe (1878), 55, 72.

143. See: Mill (1868), 125, 164; Cobbe (1878), 55, 67–8, 70, 73–6; 'The Laws Relating to Women' (1854–5), 1, 24–5; Blake (1892a), 43, 44–7; Crawford (1893), 292, 294–6, 300–1; 'The Political Disabilities of Women' (1872), 50 68–9.

144. See: 'The Law in Relation to Women' (1887), 698, 708; Dewes (1868), 114, 123; Mill (1853), 21: 103, 123; Crawford (1893), 292, 295, 301; Blake (1892a), 43, 44–7.

145. 'The Law in Relation to Women', (1887), 698, 708.

146. See: Blake (1892a), 43, 45, 47; Blake (1892b), 364, 367.

147. (1853), 21: 103, 105–6 at 105.

148. See Carol Bauer and Lawrence Ritt, *Free and Ennobled: Source Readings in the Development of Victorian Feminism* (1979), 189.

149. 'The Law in Relation to Women' (1887), 698, 708–9 at 709.

150. Blake (1892a), 43, 44–7 at 47; Cobbe (1878), 55, 79–80.

151. Ibid., 55, 58.

152. See: Blake (1892a), 43, 47; Crawford (1893), 292–3, 296–8, 303. See also Cobbe (1878), 55, 56.

153. Ibid., 55, 67–9, 70, 75–6 at 68. See also Mill (1868), 125, 166–7.

154. (1978), 328, 331–4 at 332. See also Ross (1983), 575, 577, 580–4.

155. (1878), 55, 63–4, 69, 77. See also: Blake (1892a), 43, 45; Crawford (1893), 292, 300.

156. Ibid., 292, 293, 299.

157. Ibid., 292, 293–4, 299–302.

158. See: Cobbe (1878), 55, 80, 82, 87; 'The Laws Relating to Women', (1854–5), 1, 24–5, 30–1; Mill (1868), 125, 164.

159. See: 142 H.C. Deb. cols. 175–6 (7 May 1856, Mr Muntz); 224 H.C. Deb. col. 1874 (14 June 1875, Mr Shaw-Lefevre); Kaye (1855), 536, 556–7; Kaye (1856), 233, 256; *Transactions NAPSS* 1876 (1877), 350 (Rev. C. Geldart), 352 (Mrs Louisa Lowe), 353–4 (Mr Groom Napier); but see ibid., 352 (Rev. Morris Joseph), 358 (Rev. D. Morris), 360–1 (Mr Barwick Baker, Chairman).

160. 142 H.C. Deb. col. 166 (7 May 1856).

161. See (1878), 55, 82–7.

162. s.4.

163. See: Crawford (1893), 292, 298; Cobbe (1878), 55, 85–6 and n.; 239 H.C. Deb. cols. 191–2 (29 March 1878, Earl of Kimberly).

164. See: A. K. R. Kiralfy, 'Matrimonial Tribunals and their Procedure', in Graveson and Crane (1957), 289, 307–8; Bauer and Ritt (1983a), 99, 144; Bauer and Ritt (1983b), 195–6.

165. See (1878), 55, 82.

166. Ibid., 55, 59–63, 65–6. See also: Crawford (1893), 292, 298; Shore (1874), 137, 146; Mill (1868), 125, 158–64.

167. Cobbe (1878), 55, 61, 62.

168. Quoted in Shanley (1989), 160.

169. See, for example: Blake (1892a), 43, 47–8; 'The Political Disabilities of Women', (1872), 50, 70; Mill (1868), 125, 165–8, 172–6. See also Mary Lyndon Shanley, 'Marital Slavery and Friendship: John Stuart Mill's "The Subjection of Women"', 9 *Political Theory* (1981) 229, 235–8.

170. (1868), 125, 172.

171. See: John Stuart Mill, 'The Admission of Women to the Electoral Franchise', extracted in Bauer and Ritt (1979), 216, 218–19; 'The Political Disabilities of Women', (1872), 50, 67–9; Shore (1874), 137, 145–6; Cobbe (1878), 55, 61, 64, 80; 'The Law in Relation to Women', (1887), 698, 709; Blake (1892a), 43, 44; 'Ignota' (1905), 513, 514–5, 522. See also: Pleck (1982–3), 451, 461–6; May (1978), 135, 147.

172. Lord Claud Hamilton was an exception: see 145 H.C. Deb. col. 998 (28 May 1857).

173. Ibid., col. 214 (12 May 1857).

174. 142 H.C. Deb. cols. 169, 172–3 (7 May 1856).

175. 224 H.C. Deb. col. 1870 (14 June 1875).

176. Quoted in Shanley (1989), 182–3.

177. [1891] 1 Q.B. 671, 681, 683–4.

178. See David Rubinstein, *Before the Suffragettes: Women's Emancipation in the 1890s* (1986), 56–7.

179. *The Times*, 28 March 1891 and 30 March 1891.

180. Ibid., 20 March and 17 April 1891.

181. 352 H.C. Deb. cols. 641–3 (16 April 1891).

182. Manson (1891), 244, 254; Charlotte Stopes, *British Freewomen, Their Historical Privilege* (1894), 149; Irving Browne, 'Wife-Beating and Imprisonment', 91 *Law Times* (1891), 321.

183. 'The Judicial Shock to Marriage', 171 *The Nineteenth Century* (1891), 691–5, 697–8, 700. For a biography, see Nancy Fix Anderson, *Woman against Women in Victorian England: A Life of Eliza Lynn Linton* (1987).

184. Philippa Levine, '"So Few Prizes and So Many Blanks": Marriage and Feminism in Later Nineteenth-Century England', 28 *Journal of British Studies* (1989), 150, 153.

185. *Punch, or the London Charivari*, 25 April 1891, 201; see also ibid., 28 March 1891, 156, 2 May 1891, 209 and 9 May 1891, 221.

186. 'Husband and Wife – Right of Custody', 55 *Justice of the Peace* (1891), 195.

187. 177–8 at 178.

188. 235, 239.

189. 64, 69–70.

190. 173.
191. 36–7.
192. See: Blake (1892a), 43, 44; Blake (1892b), 364, 367; Crawford (1893), 292; Stopes (1894), 149. See also J. De Montmorency, 'The Changing Status of a Married Woman', 13 *Law Quarterly Review* (1897), 187, 189.
193. Browne (1891), 321, 323. See also Manson (1891), 244, 250.
194. See Shanley (1989), 62.
195. Ibid., 80.
196. Ibid., 19.
197. Ibid., 185.

Chapter 5: Conclusion
1. Mabel Sharman Crawford, 'The Maltreatment of Wives', 139 *Westminster Review* (1893), 292, 298.
2. *A Manual of the Law Relating to Married Women* (1892), 263. See also J. L. Barton, 'The Enforcement of Financial Provisions', in R. H. Graveson and F. R. Crane, *A Century of Family Law, 1857–1957* (1957), 352, 364.
3. See (1893), 292, 294–296.
4. Ibid., 292, 301.
5. 'The Present Legal Position of Women in the United Kingdom', 163 *Westminster Review* (1905), 513, 521.
6. See The Summary Jurisdiction (Married Women) Act 1895, ss. 6, 7. Under the 1878 Act, orders for the payment of maintenance and for the custody of children could be refused or discharged on proof of the wife's adultery.
7. See 'Wife-Torture in England', 32 *Contemporary Review* (1878), 55, 87.
8. Ibid.
9. See Jane Lewis, *Women in England, 1870–1950: Sexual Divisions and Social Change* (1984), 162–73.
10. Carol Smart, *The Ties that Bind: Law, Marriage and the Reproduction of Patriarchal Relations* (1984), 21–2.
11. Leonore Davidoff and Catherine Hall, *Family Fortunes: Men and Women of the English Middle Class, 1780–1850* (1987), 454.

BIBLIOGRAPHY

Books and Theses

Anderson, M., *Family Structure in Nineteenth-Century Lancashire* (Cambridge : Cambridge University Press, 1971).

Anderson, Nancy Fix, *Woman against Women in Victorian England : A Life of Eliza Lynn Linton* (Bloomington and Indianapolis : Indiana University Press, 1987).

Backhouse, Constance, *Petticoats and Prejudice : Women and Law in Nineteenth-Century Canada* (Toronto : Women's Press, 1991).

Bacon, Francis, *Works*, 10 vols. (London : Rivington and Co., 1826).

Bacon, Matthew, *A New Abridgment of the Law*, 7 vols., 6th edn. (London : Strahan, 1807, originally 1736–66).

Baker, J. H., *An Introduction to English Legal History*, 3rd edn. (London : Butterworths, 1990).

Barbauld, Anna Laetitia (ed.), *The Correspondence of Samuel Richardson*, 6 vols. (London : R. Phillips, 1804).

Baron and Feme : A Treatise of the Common Law concerning Husbands and Wives (1700 ; repr. New York, London : Garland, 1979).

Barrett-Lennard, Thomas, *The Position in Law of Women* (London : Waterlow, 1883).

Basch, Norma, *In The Eyes of the Law : Women, Marriage and Property in Nineteenth-Century New York* (Ithaca, New York : Cornell University Press, 1982).

Bateson, Mary, *Borough Customs*, 2 vols. in *The Publications of the Selden Society*, vols. 20 and 21 (London : Quaritch, 1906).

Bauer, Carol and Ritt, Lawrence, *Free and Ennobled : Source Readings in the Development of Victorian Feminism* (Oxford : Pergamon Press, 1979).

Beale, Joseph Henry, *A Treatise on the Conflict of Laws* (New York : Baker and Voorhis, 1935).

Beard, Mary, *Women as Force in History : A Study in Traditions and Realities* (1946 ; repr. New York : Octagon Books, 1976).

Comyns, John, *A Digest of the Laws of England*, 8 vols., 5th edn. (London: Strahan, 1822, originally 1762–7).

Conley, Carolyn A., *The Unwritten Law: Criminal Justice in Victorian Kent* (Oxford: Oxford University Press, 1991).

Corin, J., *Mating, Marriage and the Status of Women* (London: Scott, 1910).

Cox, Edward, *The Principles of Punishment as Applied in the Administration of the Criminal Law by Judges and Magistrates* (London: Law Times Office, 1877).

Crane, F. R. and Graveson, R. H., *A Century of Family Law, 1857–1957* (London: Sweet and Maxwell, 1957).

Crawley, Charles, *The Law of Husband and Wife* (London: Clowes, 1892).

Cretney, Stephen Michael, *Principles of Family Law*, 4th edn. (London: Sweet and Maxwell, 1984).

Critchley, Thomas, *A History of Police in England and Wales*, 2nd edn. (Montclair, New Jersey: Patterson Smith, 1972).

Crofts, Maud Isobel, *Women Under English Law*, 2nd edn. (London: Butterworths, 1928).

Cross, Rupert, *Evidence*, (London, Butterworths, 1958).

——, and Tapper, Colin, *Cross on Evidence*, 7th edn. (London: Butterworths, 1990).

Dalton, Michael, *The Countrey Justice* (1618; repr. Amsterdam: Johnson, Theatrum Orbis Terrarum, 1975).

——, *The Countrey Justice* (London: Co. of Stationers, 1655).

Daly, Mary, *The Church and the Second Sex, With a Feminist Postchristian Introduction and New Archaic Afterwords by the Author* (Boston: Beacon Press, 1985).

Defoe, Daniel, *Moll Flanders* (1722), G. A. Starr (ed.), (Oxford: Oxford University Press, World Classics, 1981, originally 1722).

Denning, Sir Alfred, *The Changing Law* (London: Stevens, 1953).

——, *The Equality of Women* (Liverpool: Liverpool University Press, 1960).

Dicey, A. V., *Lectures on the Relation between Law and Public Opinion in England during the Nineteenth Century* (1905; repr. London: MacMillan, 1962).

Dobash, R. Emerson and Dobash, Russell, *Violence Against Wives: A Case Against the Patriarchy* (New York: Free Press, 1979).

Downer, L. J. (ed.), *Leges Henrici Primi* (Oxford: Clarendon, 1972, originally 1201–1330).

Durston, Christopher, *The Family in the English Revolution* (Oxford: Basil Blackwell, 1989).

East, Edward Hyde, *A Treatise of the Pleas of the Crown*, 2 vols. (London: Strahan, 1803).

Edwards, John Williams and Hamilton, William Frederick, *The Law of Husband and Wife* (London: Butterworths, 1883).

Ernst-Browning, William, *A Treatise of Marriage and Divorce: With the Practice and Procedure in Divorce and Matrimonial Causes* (London: Ridgway, 1879).

Eversley, William Pinder, *The Law of Domestic Relations* (London: Stevens and Haynes, 1885).

——, *The Law of Domestic Relations*, 3rd edn. (London: Steven and Haynes, 1906).

Fell, Christine, Clark, Cecily and Williams, Elizabeth, *Women in Anglo-Saxon England and the Impact of 1066* (Oxford: Basil Blackwell, 1984).

Fitzherbert, Anthony, *The New Natura Brevium* (London: Atkins, 1704, originally 1516).

——, *The New Natura Brevium*, 8th edn. (London: H. Lintot, 1755).

Forster, Margaret, *Significant Sisters: The Grassroots of Active Feminism, 1839–1939* (New York: Knopf, 1985).

Foss, Edward, *The Judges of England; with Sketches of Their Lives*, 9 vols. (1864; repr. New York: Ams Press, 1966).

Foster, Lemuel H., *The Legal Rights of Women* (1913; repr. Littleton, Colorado: Rothman, 1986).

Fox, A. Wilson, *The Earl of Halsbury, Lord High Chancellor 1823–1921* (London: Chapman and Hall, 1929).

Foxcroft, H. C., *Life and Letters of George Savile, Marquis of Halifax*, 2 vols. (London: Longmans, Green and Co., 1898).

Freeman, Michael D. A., *Violence in the Home: A Socio-legal Study* (1979; repr. Farnborough: Gower, 1980).

Fuller, Lon, *Legal Fictions* (Stanford, California: Stanford University Press, 1967).

Geary, Nevill, *The Law of Marriage and Family Relations: A Manual of Practical Law* (London, Edinburgh: Black, 1892).

George, M. Dorothy (ed.), *Catalogue of Personal and Political Satires in the British Museum*, 11 vols. (London: British Museum Publications Ltd., 1978).

Gies, Frances and Gies, Joseph, *Marriage and the Family in the Middle Ages* (New York: Harper and Row, 1989, originally 1987).

Gillis, John, *For Better, For Worse: British Marriages, 1600 to the Present* (Oxford: Oxford University Press, 1985).

Gisborne, Thomas, *An Enquiry into the Duties of the Female Sex* (London: Cadell and Davis, 1797).

Glanvil, Ranulf, *A Treatise on the Laws and Customs of the Kingdom of England*, trans. John Beame (London: Valpy, 1812, originally 1187).

Glanz, Leonore Marie, *The Legal Position of English Women Under the Early Stuart Kings and the Interregnum, 1603–1660* (Ph.D. diss.: Loyola University of Chicago, History Dept., 1973).

Goebel, Julius (ed.), *Cases and Materials on the Development of Legal Institutions* (Brattleboro, Vermont: Vermont Printing Co., 1946).

Gordon, Linda, *Heroes of Their Own Lives: The Politics and History of Family Violence* (London: Virago, 1989).

Gouge, William, *Domesticall Duties* (1622; repr. Amsterdam: Theatrum Orbis Terrarum, 1976).

Graveson, R. H., *Status in the Common Law* (London: University of London, Athlone Press, 1953).

Hale, Matthew, *The History of the Pleas of the Crown*, 2 vols. (Philadelphia: Small, 1847, originally 1678).

Hanawalt, Barbara A., *The Ties That Bound: Peasant Families in Medieval England* (Oxford: Oxford University Press, 1986).

The Hardships of the English Laws in Relation to Wives, With an Explanation of the Original Curse of Subjection Passed upon the Woman (London: Printed for J. Robert, 1735).

Hardy, Thomas, *The Mayor of Casterbridge* (1886), Martin Seymour-Smith (ed.) (1978; repr. Harmondsworth: Penguin Classics, 1987).

Haw, Reginald, *The State of Matrimony: An Investigation of the Relationship between ecclesiastical and civil marriage in England after the Reformation, with a consideration of the Laws relating thereto* (London: SPCR, 1952).

Hawkins, William, *Pleas of the Crown*, 2 vols. (1716–21; repr. London: Professional Books, 1973).

——, *Pleas of the Crown*, 2 vols., 4th edn. (London: E. Richardson & C. Lintot, 1762).

Heale, William, *An Apologie for Women* (1609; repr. New York, London: Garland, 1978).

Hecker, Eugene A., *A Short History of Women's Rights From the Days of Augustus to the Present Time. With Special Reference to England and the United States*, 2nd edn. (Westport, Connecticut: Greenwood Press, 1971, originally 1914).

Helmholz, R. H., *Marriage Litigation in Medieval England* (Cambridge: Cambridge University Press, 1974).

——, *Roman Canon Law in Reformation England* (Cambridge: Cambridge University Press, 1990).

Henderson, Edith G., *Foundations of English Administrative Law: Certiorari and Mandamus in the Seventeenth Century* (Cambridge, Massachusetts: Harvard University Press, 1963).

Heuston, R. F. V., *Lives of the Lord Chancellors 1885–1940* (Oxford: Clarendon Press, 1964).

Herrup, Cynthia, *The Common Peace: Participation and the Criminal Law in Seventeenth-Century England* (Cambridge: Cambridge University Press, 1987).

Hill, Bridget (ed.), *Eighteenth-Century Women: An Anthology* (London: Allen and Unwin, 1984).

——, (ed.), *The First English Feminist: Reflections Upon Marriage and other writings by Mary Astell* (Aldershot: Gower, 1986).

Hill, Christopher, *The World Turned Upside Down: Radical Ideas During the English Revolution* (London: Temple Smith, 1972).

Holcombe, Lee, *Wives and Property: Reform of the Married Women's Property Law in Nineteenth-Century England* (Toronto: University of Toronto Press, 1983).

Holdsworth, Sir William, *A History of English Law*, 16 vols. (1908; repr. London: Methuen, Sweet and Maxwell, 1966).

——, *Some Makers of English Law: The Tagore Lectures, 1937–1938* (1937; repr. Cambridge: Cambridge University Press, 1966).

Holmes, Thomas, *Pictures and Problems from London Police Courts* (London: Thomas Nelson, 1900).

Ingram, Martin, *Church Courts, Sex and Marriage in England, 1570–1640* (Cambridge: Cambridge University Press, 1987).

James I: *Collected Works*, (ed.) James, Bishop of Winchester and Deane of His Majesty's Chapell Royall (London, 1616).

Jenks, Edward, *A Short History of English Law From the Earliest Times to the End of the Year 1938*, 6th edn. (London: Methuen, 1949).

Jones, Ann, *Women Who Kill* (New York: Holt, Rinehart and Winston, 1980).

Jones, David, *Protest, Community and Police in Nineteenth-Century Britain* (London: Routledge and Kegan Paul, 1982).

Jones, Vivien (ed.), *Women in the Eighteenth Century: Constructions of Femininity* (London: Routledge, 1990).

Kanowitz, Leo, *Women and the Law: The Unfinished Revolution* (Albuquerque: University of New Mexico Press, 1969).

Karminski, Seymour Edward, *Some Aspects of the Development of English Personal Law in the Last Century* (Jerusalem: Magues Press, Hebrew University, 1963).

Kenny, Courtney Stanhope, *The History of the Law of England as to the Effects of Marriage on Property and on the Wife's Legal Capacity* (London: Reeves and Turner, 1879).

——, *Outlines of Criminal Law*, 4th edn. (Cambridge: Cambridge University Press, 1909).

Kent, James, *Commentaries on American Law*, 4 vols., 11th edn. (Boston: Little and Brown, 1866).

L. I., *The Lawes Resolutions of Womens Rights*, (ed.) T.E. (London: Printed for John More, 1632).

Lambarde, William, *Eirenarcha* (London: R. Newbery 1599, originally 1581).

——, *Eirenarcha* (London: Companie of Stationers, 1610).

Lasch, Christopher, *Haven in a Heartless World: The Family Besieged* (New York: Basic Books, 1977).

Lawrence, Basil Edwin, *The History of Laws Affecting the Property of Married Women in England* (London: Reeves and Turner, 1884).

The Laws Respecting Women, As They regard their Natural Rights, or their Connections and Conduct (London: Printed for J. Johnson, 1777).

Leathley, S. A., *The History of Marriage and Divorce* (London: Long, 1916).

Lewis, Jane, *Women in England, 1870–1950: Sexual Divisions and Social Change* (Sussex: Wheatsheaf Books, 1984).

Ling-Mallison, E., *Law Relating to Women* (London: Solicitors' Law Stationery Society, 1930).

Lush, Montague, *The Law of Husband and Wife Within the Jurisdiction of the Queen's Bench and Chancery Divisions* (London: Stevens, 1884).

——, *The Law of Husband and Wife*, (ed.) S. N. Grant-Bailey, 4th edn. (London: Stevens, 1933).

MacQueen, John Fraser, *The Rights and Liabilities of Husband and Wife* (London: Sweet, 1849).

——, *The Rights and Liabilities of Husband and Wife*, (ed.) Wyatt Paine, 4th edn. (London: Sweet and Maxwell, 1905).

McIntyre, Bronwyn H., *Legal Attitudes Towards Women in England, 1558–1648* (M. A. thesis: University of New Brunswick, History Dept., 1972).

McLynn, Frank, *Crime and Punishment in Eighteenth-Century England* (Oxford: Oxford University Press, 1991).

Maine, Henry Sumner, *Ancient Law: Its connection with the Early History of Society and its Relations to Modern Ideas* (London: Murray, 1930, originally 1861).

Maitland, Frederic and Pollock, Frederick, *The History of English Law before the Time of Edward I*, 2 vols. (Cambridge, Boston: at the University Press, Little and Brown, 1895).

Matthews, Joseph Bridges, *A Manual of the Law Relating to Married Women* (London: Sweet and Maxwell, 1892).

Mayhew, Henry, *London Labour and the London Poor*, 4 vols. (1851–62; repr. New York: Kelley, 1967).

Menefee, Samuel, *Wives for Sale* (Oxford: Blackwell, 1981).

Merrivale, Henry Edward, *Marriage and Divorce: The English Point of View* (London: Allen and Unwin, 1936).

Milsom, Stroud Francis Charles, *Historical Foundations of the Common Law* (London: Butterworths, 1969).

Norton, Caroline, *A Plain Letter to the Lord Chancellor on the Infant Custody Bill* (London: Ridgway, 1839).

——, *Caroline Norton's Defense: English Laws for Women in the Nineteenth Century* (1854; repr. Chicago: Academy Chicago, Academy Chicago, 1982).

Noy, William, *The Principal Grounds and Maxims with an Analysis of the Laws of England*, 3rd US from the 9th London edn. (1845, originally 1641; repr. Colorado: Rothman, 1980).

Ogden, C. K., *Bentham's Theory of Fictions*, 2nd edn. (London: Routledge and Kegan Paul, 1951, originally 1932).

Okin, Susan Moller, *Women in Western Political Thought* (Princeton: Princeton University Press, 1979).

O'Donovan, Katherine, *Sexual Divisions in Law* (London: Weidenfeld and Nicolson, 1985).

O'Neal, Capri Montgomery, *Marriage and the Status of Women as Viewed through Early Medieval Law Codes* (LL M thesis: Rice University, Houston, Texas, 1983).

O'Neil, William L., *The Woman Movement* (London: Allen and Unwin, 1969).

Parker, Stephen, *Informal Marriage, Cohabitation and the Law, 1750–1989* (London: MacMillan, 1990).

Pateman, Carole, *The Problem of Political Obligation: A Critical Analysis of Liberal Theory* (London: Wiley, 1976).

——, *The Sexual Contract* (Cambridge: Polity Press, 1988).

——, *The Disorder of Women* (Cambridge: Polity Press, 1989).

—— and Shanley, Mary Lyndon (eds.), *Feminist Interpretations and Political and Theory* (Cambridge: Polity Press, 1991).

Perkins, William, *Christian Oeconomy* (1590), in Ian Seward (ed.), *The Work of William Perkins* (Appleford: Sutton Courtenay Press, 1970), 411.

Perry, Ruth, *The Celebrated Mary Astell: An Early English Feminist* (Chicago: University of Chicago Press, 1986).

Pethick, Jane, *Battered Wives: A Select Bibliography* (Toronto: University of Toronto, Centre of Criminology, 1979).

'Philogamus', *The Present State of Matrimony: Or, The Real Causes of Conjugal Infidelity and Unhappy Marriages* (1739; repr. New York, London: Garland, 1985).

Pleck, Elizabeth, *Domestic Tyranny: The Making of Social Policy Against Family Violence from Colonial Times to the Present* (Oxford: Oxford University Press, 1987).

Pollock, Frederick and Maitland, Frederic, *The History of English Law before the Time of Edward I*, 2 vols. (Cambridge, Boston: at the University Press, Little and Brown, 1895).

Poovey, Mary, *The Proper Lady and the Woman Writer: Ideology as Style in the Works of Mary Wollstonecraft, Mary Shelley, and Jane Austen* (Chicago: University of Chicago Press, 1984).

——, *Uneven Developments: The Ideological Work of Gender in Mid-Victorian England* (London: Virago Press, 1989).

Powell, Chilton Latham, *English Domestic Relations, 1487–1653; A Study of Matrimony and Family Life in Theory and Practice as revealed by the Literature, Law and History of the Period* (Ph.D thesis: Columbia University, 1916).

Poynter, Thomas, *A concise view of the Doctrine and Practice of the Ecclesiastical Courts in Doctors' Commons, on various points relative to Marriage and Divorce*, 2nd edn. (London: Clarke, 1824).

Prater, Henry, *Cases Illustrative of the Conflict Between the Laws of England and Scotland with regard to Marriage, Divorce and Legitimacy. Designed as a Supplement to an Essay upon the Law Respecting Husband and Wife* (London: Saunders and Benning, 1835).

Prothero, G. W. (ed.), *Select Statutes and other Constitutional Documents illustrative of the Reigns of Elizabeth and James I*, 4th edn. (Oxford: Clarendon Press, 1913).

Rabkin, Peggy, *Fathers to Daughters: The Legal Foundations of Female Emancipation* (Westport, Connecticut: Greenwood Press, 1980).

Radzinowicz, Leon and Hood, Roger, *The Emergence of Penal Policy* (London: Stevens, 1986), in Leon Radzinowicz, *A History of Criminal Law and its Administration from 1750*, 5 vols. (London: Stevens, 1948–86), vol. 5.

Reeve, Tapping, *The Law of Baron and Femme* (1816; repr. Buffalo: Hein, 1981).

Reiss, Erna, *The Rights and Duties of Englishwomen* (Manchester: Sherratt and Hughes, 1934).

Rendall, Jane (ed.), *Equal or Different: Women's Politics 1800–1914* (Oxford: Basil Blackwell, 1987).

Ridley, Thomas, *View of the Civile and Ecclesiasticall Law*, 4th edn. (Oxford: H. Hall for R. Davis, 1675, originally 1607).

Risk, James E., *Marriage-Contract and Sacrament* (Chicago: Callaghan, 1957).

Roberts, Robert, *The Classic Slum*, 2nd edn. (Manchester: University of Manchester Press, 1972).

Roper, Roper Samuel Donnison, *A Treatise of the Law of Property Arising from the Relation Between Husband and Wife*, (ed.) Edward Jacob, 2 vols., 2nd edn. (London: Butterworths, 1826).

Rowbotham, Sheila, *Women Resistance and Revolution* (1972; repr. Harmondsworth: Penguin, 1980).

———, *Hidden from History*, 3rd edn. (1977; repr. London: Pluto Press, 1990).

Rubinstein, David, *Before the Suffragettes: Women's Emancipation in the 1890s* (New York: St Martin's Press, 1986).

Rudé, George, *Criminal and Victim: Crime and Society in Early Nineteenth-Century England* (Oxford: Clarendon Press, 1985).

Russell, William Oldnall, *A Treatise on Crimes and Misdemeanors*, (ed.) William Craies and Leonard Kersham, 3 vols., 7th edn. (London: Stevens, Sweet and Maxwell, 1909).

Russett, Cynthia Eagle, *Sexual Science: The Victorian Construction of Womenhood* (Cambridge, Massachusetts: Harvard University Press, 1989).

Salmon, Mary Lynn, *The Property Rights of Women in Early America: A Comparative Study* (Ph.D dissertation, Bryn Mawr College, 1980).

Schücking, Levin L., *The Puritan Family; A Social Study from the Literary Sources* (London: Routledge and Kegan Paul, 1969).

Scutt, Jocelynne, *Even in the Best of Homes: Violence in the Family* (Ringwood, Victoria: Penguin Books, Australia, 1983).

Shanley, Mary Lyndon, *Feminism, Marriage, and the Law in Victorian England, 1850–1895* (London: I. B. Tauris and Co., 1989).

———, and Pateman, Carole (eds.), *Feminist Interpretations and Political Theory* (Cambridge: Polity Press, 1991).

Sharpe, J. A. *Crime in Early Modern England, 1550–1750* (London: Longman, 1984).

———, *Early Modern England: A Social History, 1550–1760* (London: Edward Arnold, 1987).

———, *The Law of Habeas Corpus*, 2nd edn. (Oxford: Clarendon Press, 1989).

Simpson, A. W. B., *Biographical Dictionary of the Common Law* (London: Butterworths, 1984).

Sinclair, Deborah, *Understanding Wife Assault: A Training Manual for Counsellors and Advocates* (Publication funded by the Ontario Ministry of Community and Social Services, Family Violence Programme, 1985).

Smart, Carol, *The Ties that Bind: Law, Marriage and the Reproduction of Patriarchal Relations* (London: Routledge and Kegan Paul, 1984).

Smith, John Campbell, *The Marriage Laws of England, Scotland and Ireland* (London: Simpkin and Marshall, 1864).

Smith, Sir Thomas, *De Republica Anglorum*, (ed.) Mary Dewar (Cambridge: Cambridge University Press, 1982, originally 1562–5).

Soloway, R. A., *Prelates and People: Ecclesiastical Social Thought in England, 1783–1852* (London: Routledge and Kegan Paul, 1969).

Staves, Susan, *Married Women's Separate Property in England, 1660–1833* (Cambridge, Massachusetts: Harvard University Press, 1990).

Stenton, Doris May, *The English Woman in History* (London: Allen and Unwin, 1957).

Stephen, James Fitzjames, *History of the Criminal Law of England*, 3 vols. (London: MacMillan, 1883).

——, *A Digest of the Criminal Law*, 3rd edn. (London: MacMillan, 1883).

——, *A Digest of the Criminal Law*, (ed.) Herbert Stephen and Harry L. Stephen, 6th edn. (London: MacMillan, 1904).

Stetson, Dorothy M., *A Woman's Issue: The Politics of Family Law Reform* (Westport, Connecticut: Greenwood Press, 1982).

Stevenson, John, *Popular Disturbances in England 1700–1870* (London: Longman, 1979).

Stone, Lawrence, *The Family, Sex and Marriage in England, 1500–1800* (New York: Harper and Row, 1977).

——, *Road to Divorce: England 1530–1987* (Oxford: Oxford University Press, 1990).

Stopes, Charlotte, *British Freewomen, Their Historical Privilege* (London: Sonnenschein, 1894).

Swinburne, Henry, *A Treatise of Spousals or Matrimonial Contracts wherein all the questions relating to that subject are ingeniously debated and resolved* (1686; repr. New York, London: Garland, 1978).

Taylor, Barbara, *Eve and the New Jerusalem: Socialism and Feminism in the Nineteenth Century* (1983; repr. London: Virago Press, 1991).

Thomis, Malcolm I. and Holt, Peter, *Threats of Revolution in Britain, 1789–1848* (London: MacMillan Press, 1977).

Thompson, Dorothy, *The Chartists* (London: Temple Smith, 1984).

Thompson, E. P., *Customs in Common* (London: Merlin Press, 1991).

Thompson, William, *Appeal of one Half of the Human Race, Women, Against the Pretensions of the Other Half, Men, To Retain Them in Political, and Thence in Civil and Domestic Slavery* (London, Virago, 1983, originally 1825).

Thomson, David, *England in the Nineteenth Century (1815–1914)* (1950; repr. Harmondsworth: Penguin, 1963).

Tobias, J.J., *Crime and Industrial Society in the Nineteenth Century* (London: Batsford, 1967).

Townsend, Willaim, *The Lives of Twelve Eminent Judges of the Last and Present Century*, 2 vols. (London: Longman, Brown, Green and Longmans, 1846).

A Treatise of Feme Coverts: Or the Lady's Law (1732; repr. New Jersey: Rothman Reprints, 1974).

Underhill, Arthur, *The Law Reform (Married Women and Tortfeasors) Act, 1935* (London: Butterworths, 1936).

Vicinus, Martha (ed.), *Suffer and Be Still: Women in the Victorian Age* (Bloomington: Indiana University Press, 1973).

——, (ed.), *A Widening Sphere: Changing Roles for Victorian Women* (Bloomington: Indiana University Press, 1977).

Wedgwood, C. V., *The King's Peace, 1637–1641* (London: Collins, 1960, originally 1955).

Weisberg, Kelly D., *Women and the Law: The Social Historical Perspective*, 2 vols. (Cambridge, Massachusetts: Schenkman, 1982).

Wharton, J. J. S., *An Exposition of the Laws Relating to the Women of England; Showing Their Rights, Remedies and Responsibilities* (London: Longman, Brown, Green and Longmans, 1853).

Wigmore, John Henry, *Evidence in Trials at Common Law*, vol. 2 (Chadbourn rev. 1979) (Boston, Toronto: Little and Brown, 1979).

——, *Evidence in Trials at Common Law*, vol. 8 (McNaughton rev. 1961) (Boston, Toronto: Little and Brown, 1961).

Williams, Glanville, *Criminal Law, The General Part* (London: Stevens, 1953).

——, *Criminal Law, The General Part*, 2nd edn. (London: Stevens, 1961).

Williams, Merryn, *Margaret Oliphant: A Critical Biography* (London: MacMillan, 1986).

Wolfram, Sybil, *In-Laws and Outlaws: Kinship and Marriage in England* (London: Croom Helm, 1987).

Wollstonecraft, Mary, *A Vindication of the Rights of Women*, (ed.) Carol Poston (New York: Norton, 1975, originally 1792).

Articles and Conference Papers

Backhouse, Constance, ' "Pure Patriarchy": Nineteenth-Century Canadian Marriage', 31 *McGill Law Journal* (1896), 264.

Baker, J. H., 'Male and Married Spinsters', 21 *American Journal of Legal History* (1977), 255.

Bart, J. T. (Rev.), 'On the Adoption of Punishment to the Causes of Crime', *Transactions NAPSS* (1857) (London: Parker, 1858), 315.

Basch, Norma, 'Invisible Women: The Legal Fiction of Marital Unity in Nineteenth Century America', 5 *Feminist Studies* (1979), 346.

——, 'Book Review of Peggy Rabkin, Fathers to Daughters: The Legal Foundations of Female Emancipation', 26 *American Journal of Legal History* (1982), 26.

——, 'Equity v. Equality: Emerging Concepts of Women's Political

Status in the Age of Jackson', 3 *Journal of the Early Republic* (1983), 297.

Bates, Frank, 'Wives as Witnesses', 47 *Journal of Criminal Law* (1983), 123.

Bauer, Carol and Ritt, Lawrence, ' "A Husband is a Beating Animal", Frances Power Cobbe Confronts the Wife-Abuse Problem in Victorian England', 6 *International Journal of Women's Studies* (1983a), 99.

——, 'Wife-Abuse, Late Victorian English Feminists, and the Legacy of Frances Power Cobbe', 6 *International Journal of Women's Studies* (1983b), 195.

Beattie, John M., 'The Criminality of Women in Eighteenth-Century England', 8 *Journal of Social History* (1974–5), 80.

Birrell, Augustine, 'Woman Under the English Law', 184 *Edinburgh Review* (1898), 322.

Blake, Matilda, 'Are Women Protected?', 137 *Westminster Review* (1892a), 43.

——, 'The Lady and the Law', 137 *Westminster Review* (1892b), 364.

Bonfield, Lloyd, 'Marriage, Property and the "Affective" Family', 1 (2) *Law and History Review* (1983), 297.

Bowker, Margaret, 'Marriage and the Role of Women in English History', 31–41 *Quis Custodiet* (1971–3), 76.

Boyle, Christine, 'Violence Against Wives – The Criminal Law in Retreat?', 31 *Northern Ireland Legal Quarterly* (1980), 35.

Brennan, Teresa and Pateman, Carole, ' "Mere Auxiliaries to the Commonwealth": Women and Liberalism', 27 *Political Studies* (1979), 183.

Browne, Irving, 'Wife-Beating and Imprisonment', 91 *Law Times* (1891), 321.

Browne, Matthew (pseud.), 'The Subjection of Women', 14 *Contemporary Review* (1870), 273.

Buckstaff, Florence Griswold, 'Married Women's Property in Anglo-Saxon and Anglo-Norman Law and the Origin of the Common-Law Dower', 4 *Annals of the American Academy of Political and Social Science* (1893–4), 233.

Campbell, Ruth, 'Sentence of Death by Burning for Women', 5–6 *Journal of Legal History* (1984–5), 43.

Cavanagh, Barbara, ' "A Little Dearer Than His Horse": Legal Stereotypes and the Feminine Personality', 6 *Harvard Civil Rights – Civil Liberties Law Review* (1971), 260.

Clark, Anna, 'Humanity or Justice? Wifebeating and the law in the eighteenth and nineteenth centuries', in Carol Smart (ed.), *Regulating Womenhood: Historical Essays on Marriage, Motherhood and Sexuality* (London: Routledge, 1992). 187.

Cobbe, Frances Power, 'Criminals, Idiots, Women and Minors', 78 *Fraser's Magazine* (1868), 777.

——, 'Wife-Torture in England', 32 *Contemporary Review* (1878), 55.

Cornwallis, Caroline, 'The Property of Married Women', 66 *Westminster Review* (1857), 42.

'Corporal Punishment for Wife Beating', 2 *Central Law Journal* (1875), 134.

Cowley, David, 'Marital Rape – Waiver of Injunction: *R*. v. *Reeves*', 48 *Journal of Criminal Law* (1984), 352.

Crawford, Mabel Sharman, 'Maltreatment of Wives', 139 *Westminster Review* (1893), 292.

Davidoff, Leonore, 'Mastered for Life: Servant and Wife in Victorian and Edwardian England', 7 *Journal of Social History* (1974), 406.

Davidson, Terry, 'Wife-beating: A Recurring Phenomenon Throughout History', in Maria Roy (ed.), *Battered Women: A Psychosociological Study of Domestic Violence* (New York: Van Nostrand Reinhold, 1977), 2.

Davies, Kathleen M., 'Continuity and Change in Literary Advice on Marriage', in R. B. Outhwaite (ed.), *Marriage and Society: Studies in the Social History of Marriage* (London: Europa Publications, 1981), 58.

Davis, Jennifer, 'A Poor Man's System of Justice: The London Police Courts in the Second Half of the Nineteenth Century', 27 *Historical Journal* (1984), 309.

——, 'The London Garrotting panic of 1862: A Moral Panic and the Creation of a Criminal Class in Mid-Victorian England', in V. A. C. Gatrell, Bruce Lenman and Geoffrey Parker (eds.), *Crime and the Law: The Social History of Crime in Western Europe since 1500* (London: Europa Publications, 1980), 190.

——, 'Prosecutions and Their Context: The Use of the Criminal Law in Later Nineteenth-Century London', in Douglas Hay and Francis Snyder (eds.), *Policing and Prosecution in Britain, 1750–1850* (Oxford: Clarendon Press, 1989), 397.

De Montmorency, J., 'The Changing Status of a Married Woman', 13 *Law Quarterly Review* (1897), 187.

Dewes, Alfred, 'The Injustice of the English Law as it Bears on the Relationship of Husband and Wife', 9 *Contemporary Review* (1868), 114.

Dietrich, Sheila C., 'An Introduction to Women in Anglo-Saxon Society (c. 600–1066)', in Barbara Kanner (ed.), *The Women of England from Anglo-Saxon Times to the Present: Interpretative Bibliographical Essays* (London: Mansell, 1980), 32.

Dobash, Emerson R. and Dobash, Russell, 'Wives: The "Appropriate" Victims of Marital Violence', 2 *Victimology* (1977–8), 426.

——, 'Community Response to Violence Against Wives: Charivari, Abstract Justice and Patriarchy', 28(5) *Social Problems* (1981), 563.

Donahue, Charles, 'What Causes Fundamental Legal Ideas? Marital Property in England and France in the Thirteenth Century', 78 *Michigan Law Review* (1979), 59.

Dubois, Ellen, 'The Radicalism of the Woman Suffrage Movement: Notes Toward the Reconstruction of Nineteenth-Century Feminism', 3 *Feminist Studies* (1975), 63.

Edwards, J., 'Compulsion, Coercion and Criminal Responsibility', 14 *Modern Law Review* (1951), 297.

Edwards, Valerie, 'The Case of the Married Spinster: An Alternative Explanation', 21 *American Journal of Legal History* (1977), 260.

Eisenberg, Susan E. and Micklow, Patricia L., 'The Assaulted Wife: "Catch 22" Revisited', 2–3 *Women's Rights Law Reporter*, 138.

Fellows, Alfred, 'Changes in the Law of Husband and Wife', 22 *Law Quarterly Review* (1906), 64.

Fenberg, Matilda, 'Blame Coke and Blackstone', 33–4 *Women Lawyers' Journal* (1947–8), 7.

Finesmith, Barbara K., 'Police Responses to Battered Women: A Critique and Proposals for Reform', 14 *Seton Hall Law Review* (1983), 74.

Flitcraft, Anne, Frazier, William and Stark, Evan, 'Medicine and Patriarchal Violence: The Social Construction of a "Private Event"', 9 *International Journal of Health Services* (1979), 461.

Freeman, Jo, 'Legal Basis of Sexual Caste System', 5 *Valparaiso University Law Review* (1971), 203.

Freeman, Michael, D. A., 'Violence Against Women: Does the Legal System Provide Solutions or Itself Constitute the Problem?', 3 *Canadian Journal of Family Law* (1980), 377.

——, 'Legal System, Patriarchal Ideologies and Domestic Violence: A Case Study of the English Legal System', 4 *Research in Law, Deviance and Social Control* (1982), 131.

——, 'Legal Ideologies, Patriarchal Precedents, and Domestic Violence', in M. D. A. Freeman (ed.), *The State, the Law and the Family* (London, New York: Tavistock, 1984), 51.

Garner, J. F., 'The Defence of Coercion', [1954] *Criminal Law Review*, 448.

Gatrell, V. A. C., 'The Decline of Theft and Violence in Victorian England', in V. A. C Gatrell, Bruce Lenman and Geoffrey Parker (eds.), *Crime and the Law: The Social History of Crime in Western Europe since 1500* (London: Europa Publications, 1980), 238.

Gavigan, Shelley, 'Petit Treason in Eighteenth Century England:

Women's Inequality Before the Law', 3 *Canadian Journal of Women and the Law* (1989–1990), 335.

Gayford, J.J., 'Battered Wives One Hundred Years Ago', 219 *The Practitioner* (1977), 122.

Griew, Edward, 'Common Assault and the Statute Book', [1983] *Criminal Law Review*, 710.

Hall, Catherine, 'The Early Formulation of Victorian Domestic Ideology', in Sandra Burman (ed.), *Fit Work for Women* (London: Croom Helm in Association with Oxford University Women's Studies Committee, 1979), 15.

Hammerton, A. James, 'Victorian Marriage and the Law of Matrimonial Cruelty' (Paper presented at the Law and History Conference, La Trobe University, Melbourne, May 1987).

Haskins, George L., 'The Estate by the Marital Right', 97 *University of Pennsylvania Law Review* (1949), 345.

Hay, Douglas, 'Property, Authority and Criminal Law', in Douglas Hay et al. (eds.), *Albion's Fatal Tree: Crime and Society in Eighteenth-Century England* (New York: Pantheon Books, Random House, 1975), 17.

——, 'Poaching and the Game Laws on Cannock Chase', in Douglas Hay et al. (eds.), *Albion's Fatal Tree: Crime and Society in Eighteenth-Century England* (New York: Pantheon Books, Random House, 1975), 189.

——, 'Contempt by Scandalizing the Court: A Political History of the First Hundred Years', 25 *Osgoode Hall Law Journal* (1987), 431.

Holmes, Oliver Wendell, 'Agency', 4 *Harvard Law Review* (1891), 345.

Hooper, Carol-ann, 'Child sexual abuse and the regulation of women: Variations on a theme', in Carol Smart (ed.), *Regulating Womenhood: Historical Essays in Marriage, Motherhood and Sexuality* (London: Routledge, 1992), 53.

Hughes, Marija Matich, 'And then there were two', 23 *Hastings Law Journal* (1971–2), 233.

'Husband and Wife – Right of Custody', 55 *Justice of the Peace* (1891), 195.

'The Husband's Dominion Over His Wife', 65 *Law Journal* (1928), 182.

Ingram, Martin, 'Ridings, Rough Music and the "Reform of Popular Culture" in Early Modern England', 105 *Past and Present* (1984), 79.

Johnston, John D., 'Sex and Property: Tradition, The Law School Curriculum, and Developments Towards Equality', 47 *New York University Law Review* (1972), 1034.

Kahn-Freund, Otto, 'Inconsistencies and Injustices in the Law of Husband and Wife', 15 *Modern Law Review* (1952), 133.

Kaye, J. W., 'The Non-Existence of Women', 23 *North British Review* (1855), 536.

——, 'Outrages on Women', 25 *North British Review* (1856), 233.

Kerber, Linda K., 'From the Declaration of Independence to the Declaration of Sentiments: The Legal Status of Women in the Early Republic, 1776–1848', 6 *Human Rights* (1976–7), 115.

Kittel, Ruth, 'Women Under the Law in Medieval England, 1066–1485', in Barbara Kanner (ed.), *The Women of England From Anglo-Saxon Times to the Present: Interpretative Bibliographical Essays* (London: Mansell, 1980), 124.

Lambertz, Jan, 'Feminists and the Politics of Wife-Beating', *Feminism in the Twentieth Century* (Aldershot: Edward Elgar, 1990), 25.

Lanham, David, 'Hale, Misogyny and Rape', 7 *Criminal Law Journal* (1983), 148.

'The Law in Relation to Women', 128 *Westminster Review* (1887), 698.

'The Laws of Marriage and Divorce', 82 *Westminster Review* (1864), 442.

'The Laws Relating to Women', 20–1 *Law Review* (1854–5), 1.

Le Pauw, Linda Grant, 'Women and the Law: The Colonial Period' 6 *Human Rights* (1976–7), 107.

'A Letter from Wisbech: Of two Murders on Account of Jealousy', 19 *Gentleman's Magazine* (Nov. 1749), 486.

Lewis, Jane, 'The Working-Class Wife and Mother and State Intervention, 1870–1918', in Jane Lewis (ed.), *Labour and Love: Women's Experience of Home and Family, 1850–1940* (1986; repr. Oxford: Basil Blackwell, 1989), 99.

Levine, Philippa, '"So Few Prizes and So Many Blanks": Marriage and Feminism in Later Nineteenth Century England', 28 *Journal of British Studies* (1989), 150.

Levy, Philip, 'More Equal Than Others?', 142 *New Law Journal* (13 March 1992), 355.

Linton, E. Lynn, 'The Judicial Shock to Marriage', 171 *The Nineteenth Century* (1891), 691.

Lowman, John, 'Comment: The Dangers of Feminist Correctionalism: Some Thoughts About the Criminalization of Family Violence Offenders', 2 *Canadian Criminology Forum* (1981), 158.

Lush, Montague, 'Changes in the Law Affecting the Rights, Status and Liabilities of Married Women', in *A Century of Law Reform: Twelve Lectures on the Changes in the Law of England During the Nineteenth Century* (London: MacMillan, 1901), 342.

McGregor, O. R., 'The Social Position of Women in England, 1850–1914: A Bibliography', 6 *British Journal of Sociology* (1955), 48.

Maidment, Susan, 'The Law's Response to Marital Violence in England and the USA', 26 *International and Comparative Law Quarterly* (1977), 403.

Mallett, Phillip, 'Women and Marriage in Victorian Society', in Elizabeth M. Craik (ed.), *Marriage and Property* (Aberdeen: University of Aberdeen Press, 1984).

Manchester, A. H., 'Marital Violence and the Act of 1878', in Geoffrey Hand and Jeremy McBride (eds.), *Droit Sans Frontieres: Essays in Honour of L. Neville Brown* (Birmingham: Holdsworth Club, 1991), 131.

Manson, Edward, 'Marital Authority', 7 *Law Quarterly Review* (1891), 244.

Marshall, David, 'Coercion is the Oppression of Wives: An Introduction to the History of a Criminal Law Defence' (University of Keele, Centre for Criminology: Occasional Paper No. 2, 1987).

May, Margaret, 'Violence in the Family: An Historical Perspective', in J. P. Martin (ed.), *Violence in the Family* (Chichester: Wiley, 1978), 135.

Myer, Marc A., 'Land Charters and the Legal Position of Anglo-Saxon Women', in Barbara Kanner (ed.), *The Women of England from Anglo-Saxon Times to the Present: Interpretative Bibliographical Essays* (London: Mansell, 1980), 57.

Mill, Harriet Taylor, 'Enfranchisement of Women', 55 *Westminster Review* (1851), 149.

Mill, John Stuart, 'Remarks on Mr Fitzroy's Bill for the More Effectual Prevention of Assaults on Women and Children' (1853), in John Robson (ed.), *Essays on Equality, Law and Education*, 21 vols. (Toronto: University of Toronto Press, 1984), vol. 21, 103.

——, 'The Subjection of Women' (1868), in Alice S. Rossi (ed.), *Essays on Sex Equality* (Chicago: University of Chicago Press, 1970), 125.

Minor, Iris, 'Working-class Women and Matrimonial Law Reform, 1890–1914', in David Martin and David Rubinstein (eds.), *Ideology and the Labour Movement* (London: Croom Helm, 1979), 103.

Minton-Senhouse, R. M., 'Married Women: An Historical Sketch', 131 *Westminster Review* (1889), 355.

Mitchell, Juliet, 'Women and Equality', in Juliet Mitchell and Anne Oakley (eds.), *The Rights and Wrongs of Women* (1976; repr. Harmondsworth: Penguin, 1979), 379.

Mohr, James C., 'Feminism and the History of Marital Law: Basch and Stetson on the Rights of Wives', (1984) *American Bar Foundation Research Journal*, 223.

Mohr, Johanns, W., 'The Future of the Family, the Law and the State' (Keynote address to the People's Law Conference on the Family and the Law: Ottawa, April 1984).

Morris, N. and Turner G., 'Two Problems in the Law of Rape', 2 *University of Queensland Law Review* (1956), 247.

'Mr Mill on the Subjection of Women', 106 *Blackwood's Magazine* (1869), 309.

Mueller, Gerhard O. W., 'Inquiry into the State of a Divorceless Society: Domestic Relations Law and Morals in England from 1600–1857', 18 *University of Pittsburg Law Review* (157), 545.

Newman, F. W. (attrib.), 'Corporal Punishment, and Penal Reformation', 71 *Fraser's Magazine* (1865), 154.

O'Donovan, Katherine, 'The Male Appendage – Legal Definitions of Women', in Sandra Burman (ed.), *Fit Work for Women* (London: Croom Helm in Association with Oxford University Women's Studies Committee, 1979), 134.

Okin, Susan Moller, 'Patriarchy and Married Women's Property in England: Questions on Some Current Views', 17(2) *Eighteenth-Century Studies* (1983–4), 121.

Oliphant, Margaret, 'The Laws Concerning Women', 79 *Blackwood's Edinburgh Magazine* (1856), 379.

——, 'The Condition of Women', 83 *Blackwood's Edinburgh Magazine* (1858), 138.

O'Neil, M. J., 'A Little Help From our Friends: Citizen Predisposition to Intervene in Spouse Abuse', 1 *Law and Policy Quarterly* (1979), 177.

Oppenlander, Nan, 'The Evolution of Law and Wife Abuse', 3 *Law and Policy Quarterly* (1981), 382.

Pace, P. J., 'Marital Coercion – Anachronism or Modernism?', [1979] *Criminal Law Review*, 82.

Paley, Ruth, 'The Crown Side of the Court of King's Bench: Litigants and Litigation in Hanoverian London' (Unpublished paper, 1991).

Paley, Ruth, 'Londoners and the King's Bench (Crown Side) in the Eighteenth and Early Nineteenth Centuries' (Paper presented at the British Legal History Conference, Oxford, July 1991).

Pastoor, Maria K., 'Police Training and the Effectiveness of Minnesota "Domestic Abuse" Laws', 2 *Law and Inequality* (1984), 53.

Pateman, Carole, '"God Hath Ordained to man a Helper": Hobbes, Patriarchy and Conjugal Right', in Mary Lyndon Shanley and Carole Pateman (eds.), *Feminist Interpretations and Political Theory* (Cambridge: Polity Press, 1991), 53.

——, and Brennan, Teresa, '"Mere Auxiliaries to the Commonwealth": Women and Liberalism', 27 *Political Studies* (1979), 183.

Perry, Thomas Erskine, 'Rights and Liabilities of Husband and Wife', 105 *Edinburgh Review* (1857), 181.

'The Personal Liberty of Married Women', 90 *Law Times* (1890–1), 386.

'Personal Relations of Husband and Wife', 55 *Justice of the Peace* (1891), 211.

Pleck, Elizabeth, 'Feminist Responses to "Crimes Against Women", 1868–1896', 8 *Signs* (1982–3), 451.

'The Political Disabilities of Women', 97 *Westminster Review* (1872), 50.

Pulling, Alexander, 'What Legislation is Necessary for the Repression of Crimes of Violence?' and Discussion, *Transactions NAPSS* (1876) (London: Longmans and Green, 1877), 345.

'Rape: Case and Comment (*R. v. Roberts*)', [1986] *Criminal Law Review*, 188.

Reade, William, 'Our Judges, Our Persons, and Our Purses', 24 *Law Magazine and Review* (3rd Ser.) (1867–8), 118.

'Remarks on a Pamphlet intitled, The Hardships of the English Laws Relating to Wives; in an humble Petition to his Majesty', 6 *The Gentleman's Magazine* (1736), 648.

Ross, Ellen, ' "Fierce Questions and Taunts": Married life in Working-Class London, 1840–1914', 8 *Feminist Studies* (1983), 575.

Rowe, G. S. 'Femes Covert and Criminal Prosecution in Eighteenth-Century Pennsylvania', 32 *American Journal of Legal History* (1988), 138.

Rubinstein, David, 'Lunatic or Heroine', *New Society* (25 April 1986), 10.

Russell, Bertrand, 'Rights Husbands Had Once', *Sunday Referee* (15 December 1935), 12.

Scutt, Jocelynne, 'Consent in Rape: The Problem of the Marriage Contract', 3 *Monash University Law Review* (1977), 255.

Shanley, Mary Lyndon, 'Marriage Contract and Social Contract in Seventeenth Century English Political Thought', 32 *Western Political Quarterly* (1979), 79.

——, 'Marital Slavery and Friendship: John Stuart Mill's "The Subjection of Women"', 9 *Political Theory* (1981), 229.

——, ' "One Must Ride Behind": Married Women's Rights and the Divorce Act of 1857', 25 *Victorian Studies* (1982), 355.

Sheehan, Michael, 'Influence of Canon Law on the Property Rights of Married Women in England', 25 *Medieval Studies* (1963), 109.

Sheldon, Amos, 'The Subjection of Women', 93 *Westminster Review* (1870), 63.

Shore, Louisa Catherine, 'The Emancipation of Women', 102 *Westminster Review* (1874), 137.

Staves, Susan, 'Where is History but in Texts? Reading the History of Marriage', in John. M. Wallace (ed.), *The Golden and the Brazen World: Papers in History and Literature* (Berkeley: University of California Press, 1985), 125.

Stedman, Bierne, 'Right of Husband to Chastise Wife', 3 *Virginia Law Register* (N.S.) (1917), 241.

Stone, O. M., 'When a Wife May Testify', 14 *Modern Law Review* (1951), 341.

Storch, Robert, 'The Policeman as Domestic Missionary: Urban Discipline and Popular Culture in Northern England, 1850–1880', 9 *Journal of Social History* (1976), 481.

Sutton, Jo, 'Modern and Victorian Battered Women: A Look at an Old Pattern', in University of Bradford, Occasional Paper No. 4, *Battered Women and Abused Children* (Bradford: University of Bradford Issues Publications, 1979), 9.

Taylor, William, 'On Criminal Offences and the Repression of Crime', *Transactions NAPSS* (1984) (London: Longmans and Green, 1875), 353.

Thomas, Keith, 'Women and the Civil War Sects', 13 *Past & Present* (1958), 42.

——, 'The Double Standard', 20 *Journal of the History of Ideas* (1959), 195.

Thompson, Dorothy, 'Women and Nineteenth-Century Radical Politics: A Lost Dimension', in Juliet Mitchell and Anne Oakley (eds.), *The Rights and Wrongs of Women* (1976; repr. Harmondsworth: Penguin, 1983), 112.

——, 'Women, Work and Politics in Nineteenth-Century England: The Problem of Authority', in Jane Rendall (ed.), *Equal or Different: Women's Politics 1800–1914* (Oxford: Basil Blackwell, 1987), 57.

Thompson, Edward P., 'Rough Music: Le Charivari Anglais', 27 *Annales Economies Societes Civilization* (1972), 285.

Tierney, Kathleen J., 'The Battered Women Movement and the Creation of the Wife Beating Problem', 29(3) *Social Problems* (1982), 207.

Tomes, Nancy, '"A Torrent of Abuse": Crimes of Violence Between Working-Class Men and Women in London, 1840–1875', 11 *Journal of Social History* (1978), 328.

Underdown, D. E., 'The Taming of the Scold: the Enforcement of Patriarchal Authority in Early Modern England', in Anthony Fletcher and John Stevenson (eds.), *Order and Disorder in Early Modern England* (Cambridge: Cambridge University Press, 1985), 116.

Walters, Margaret, 'The Rights and Wrongs of Women: Mary Wollstonecraft, Harriet Martineau, Simone de Beauvoir', in Juliet Mitchell and Ann Oakley (eds.), *The Rights and Wrongs of Women* (1976; rpt. Harmondsworth: Penguin, 1983), 304.

Weiner, Carol Z., 'Sex Roles and Crime in Late Elizabethan Hertfordshire', 8 *Journal of Social History* (1975), 38.

——, 'Is a Spinster an Unmarried Woman?', 20 *American Journal of Legal History* (1976), 27.

Westman, Barbara Hanawalt, 'The Peasant Family and Crime in Fourteenth-Century England', 13(2) *Journal of British Studies* (1974), 1.

Williams, Glanville, 'The Legal Unity of Husband and Wife', 10 *Modern Law Review* (1947), 16.

Williams, John, 'Marital Rape', 15 *Family Law* (1985), 99.

Wilson, Joan H., 'The Legal Status of Women in the Late Nineteenth and Early Twentieth Centuries', 6 *Human Rights* (1976–1977), 125.

Wolfram, Sybil, '"Husband and Wife are one Person: the Husband" (Nineteenth-century English Aphorism)', in A-J. Arnaud and E. Kingdom (eds.), *Women's Rights and the Rights of Man* (Aberdeen: Aberdeen University Press, 1990), 158.

Wolstenholme Elmy, Elizabeth C. ('Ignota'), 'The Present Legal Position of Women in the United Kingdom', 163 *Westminster Review* (1905), 513.

——, 'Judicial Sex Bias', 149 *Westminster Review* (1898), 147, 279.

'Woman's Law: Mrs Norton's Letter to the Queen', 23 *Law Review* (1855–6), 334.

Zainaldin, Jamil S., 'The Emergence of a Modern American Family Law: Child Custody, Adoption, and the Courts, 1796–1851', 73 *Northwestern University Law Review* (1979), 1038.

Official Documents

'Royal Commission on Divorce and Matrimonial Causes: Minutes of Evidence' (c. 1604) *Sessional Papers H.C. (1852–3), vol. 40.*

'Report from the Select Committee of the House of Lords on the Divorce and Matrimonial Causes Bill ... together with the Proceedings of the Committee', Sessional Papers H.L. (1856), vol. 24, 181.

'Report to the Secretary of State for the Home Department on the State of the Law Relating to Brutal Assaults etc.' (C. 1138), *Sessional Papers H.C.* (1875), vol. 61, 29.

'A Bill for the Better Protection of Women and Children in England from Crimes of Violence', *Sessional Papers* H.C. (1882), vol. 6, 755.

'Royal Commission on Divorce and Matrimonial Causes' (cd 6478–82), *Sessional Papers* H.C. (1912–13), vols. 18–20.

Criminal Law Revision Committee: *Fifteenth Report*, Sexual Offences (Cmnd 9213), (1984).

Law Commission: Working Paper No. 103, *Criminal Law: Binding Over: The Issues* (1987).

INDEX